SUSTAINABLE RURAL DEVELOPMENT FOR DISASTER MITIGATION

Pradeep Chaturvedi

CONCEPT PUBLISHING COMPANY, NEW DELHI-110 059

ISBN: 81-7022-633-3

First Published 1997, 2004

Published and Printed by
Ashok Kumar Mittal
Concept Publishing Company
A/15-16, Commercial Block, Mohan Garden
New Delhi-110 059 (INDIA)
Phones : 25351460, 25351794 *Fax* : 091-11-25357103
Email : publishing@conceptpub.com

"More effective prevention strategies would save not only tens of billions of dollars, but save tens of thousands of lives. Funds currently spent on intervention and relief could be devoted to enhancing equitable and sustainable development instead, which would further reduce the risk for war and disaster. Building a culture of prevention is not easy. While the costs of prevention have to be paid in the present, its benefits lie in a distant future. moreover, the benefits are not tangible; they are the disasters that did NOT happen."

— Kofi Annan,
U.N. Secretary General

भारतीय लोक प्रशासन संस्थान
इन्द्रप्रस्थ एस्टेट, रिंग रोड, नई दिल्ली–110 002, दूरभाष : 2370240 (15 लाइन)
INDIAN INSTITUTE OF PUBLIC ADMINISTRATION
Indraprastha Estate, Ring Road, New Delhi 110 002

Dr. P.L. Sanjeev Reddy, *IAS* (Retd.)
(Former Secretary to Govt. of India)
Director, IIPA

Tel. : 011-23702434 (Off.)
011-23766000 (Res.)
011-2376800

Foreword

A disaster is an event which gives rise to casualties, loss of property, damage to infrastructure, essential services and means of livelihood, on a scale which the affected community cannot cope with unaided. Disasters ruin years of investment in the development process. A disaster places new demands on society for reconstruction and reabilitation.

India due to its vast territory, large population, typical geological and geo-morphological structures and variable geo-climatic condition is exposed to multiple hazards. Though the hazards are common in both rural and urban areas, the adverse impacts of these hazards are much more visible in villages. Poverty, illiteracy, increasing demographic pressure, unemployment, changing socio-economic conditions lead to increased vulnerability of Indian rural society to natural disasters. Besides causing tremendous loss to life and property, these disastrous events triggered by natural hazards threaten development and poverty alleviation initiatives in rural areas.

In spite of various efforts at the government and non-government level, the severity of the adverse impact of natural disasters has been increasing. The reason is that in the existing disaster management scenario, the emphasis is more on disaster response, rather than on preparedness and mitigation.

All countries are faced with the basic problem of allocating limited and finite resources to different uses. Using limited resources in one direction decreases resources availability for use in other direction.

Mitigation measures would decrease the impact of a disaster & minimize damage. Examples include the enforcement of building codes, land use regulations that disallow people to settle on vulnerable sites, protection of power supplies, investments in infrastructure away from disaster prone areas and soil conservation.

In this manuscript the authors discuss the various factors responsible for increased vulnerability to natural disasters in rural India and analyze the prevailing disaster management systems, as also their problems and shortomings. A critical review and analysis of the secondary and primary data reveals that for effective management of the disaster, the rural communmity should be involved in the preventive aspects for risk and vulnerability reduction. Disaster management in rural areas should aim to make the society resilient to adverse impact of natural hazards through an on-going process that does not focus on a sporadic and solitary disaster event. Efforts in the field of disaster management will have an enduring impact only when they are conducted in-concert with normal development process. In this prespective, the book rightly suggests that rural development should be linked to disaster management and concludes that sustainable rural development can significantly reduce the risk to natural disasters. The book also discusses in detail the dovetailing of various on-going developmental schemes in rural areas to achieve this target. The role of panchayat as the implementing agency for these programmes/ schemes has been rightly highlighted for effective results in the field of disaster management.

I am confident that the rich information and sound suggestions provided in the book would be of great relevance and use for the planners, implementers and the people of the country.

Dr. P.L. Sanjeev Reddy
IAS (Retd.)
Director, IIPA

New Delhi

R.K. SINGH, *IAS*
Joint Secretary (DM)

Tel: 23093178

सत्यमेव जयते

गृह मंत्रालय
भारत सरकार
नार्थ ब्लाक, नई दिल्ली–110001
MINISTRY OF HOME AFFAIRS
GOVERNMENT OF INDIA
NORTH BLOCK, NEW DELHI-110001

Preface

"India is a land of villages" is as true as it was 55 years ago when the country won its freedom from colonial rule. Despite rapid urbanization in the recent past, the majority of the country's population still lives in villages and is primarily dependent on agriculture. The majority of the rural population is stricken by poverty, unemployment/under employment; illiteracy, poor health and low life expectancy. After more than fifty-five years of independence, more than 27% of rural population is forced to survive below poverty line. Natural disasters cause further deterioration in their condition and negate any efforts to get out of the poverty cycle. Due to their increased vulnerability, the rural population is much more adversely affected by the impact of natural disasters. Poverty and hazard vulnerability are integrally linked and mutually reinforcing.

The present book has made a conscious attempt to delineate the factors responsible for increased vulnerability of rural population, especially the rural poor to natural hazards. After critically analyzing the existing disaster maagement policies and its implementation in rural areas, the book concludes that it is a comprehensive and sustainable rural development approach that can reduce the frequency, intensity and the overall adverse impacts of natural hazards on rural society. Sustainable and integrated management of natural resources, including afforestation, water management and appropriate land use will increase the resilience of rural communities to natural hazards by reversing the current trends of natural environmental degradation.

The book emphasizes the need to link disaster management with development, suggesting various ways in which disaster risk of the rural society can be reduced as part of developmental policies. For this, it is necessary that the objective of disaster management must expand beyond the pattern of traditional response to natural disasters and link it to an ongoing process that does not focus only on the immediate disaster. In order to ensure that the development process integrates disaster mitigation concerns, it will be necessary that disaster management and development are to be managed by the same authority. In such circumstances, the Panchayats or local self governments may be the best choice. The vital strength of the PRIs is that they are working at the grass root level in accordance with the people's need and aspirations, which is basically required for a successful long terms strategy of disaster management in rural areas.

The book will encourage various sections of the society to think over the issue of linkage between poverty and disaster management in rural areas. It is hoped that the book will be of utility and help to the policy makers, planners and researchers.

31st October, 2003 **(R.K. Singh)**

Acknowledgements

The present book is an outcome of extensive study of primary and secondary data. During the course of this work, intensive discussions, interviews and meetings were held with various stakeholders. We express our gratitude to each and every individual who spared their valuable time and suggestions in completing the work.

First of all we feel immense pleasure in offering our most sincere gratitude to Dr. P. L. Sanjeev Reddy, Director of IIPA, for his encouragement and fruitful suggestions, which helped us in completing the book.

Our sincere thanks are due to Shri M. Nambiar, Executive Director of National Institute of Disaster Management for his inspiration. The guidance and advice given by Shri Anil Sinha, former Executive Director have been of immense value for us.

The authors also feel grateful to their friends and colleagues for their help in many ways. Thanks are due to Mrs. Pratiba, Mr. Rajesh Patel, Dr. N. Satish Chandra, Mr. Michael Shiromany, Mr. A. K. Singh, Mr. R. B. S. Rawat, Mr. B. A. Khan, Mr. Dipankar Guha, Dr. S. Saran, Dr. V.K. Bahuguna, Mr. K. N. Kandwal, Ms. Tanushree, Mr. Kanishk Singh, Mr. Bodh, Mr. Bharat Lal, Dr. S.P.Sati, Mr. Anil Kashyap, Mr. V. S. Lal and Mr. A. K. Das, for their assistance in many ways in completing the work.

We are also highly indebted to our colleagues and staff of NCDM of IIPA, mainly Mr. Amir Ali Khan, Mr. Rahul Kaushik, Dr. A. D. Kaushik, Mr. C.S. Raut, Mr. Amar, Mr. Pyare Lal, Mrs. Krishna, Mrs. Santosh, Ms. Megha, Mr. Trilochan Singh, Mr. Ahmed Kamal, Mr. Manoj and Mr. Vijay.

The cooperation and assistance of our family members were equally important and need due acknowledgement.

Dr. Satendra

New Delhi **Prof. Vinod K. Sharma**

Contents

List of Tables

List of Figures

1
Disaster — An Introduction

A disaster may be defined as "an event' concentrated in time and space which threatens a society or a relatively self-sufficient sub-division of a society with major unwarranted consequences as a result of the collapse of precautions, which had hitherto been culturally accepted as adequate" (Turner, 1976).

The World Health Organisation (WHO) describes disaster as an occurrence that causes damage, economic destruction, loss of human life and deterioration in health and health services on a scale sufficient to warrant an extraordinary response from outside the affected community or the area.

Another definition of the disaster (Sinha, P.C., 1998) is that it is "an occurrence arising with little or no warning, which causes or threatens serious disruption of life, and perhaps death or injury to large numbers of people, and requires therefore a mobilisation of efforts in excess of that normally provided by the statutory emergency services".

Disasters are also assessed as an event "that produces the conditions whereby the continuity of the structure of and process of social units become problematic....." (Dynes, R.R.,1998).

Thus the word "disaster" has been defined contextually by various authorities. However for convenience, disasters may be termed as extreme events which cause great loss to life and property. They pose a serious threat to the normal life as well as the process of development and strike with sudden violence, tearing bodies, destroying lives and structures and throwing apart families. Natural disasters, which are both sudden and powerful, damage national economy and cause hardships to a large section of the population. They are the single largest concern for most of the nations as they take a heavy toll of human life, destroy belongings and infrastructures and have far-reaching economic and social consequences for communities. Thus, the impact of disasters on human life is multi-dimensional, affecting it in all aspects - domestic, social, economic, etc.

Types and Groups of Disasters

In general, on the basis of their origin, disasters have been categorised as natural or man-made. However there is no clear cut boundary and it is observed that in most of the cases disasters have a hybrid origin. A natural disasters may be initiated or accelerated by the man induced activities as is in the case of landslide, drought, flood etc. *The Indian Encyclopedia of Disaster Management*, edited by P. C. Sinha categorised sixteen types of disasters on the basis of their origin as follows:

S.N.	Disaster Type	Natural	Man-made	Hybrid
1	Avalanche/ Rock-fall	Yes	No	Yes
2	Air transport	No	Yes	Yes
3	Road transport	No	Yes	Yes
4	Marine transport	No	Yes	Yes
5	Rail transport	No	Yes	Yes
6	Climatic	Yes	No	Yes
7	Drought	Yes	Yes	Yes
8	Famine	Yes	Yes	Yes
9	Epidemic	Yes	No	Yes
10	Plague	Yes	Yes	Yes
11	Earthquake	Yes	No	No
12	Fire	Yes	Yes	Yes
13	Explosion	No	Yes	Yes
14	Flooding	Yes	No	Yes
15	Mining	No	Yes	Yes
16	Volcanic activity	Yes	No	Yes

The High Power Committee on Disaster Management (HPCDM), constituted in 1999 at the behest of the Prime Minister to suggest the institutional reforms and preparedness of Disaster Management Plans at the National, State and District levels, has identified 31 various disasters and categorised them into five major sub-groups, primarily based on their origin :

Disasters Identified by the High Powered Committee

I. Water and climate related disasters

1. Floods and drainage management
2. Cyclones
3. Tornadoes and hurricanes
4. Hailstorm
5. Cloud burst
6. Heat wave and cold wave
7. Snow avalanches
8. Droughts
9. Sea erosion
10. Thunder and lightening

II. Geologically related disasters

1. Landslides and mudflows
2. Earthquakes
3. Dam failures/Dam bursts.
4. Mine fires

III. Chemical, Industrial and Nuclear related disasters

1. Chemical and Industrial disasters
2. Nuclear disasters

IV. Accident related disasters

1. Forest fires
2. Urban fires
3. Mine flooding
4. Oil spills
5. Major building collapse
6. Serial bomb blasts
7. Festival related disasters
8. Electrical disasters and fires
9. Air, road and rail accidents
10. Boat capsizing.
11. Village fire

V. Biologically related disasters

1. Biological disasters and epidemics

2. Pest attacks
3. Cattle epidemics
4. Food poisoning

Managing Disasters and Disaster Management Cycle

Most of the disasters are not completely unavoidable and hence they are to be faced. The best approach to minimise the impacts of these disasters is to manage them in a better and scientific way. The damage from natural hazards can be minimised by introducing appropriate preparedness measures - including both early warning and preparedness on the part of vulnerable community. In general, there are three stages in disaster management, namely, pre-disaster, emergency and post-disaster. The pre- disaster stage includes reducing the vulnerability or susceptibility of a society or community to ensure minimal losses in the case of a disaster. The emergency stage refers to fulfil the needs and provisions of the victims affected by a natural hazard. The most important phase of disaster starts with the passing of the emergency phase and it covers the rehabilitation of the affected communities. Rehabilitation does not merely mean rebuilding/ repairing the houses, roads, etc. or financial assistance to affected population but it has much wider implications. In true sense it aims at total reconstruction of physical and social infrastructure as well as economic and social upliftment of the people. This aspect of rehabilitation is very much desired in a region where disasters are very common and frequent accentuate features.

Due to various factors, both natural and anthropogenic, India is very prone to natural disasters. The number and magnitude of adverse impact of these disasters are increasing every year due to combined effects of adverse weather, population growth, urbanisation, environmental degradation including deforestation and so on. As a result the country is facing one or the other type of disasters like earthquakes, landslides, floods, drought, forest fires, etc. very frequently. Though at the time of disaster, various rescue and relief operations are carried out and plans for long- term strategies are formed, yet the long-term strategies are easily forgotten as memory fades. Till now the approach adopted traditionally in the country for disaster management has been marked with the activities mainly focused on disaster relief. It is observed that disaster management is just like fire fighting and very negligible conscious attempt is made for long- term strategies. Partial failure of the administration and other agencies to counter the situation results in further deterioration of the condition. Unemployment, diseases, scarcity of livelihood, food and water shortage, shelter/housing problem, failure of communication and other infrastructures, environmental degradation, etc., are some major problems which are being faced due to one or the other form of disaster in the country. In recent past, the intensity and severity of disasters have increased many times, mainly due to increasing population pressure and various other man-made/natural factors and subsequently the problem of rehabilitation has become more serious. This increasing trend in the losses, clearly show that the existing policy and approach to disaster management in the country is not much suited in the existing situation and need thorough review and modification. The SWOT analysis (based on primary and secondary data) of the existing policy and its implementation clearly states many strengths and opportunities, which are to be identified, explored and properly used while devising new policy for disaster management in the country.

Realising the seriousness of the problem and its adverse impact on the socio-economic status of the people in the recent past, there is a perceptible shift in focus from relief to preparedness and prevention. This shift in approach has brought a significant positive change in the field of disaster management, which is clearly reflected in the Disaster Management Cycle—the basis of new thinking in this field.

The Disaster Management Cycle

Disaster management in general comprises of three main stages—pre-disaster, emergency and post- disaster.

1. ***Pre-disaster:*** The stage refers to preparedness and mitigation aspects mainly with the objectives to reduce the potential risks for human, material, or environmental losses caused by hazards and to ensure that these losses are minimised when the disaster actually strikes.
2. ***Emergency:*** The stage covering the relief, rescue, check on epidemic spread, and loss assessments basically aims to ensure

that the needs and provisions of victims are met to alleviate and minimise suffering.

3. ***Post-disaster:*** This important stage of disaster management starts immediately after the actual phase of disaster is over. With the sole objective of rehabilitation of disaster affected people this stage is geared to achieve rapid and durable recovery, which does not reproduce the original vulnerable conditions.

In general the disaster management is looked as rescue, relief and rehabilitation of the affected population and other physical amenities. However this traditional approach of disaster management does not cover the true spirit of disaster management, which requires that in reality the process must start much before a disaster actually strikes. In real sense the disaster management is a continuous process that covers many important aspects ultimately leading to reduction of vulnerability and susceptibility of region and society from natural hazards.

A successful disaster management planning encompasses the complete realm of activities and situations that occur before, during and after the disasters. All these stages of disaster management, i.e., preparedness and mitigation, disaster, emergency, rehabilitation and reconstruction are in fact cyclical and overlap, referring to disaster management cycle, shown in the Fig. 1.1.

Traditionally in the Disaster Management Cycle, the disaster is seen as the trigger for every thing else occurred in a cyclical sequence of action and back to disaster again. These various stages of cycle refer to various actions taken during that particular event. However there is no clear cut boundary line and the actions of one stage overlap with the other stage. The various stages of Disaster Management Cycle are defined as follows.

1. The disaster

This refers to the "real-time" of the event of a hazard affecting elements at risk. The duration of the event depend on the type of disaster : ground shaking may occur only for few seconds during an earthquake while drought may take place over a prolonged period.

2. Emergency/relief

This stage which includes issue such as warning, action for evacuation, taking people to safer areas, rendering medical aid to the needy, setting

Fig. 1.1 : Disaster Management Cycle and its components

up control rooms, putting the contingency plan in action, etc. to the needy, assessment of loss, restoration of communication, disbursement of assistance in cash or kind is the immediate response to any disaster.

3. Rehabilitation/reconstruction

The stage in general describes the activities that encompass the activities with aim to revive the situation in term of physical, social and economic aspects. In the disaster-prone areas, rehabilitation should not be simply viewed as only shifting of people from one place to another and resettling them. The rehabilitation here does not merely means providing financial support or rebuilding/repairing/retreating the damaged houses, etc., instead it is to be focussed on overall development of the region. Four essential aspects of successful rehabilitation / reconstruction are:

- Politico-administrative will for rehabilitation.
- The rehabilitation should be acceptable to the community

i.e. to be formulated considering the local needs of the people, their culture and traditions. This aspect of rehabilitation also covers the revival / strengthening of educational system and health facilities and rehabilitation of vulnerable groups of the society.

- The rehabilitation plan is required to consider various economic aspects related to the livelihood of the people affected by the disasters.

- For successful and sustainable rehabilitation plan, the environmental aspect is of very crucial and strategic importance. A rehabilitation plan devoid of the environmental aspect is bound to fail in fragile and unstable zones.

4. Pre-disaster including preparedness and mitigation

This stage includes preparedness and mitigation with objectives to minimise the impact of hazard and make the society resilient against them. The preparedness for disaster in general comprises of:

– Preparing hazard zonation maps and predictability
– Preparing disaster preparedness plan
– Land use and exploitable zones
– Preparedness through IEC.

The mitigation covers different aspects that reduce the impact of disasters and which are to be taken before the disaster. Various measures to be taken in this regard are—

- Construction of disaster resistant houses and retrofitting of weak structures,
- Reduce population pressure in sensitive zones,
- Increasing people's awareness, etc.

Disaster Management Bicycle

The disaster management cycle describes most of the programmes and projects, which are inter-linked and overlapping, undertaken on account of disaster occurrence. However this traditional approach of disaster management cycle is not covering other activities, which directly or indirectly influence the disaster management. These activities or group of activities although form an integral part of disaster management cycle but they work on a parallel line. In his book, "Development in Disaster prone Places" James Lewis (1999), while discussing this issue has rightly mentioned

> *"This disaster cycle still appears in descriptions of programmes and projects undertaken on account of natural disaster occurrence.*
> *What the self centric " disaster cycle " did not acknowledge was that there were other sectors of activity outside of the cycle. Not every thing that happened or that was undertaken, subscribe to the contexts for the impacts of natural disasters themselves. Development or 'change' was also taking place - of its own inevitable volition or in a planned and programmed way. Where did ' development appear in the ' disaster cycle'?"*

Fig. 1.2: Disaster Bicycle - Where it is heading to ....

He further argues that the disaster cycle is not one cycle, instead it is a disaster bicycle. However the speciality with this bicycle is that it is not driven by the single authority, and it is where the confusion starts. The activities of this cycle of events are implemented by various sectors and are not inter-related. This situation creates utmost confusion in the planning and leads to disastrous activities. In other words, in the present context, the disaster management has become separated from the development, making society and the region more vulnerable and susceptible to natural disasters.

In such situation it can be visualised that for effective management of disaster, development is to be taken as the second cycle of the disaster management bicycle (Fig 1.2). These two cycles of the bicycle are either driven by the same authority, if not possible at least with good coordination and correlation.

Disaster Mitigation and Prevention : Recent Initiatives

Keeping in view the new developments and initiatives, the disaster management setup in India is trying to orient itself towards a strong focus on preventive approaches, mainly through administrative reforms and participatory methods. Preparedness measures such as training of role players including the community, development of advanced forecasting systems, effective communications, and above all a sound and well networked institutional structure involving the government organisations, academic and research institutions, the armed forces and the non-governmental organisations have greatly contributed to the overall disaster management in the country. The approach of reducing community vulnerability for reducing disasters has paid rich dividends. The first step in this direction has been of identification of vulnerable communities. Those communities periodically exposed to natural hazards, and within them, those with low levels of coping powers, such as economically weaker sections, are the first focus of preparedness efforts. Marginal sections of rural communities and dwellers of informal settlements and slums in urban areas fall within this class.

Efforts in the direction of integrating disaster prevention into habitat planning processes are one of the most viable disaster prevention means. The general direction of current efforts is one of the multi-pronged approaches of mobilisation of community perceptions towards a culture of prevention of natural disasters. Along with this, the increase in the number of natural disasters during the last three decades, there has been a growing awareness of the relation between the declining quality of the earth's environment and the frequency and severity of natural catastrophes. It is becoming increasingly evident now that relatively smaller investment in disaster preparedness can save thousands of lives and vital economic assets, as well as reduce the cost of overall relief assistance.

Giving due consideration and serious thought to new emerging approaches in disaster management, a number of initiatives have already been taken up within the country towards influencing policy level changes in building a nation-wide culture of preparedness and mitigation. The High Powered Committee on Disaster Management (HPC) has propagated the idea of holistic, comprehensive and integrated approach towards disaster management and mitigation. The HPC had already submitted its report with its recommendations to the Government in 2001. It has advocated for ushering in a new culture of prevention which is based upon the cultures of "Preparedness, Quick Response and Strategic Thinking". The formation of Working Group (HPC stands converted) is an indication towards a renewed commitment of the government towards disaster mitigation. This working group has also submitted recently its report to government.

The Government of India, after the Gujarat earthquake, has established a National Committee on Disaster Management (NCDM), headed by the Prime Minister, to provide a forum to political parties of all shades to share and discuss the issues related to disaster management and mitigation. This Committee is supposed to suggest the institutional and legislative measures to strengthen the existing disaster management structure of the country.

In addition to this, the most sensible efforts at government level has been the initiatives taken by Planning Commission. The Planning Commission has incorporated, for the first time, disaster management as one of its areas of concern. A chapter titled "Disaster Management: The Development Perspective" has been included in the Tenth Plan document to make the whole gamut of planning process sensitive to various dimensions of disaster management and influencing upon the disaster prevention, reduction and mitigation concerns in the process of development. The inclusion of a separate chapter on Disaster Management is considered to be one of the most important development triggered by the HPC on Disaster Management. The Tenth Plan document and especially the chapter on Disaster Management will inform, guide and provide specific strategies to all state governments. It is expected and hoped that over the years, this would go a long way in tackling disasters on a long-term basis. It also sets out the broad parameters and strategies for information dissemination and research initiatives, capacity building, education and training, community level initiatives and institutional arrangements.

The Tenth Plan also addresses the community-based disaster preparedness and management by way of strengthening and capacity building of Panchayati Raj Institutions (PRIs) and Urban Local Bodies (ULBs). A special mention has been made about the role of the youth in disaster management, not only through educational institutions but through youth movements like Nehru Yuvak Kendra Sangathan (NYKS), National Cadet Corps (NCC), National Service Scheme (NSS), Bharat Scouts & Guides (BS&G), etc.

In addition to these initiatives, some more new ideas and projects are being introduced in the existing Disaster Management System in the country, with a sole objective to make it more effective. Some of them, which can play very effective role while managing disasters, are discussed in the succeeding text.

SPHERE: It has been a common observation that during a disaster, while providing assistance to the affected population, minimum standards of relief are very rarely considered. Minimum standards of relief here not only means the food requirements of the victims but also refers to the health and immediate First Aid facilities, looks at the drinking water and sanitation needs, shelter requirements, and providing food.

The SPHERE Project is for Humanitarian Charter and Minimum Standards in Disaster Response. The SPHERE Project was initiated by the agency network, Steering Committee for Humanitarian Response (SCHR) and Inter Actions in 1997 to develop a humanitarian charter and an associated set of minimum standards. The humanitarian Charter and Minimum Standards reflect the determination of agencies to improve, both, the effectiveness of their assistance and accountability to their stakeholders. The standards are designed with this in mind and each standard is accompanied by a series of indicators. These are important not only to design and implement programmes, but also to provide a way for disaster affected people, agency staff, donors, the public and others to review the provision of assistance. The Humanitarian charter and Minimum Standards thus contribute to a practical framework for accountability. Cooperation between all humanitarian actors features strongly in the minimum standards.

Infact, minimum standards of relief laid out by the SPHERE project are a valuable effort and need to be reviewed and adapted for applicability to the Indian context. When addressing the relief requirements of the disaster victims, focus is to be placed on the special needs of the vulnerable population i.e. children, women, aged and the disabled.

The Minimum Standards apply to any situation where people's normal means of support for life with dignity have failed, whether as a result of a normal or human-made disaster, in any country or any continent. The standards provide a description of what people have a right to expect for humanitarian assistance and specify the minimum acceptable levels to be attained in water supply, sanitation, nutrition, food aid, shelter, site planning and health services. They have been made as "specific" as possible, but are intended to be adaptable to different emergency situations. This document (humanitarian charter) may be useful for disaster affected populations and other stakeholders including coordinating bodies, local authorities, institutional donors, individual donors, scholars and journalists. The achievements of minimum standards depends on a range of factors which may be either within the control and remit humanitarian agencies or others, particularly those relating to political situation, security and protection lie outside their control. The Humanitarian Charter and Minimum Standards were produced as an extensive and sustained cooperation between agencies/individuals to meet fundamental human needs of people affected by disaster in way that respect their dignity & rights.

Incident Command System

The Incident Command System (ICS) is a model tool for command, coordination and use of resources at the site of the incident i.e. disaster. The system was first established in 1970 after a major forest fire in southern California. ICS is based on the management and direction tools that Experts and Disaster Managers are already aware of. In India also ICS has been adapted as a disaster response mechanism. It has considerable flexibility and can grow or shink to meet different needs, and makes it a very cost-effective and efficient management system. This system can be applied to a wide variety of disaster situations. The organization of the ICS is built around five major management activities viz.

Command	—	Sets objectives and priorities
	—	Has overall responsibility of the incident or event
Operations	—	Conducts tactical operations to carry out the plan
	—	Develops tactical objectives
	—	Organisation
	—	Directs all resources
Planning	—	Develops the action plan to accomplish the objectives
	—	Collects and evaluates information
	—	Maintains resource status
Logistics	—	Provides support to meet incident needs
	—	Provides resources and all other services needed to support the incident
Finance/ Administration	—	Monitors costs related to incident
	—	Provides accounting
	—	Procurement time
	—	Recording cost analyses

ICS is therefore an effective model for centralized management. In the ICS model the base of operations for response to a disaster i.e. incident is recognized as Command Centre (CC). Upon activation of a plan, the Incident Commander establishes the CC and initiates ICS.

The staffing positions in the ICS is as follows:

— Incident Commander
— Incident Officer
— Safety Officer
— Intra-agency Coordinator
— Operations Officer

— Planning Officer
— Logistics Officer
— Finance Officer
— Operation Teams
  — Damage Assessment
  — Search & Rescue
  — Medical Assistance
  — Donation Management
  — Restoration each ESF (Emergency Support Functions)
  — Relief Camps Team

The Indian Earthquake Safety Initiative

Around 54 per cent area of the Indian Institute of Public Administration territory is prone to earthquakes. Some of the major cities of the country fall in this seismically active zone. These cities, due to higher population densities and other developments are very much susceptible to adverse impacts of earthquakes. A major earthquake in such area may result into havoc. Keeping this in view, the project—IndESI has been started in India with USAID. The project aims to assess earthquake risk of 20 most vulnerable cities of India. It is a cooperative agreement between USAID and Geo-Hazard International (GHI). This project is initiated to reduce the consequences of earthquakes in India's major cities by strengthening the capacity of local organizations to prepare for and respond to earthquakes and to identify those activities with greatest risk, raise awareness about this risk and to be implemented in a "Self-sustainable" manner. IndESI is to strengthen the capacity of the national and local governments, and of NGOs to prepare for and respond to future earthquakes. It has also to launch potentially self-sustaining mitigation activities by local organizations in 5 of the project cities. IndESI evaluates a city's earthquake risk, the sources of that risk and effectiveness of various mitigation options. The evaluation method of IndESI is done through the data collected from local studies of Seismology, Soil and Land-types, City Planning, Building Inventory, School Buildings, Emergency Response, City Medical Preparedness, Hospital Preparedness and Fire Preparedness. The organizations like GHI, SEEDS, UNCRD, NCDM and Policy and Technical Advisory Groups are actively involved in IndESI.

Standard Operating Procedure (SOP)

In general, disaster in an area results into a state of shock and confusion. To recover from this state takes some time; which is very precious and crucial, as far as the rescue and relief operations are concerned.

Standard Operation Procedure (SOP) or Trigger Mechanism (tm) has been envisaged as a preparedness plan whereby the receipt of a signal of an impending disaster would simultaneously energise and activate the procedure for response and mitigation without loss of crucial time. SOP would entail all the Disaster Managers to know in advance the task assigned to them. Identification of available resources including manpower, material, equipment and adequate delegation of financial and administrative powers are pre requisites to successful procedure of SOP or TM.

SOP is a process to ensure the implementation of response activities on ground after a disaster. Response activities such as evacuation, search and rescue, temporary shelter, food, clothing, drinking water, health and sanitation, communications, accessibility and public information which are important units of Disaster Management would follow on the activation of the Trigger Mechanism. Trigger Mechanism (tm) and SOP, two view points are in essence the same.

The response activities are common to all types of disasters and require sub-division and preparation of sub-action plans by each specified authority. Some aspects of SOP or TM for the Disasters managers are to:

- Evolve an effective signal/warning procedure
- Identify activities and their levels along with sub activities under each activity
- Specify authorities for each level of activity and sub-activity.
- Determine the response time for each activity.
- Workout individual plans of each specified authority to achieve activation as per the response time.
- Have Quick Response Teams for each specified authority as well as alternative plans & contingency measures.

- Provide appropriate administrative and financial delegation to make the response procedure functionally viable.
- Undergo preparedness drills

This SOP or TM has been incorporated by the High Powered Committee (HPC) as an emergency quick response mechanism or procedure, which would spontaneously set the vehicle of management into motion on the road to disaster mitigation process at national & state levels.

2
DISASTERS - GLOBAL TREND

Disasters in World

Disasters, natural or man-made are common through out the world. However their adverse impact on the land and society are not uniform. While on one hand the developing countries are worst affected in terms of fatality, on other hand the developed countries observe tremendous property loss due to these catastrophes. The major loss due to disasters is observed in terms of human life loss. The figures in the table 2.1 elaborate about the fatality caused due to various forms of disasters in five continents. The figures clearly reveal that between 1973 and 1997, i.e., in a quarter century, average annual human life loss has been maximum in most undeveloped continent of Africa followed by Asia (Fig. 2.2).

This clarifies that the loss due to hazard is a direct function of the vulnerability or susceptibility of the people and the region, where it strikes. Along with natural causes, the poor people of the developing countries, are more vulnerable to the adverse impact of hazards and consequently at more risk due to various human induced factors (to be discussed in succeeding text).

Fig. 2.1 : Relation between Natural Disasters and Human being

Table 2.1 : Life Loss, continentwise due to disasters (between 1973 and 1997)

	Africa	America	Asia	Europe	Oceania	Total
1973-1977	84413	8519	68454	2318	107	163811
1978-1982	1436	3172	16529	1406	35	22579
1983-1987	115269	10853	17073	2302	189	145686
1988-1992	12272	5248	63345	2352	138	83445
1993-1997	7919	3065	19078	1996	149	32206
1973-1997	44262	6171	36914	2075	124	89546

Source : World Disaster Report, 1999

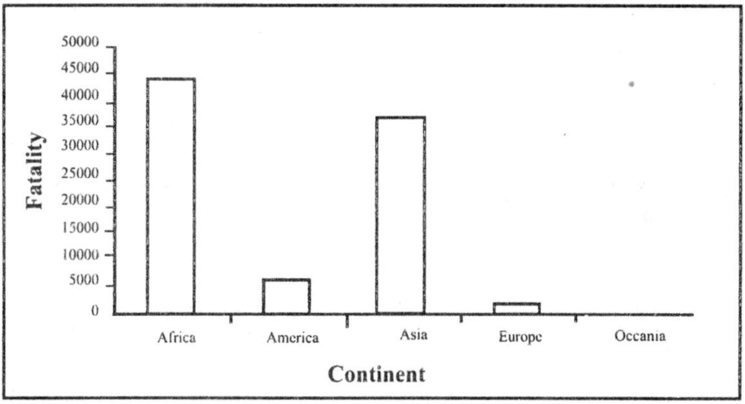

Fig 2.2: Annual average number of people killed by region and period. Average number of fatalities are maximum in developing continents i.e. Asia and Africa.

Source : World Disaster Report, 1999.

Trend in Economic Losses

In the second half of the 20th century, more than 200 worst natural disasters hit different parts of the world and claimed the lives of 1.4 million people. The major causalities (around 90% in total) were due to two types of disasters, i.e., flood and wind storm. The economic losses were primarily due to the earthquake, flood and windstorm (35 per cent, 30 per cent and 28 per cent respectively). (Table 2.2)

Table 2.2 : Number of disasters and economic losses and their trend in the second half of 20th century

	Decade 1950-1959	Decade 1960-1969	Decade 1970-1979	Decade 1980-1989	Decade 1990-1999
Number	20	27	47	63	82
Economic Losses (in US billion $)	38.5	69	124.2	192.9	535.8

	Factor 90s:80s	**Factor 90s:70s**	**Factor 90s:60s**	**Factor 90s:50s**
Number	1.3	1.7	3.0	4.1
Economic Losses	2.8	4.3	7.8	13.9

Source : Munichener Ruck of Munich Re Groups Report.

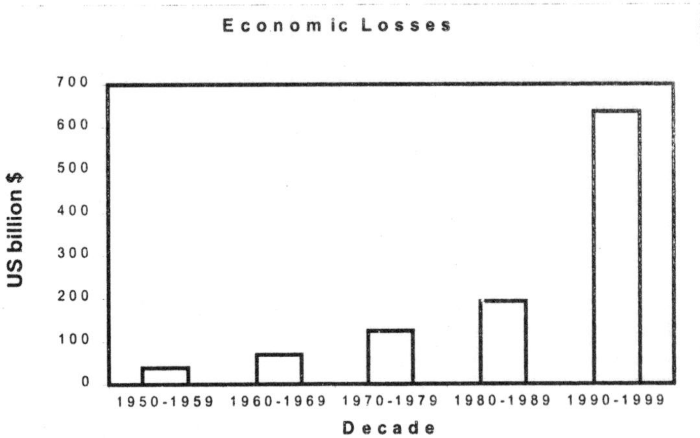

Fig. 2.3 : Economic losses due to disasters during the last five decades.

1. During the 20th century there has been significant increase in the number and quantum of economic losses due to natural catastrophes.
2. In numerical value while the number of natural catastrophe during the decade 1990-99 has been 4.1 times more, the economic loss during the same period has increased 13.9 times.
3. While the maximum fatalities were observed in developing countries, the developed countries experienced the major economic losses.

World Disasters : Some Facts and Figures

In its special issues "topics-2000" and "topics-2001", the Munichener Ruck of Munich Re Group, Germany and World Disaster Report-2002, published by International Federation of Red Cross and Red Crescent Societies have brought many important facts and figures about the disasters throughout the world (Annexure II to X). The most significant among them are as follows:

1. During the last fifty years there were about 234 natural catastrophes. Numberwise the windstorms have been maximum (89 in numbers) followed by earthquakes (68) and floods (63).
2. Out of estimated 1.4 million fatalities, the earthquakes were on the top claiming around 47 per cent of the total casualties, followed by wind storms and floods (45 and 7 per cent respectively) (Fig. 2.4).

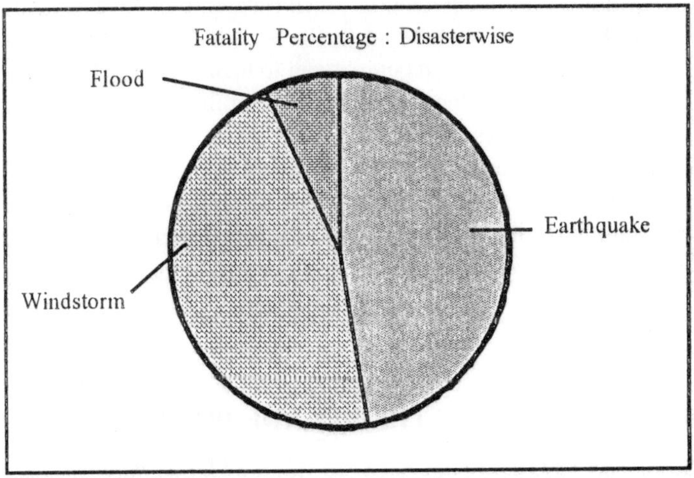

Fig. 2.4 : Fatality due to disasters, phenomenonwise.

3. Out of these three most common types of natural catastrophes, the earthquakes caused maximum economic loss claiming around 35 per cent of the total (Fig 2.5).

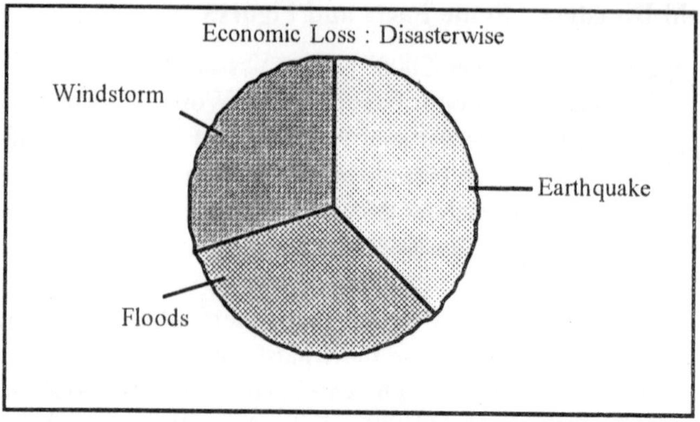

Fig. 2.5 : Economic losses due to various disaster phenomena.

4. The floods and the windstorm have been at number two and three respectively, causing around 30 and 28 per cent of the loss.
5. The most significant feature, which is clear from the data analysis is that losses to human and cattle life had been much higher in developing countries in comparison to their western counterparts. The reason being the increased vulnerability of the poor people of these countries.
6. During the second half of the last century, a significant increase has been observed in the number as well as in losses due to natural hazard . In comparison to the first decade of half century, i.e., the decade 1950-59, the last decade 1990-1999 has shown an increase of 4.1 times in number and 13.9 times more in term of economic losses.

DISASTERS DURING THE DECADE 1992-2001

The decade 1992-2001 has been the worst as far as the disasters are concerned. During this period, 6,22,363 people lost their lives due to one or the other form of disasters. Economically also the decade proved very disastrous and properties almost worth US$ 6,94,424 million were damaged by these disasters. World Disaster Report 2002 compiled different data about the various forms of disasters through out the world. The compiled data depict many significant features, being discussed in the succeeding section of the chapter.

I. Disasters by Continent and by Year:

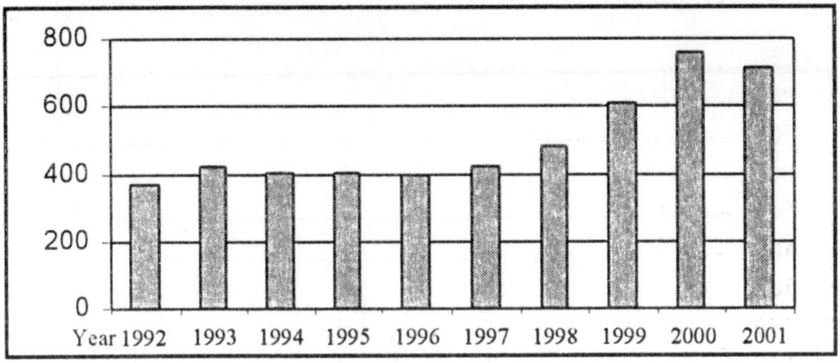

Fig. 2.6 : Number of disasters, year-wise.

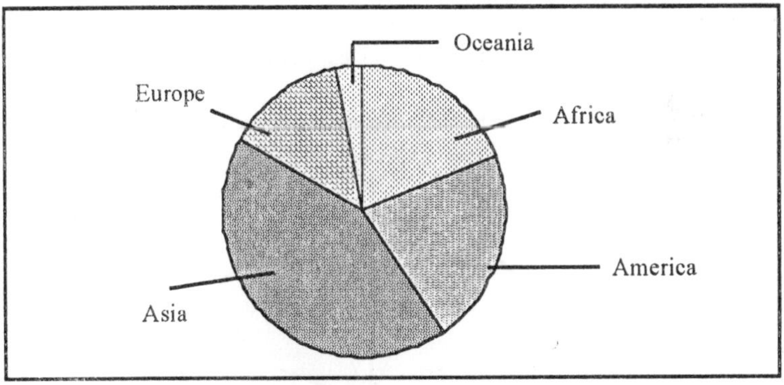

Fig. 2.7 : Number of disasters by continent

1. In all, 4,989 disasters did hit the world during the last decade.
2. During the decade, continent-wise Asia was the worst affected (total 2,128 disasters) (Fig. 2.7).
3. America was the second worst affected with total 1,071 disasters.
4. The number of disasters showed an increasing trend during the decade (Fig. 2.6) (368 in 1992 to 712 in 2001).
5. Year 2000 was marked by maximum number of disasters.
6. Development-wise the countries classified as the Medium Human Development (MHD) Index, were hit by the maximum number of disasters followed by countries with High Human Development (HHD) Index.
7. Asia remains the continent, most frequently struck by disasters, with 42.6 per cent of the total number of recorded events during the decade 1992- 2001 (Fig. 2.7).
8. Countries classed as MHD accounted for more than half of the decade's disasters.

II. People Killed by Disasters, by Continent, by Year and by Development

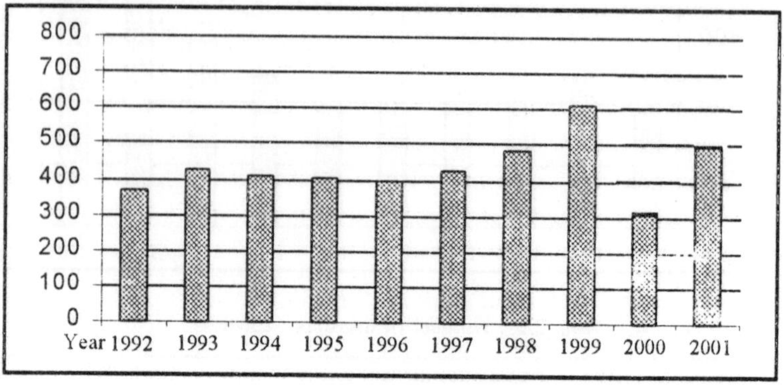

Fig. 2.8 : People killed, year-wise

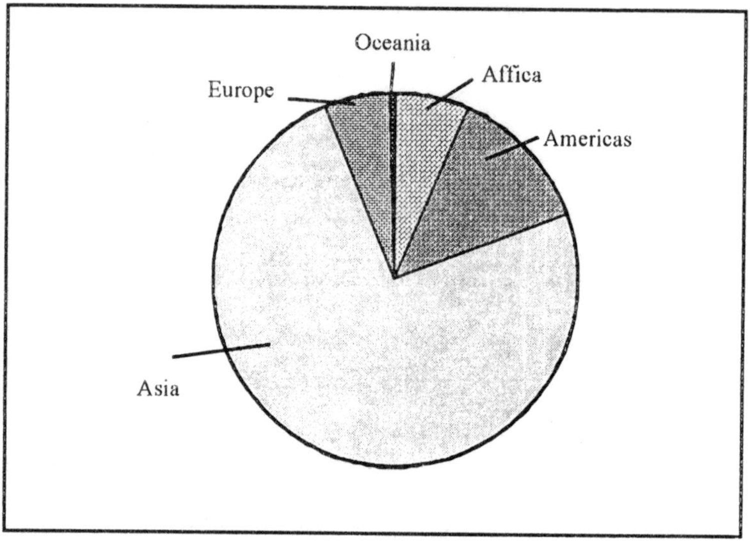

Fig. 2.9 : People killed, continent-wise

1. During the decade around 6,22,363 people were killed by various forms of disasters through out the world.

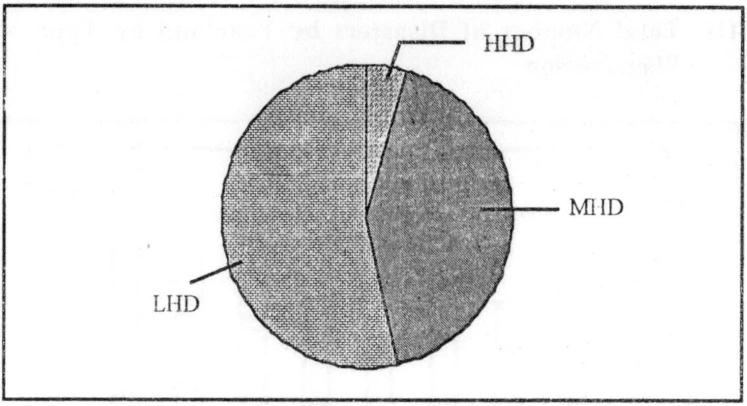

Fig. 2.10 : People killed in various development categories.

2. Out of the total number of people killed, 74.5 per cent are from Asia alone (Fig. 2.9).

3. There has been an increasing trend in death toll from 1992 to 1999. However the year 2000 and 2001 showed comparatively a decreasing trend (Fg. 2.8).

4. A significant link has been observed in the development and death toll. Though the Low Human Development (LHD) countries are hit by only 1/5th of total number of disasters, the death toll in these countries has been more than half of the world (Fis. 2.10).

5. On an average thirteen times more people died per reported disaster in LHD countries.

6. With HHD countries , the life loss has been very less, i.e., only 4.4 per cent of the total death toll in the world.

III. Total Number of Disasters by Year and by Type of Phenomenon

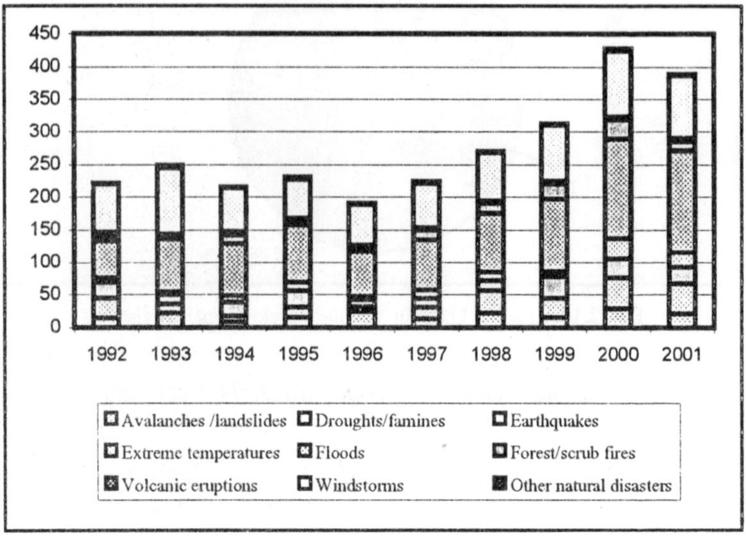

Fig. 2.11 : Total number of disasters during decade 1992-2001

1. Out of total around 4,989 disasters, around 1/5th, i.e., total 963 have been flood related (Fig. 2.11).
2. Windstorm, with total number of 783 has been second in position.
3. The floods showed a continuous increase in the number since 1992.
4. The total number of technological disasters increased significanly during the decade and almost doubled (147 in 1992 to 323 in 2001).
5. Although the number of hydro-meteorological disasters since 1996 has more than doubled, the year 2001 saw a slight decline in numbers.
6. The extreme temperature related events have shown tremendous increase in the number of events since 1992 (7 in 1992 to 31and 22 during the years 2000 and 2001 respectively).

IV. Total Number of People Killed by Disasters, by Type of Phenomenon and by Year

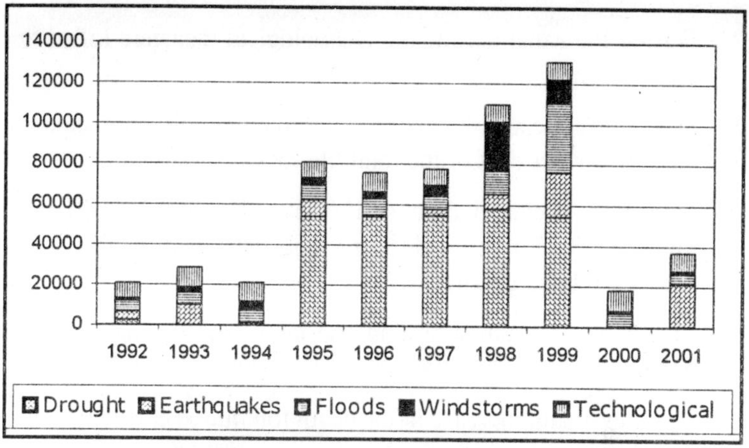

Fig. 2.12 : Number of people killed by year

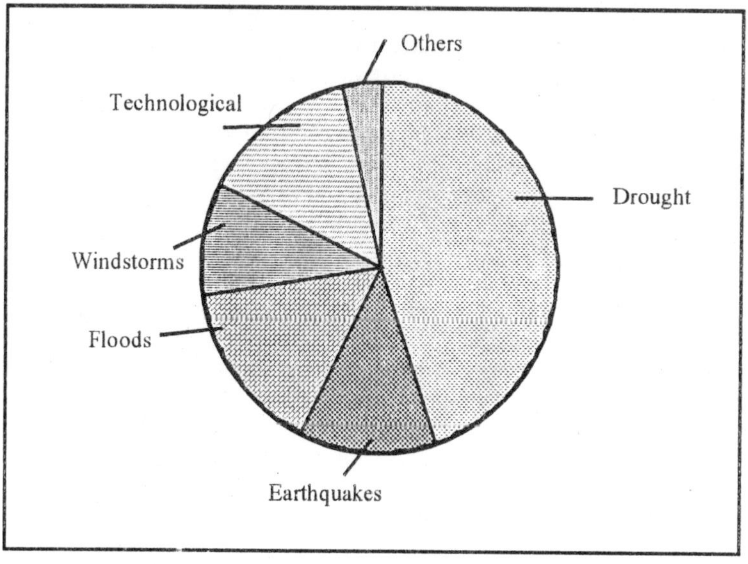

Fig. 2.13 : Percentage fatality due to type of phenomenon

1. During the decade, natural disasters (hydro-meteorological and geo-physical disasters) killed a reported 534, 416 persons, accounting for more than 86 per cent of the total death toll .
2. During the same decade the technological disasters killed 86, 947 persons.
3. During the decade, the hydro-meteorological disasters claimed around 71 per cent of the total life loss.
4. During the decade maximum life loss has been due to drought, i.e., total 2,77,574 people were reported killed by this water scarcity related disaster.
5. Floods alone claimed around one lakh lives during the same period.
6. The significant increase in the death toll due to earthquake has been as a result of massive life loss during the Gujarat tremors in the year 2001.
7. The drought claimed more than half of life lost in the five consecutive years from 1995 to 1999.

V. Disaster Estimated Damage Yearwise by Type of Phemomenon

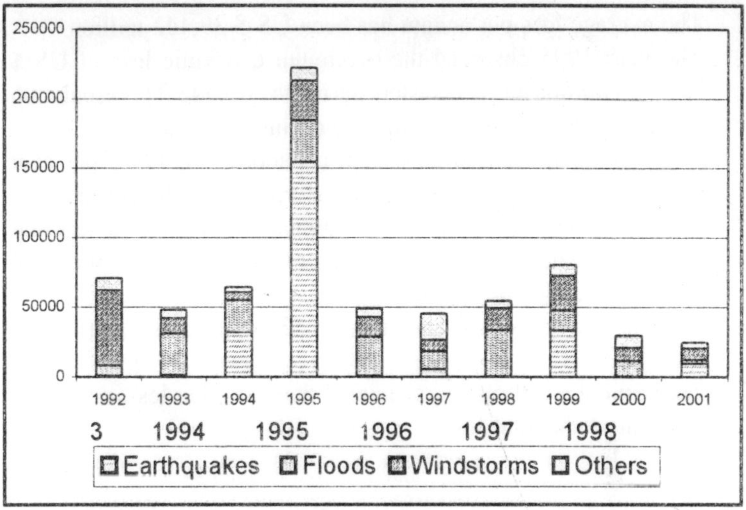

Fig. 2.14 : Damage in US million $ by different types of disasters

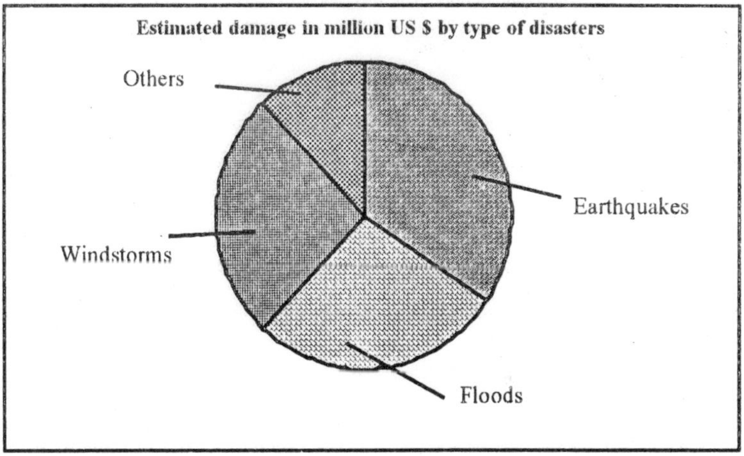

Fig. 2.15 : Percentage property damage by different categories of disasters

1. During the decade there was total US $ 6,94,424 million (2001 pricing) loss due to various forms of disasters through out the world
2. The average loss per annum has been US $ 39,442 million.
3. The year 1995 observed the maximum economic loss of US $ 222,539 million due to disasters during the decade. This escalation in loss has been due to earthquake during the year.
4. The earthquake caused maximum economic loss (34.2 per cent of the total loss by all types of disasters) during the decade.
5. Next to earthquake it was the hydro-meteorological disasters that claimed the heavy economical loss of 64 per cent of the total economic loss of the decade.
6. Flood and windstorm claimed about 53 per cent loss during the decade.
7. The technological disasters claimed the minimum loss, only 1.44 per cent of the total loss.

VI. Total Number of People killed by Disasters, Continent-wise and by Phenomenon

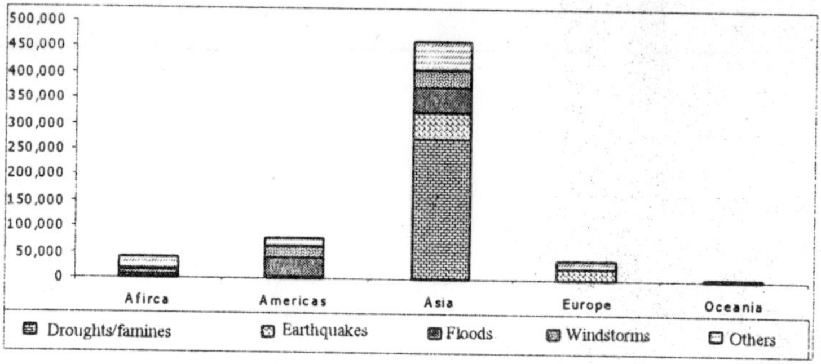

Fig. 2.16 : Number of people killed continentwise and by phenomenon

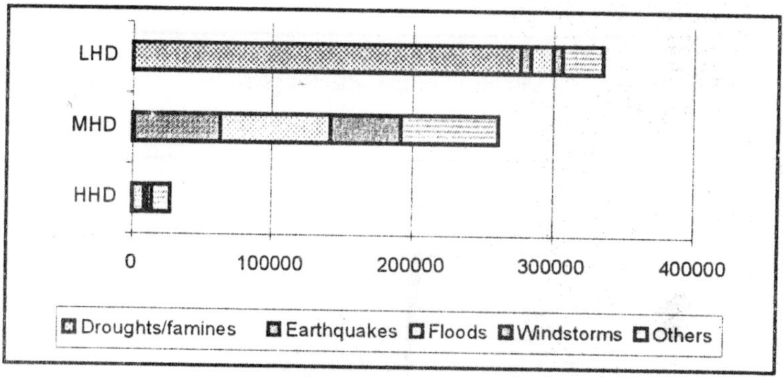

Fig. 2.17 : Number of people killed by development categories and by phenomenon

1. Asia remains the most affected continent by both natural (39 per cent) and technological disasters (47 per cent). In both Africa and Asia, technological disasters outnumbered natural catastrophes
2. Out of total death toll during the decade around 44.6 per cent were due to drought or famine.
3. About 74.5 per cent of the total people killed are from Asia alone (Fig. 2.16).
4. Around 99.6 per cent of the total death toll due to drought or famine disasters is reported from the LHD countries (Fig 2.17).
5. In general the maximum death toll from other forms of disasters (more than 50 per cent) has been reported from LHD countries.
6. The death toll due to earthquakes, floods, windstorms and technological disasters were maximum in the MHD countries (79.7, 81.5, 82.9 and 59.3 per cent respectively).
7. The minimum life loss has been in HHD countries which accounted for only 4.4 per cent of the total life loss.

VII. Total Number of People Reported Affected by Disasters, Continentwise and Yearwise

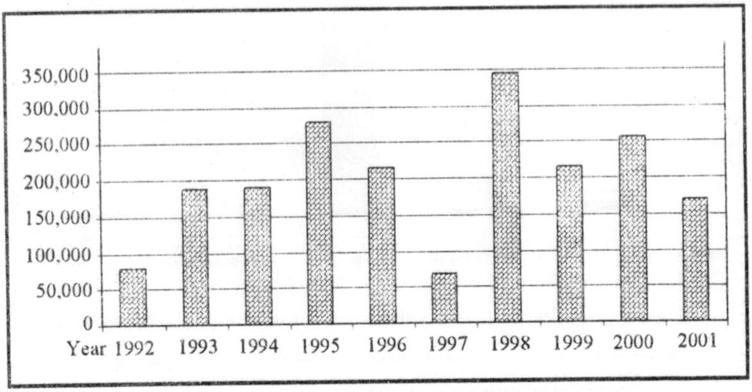

Fig. 2.18 : Total number of people affected year-wise by disasters

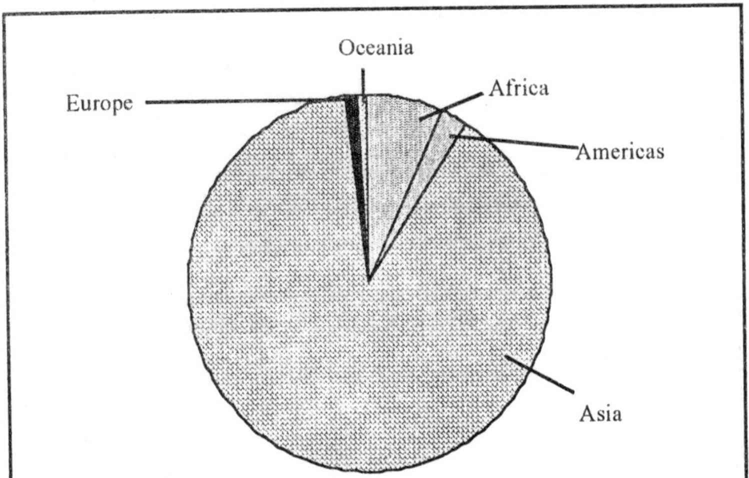

Fig. 2.19 : Number of people affected, continent-wise

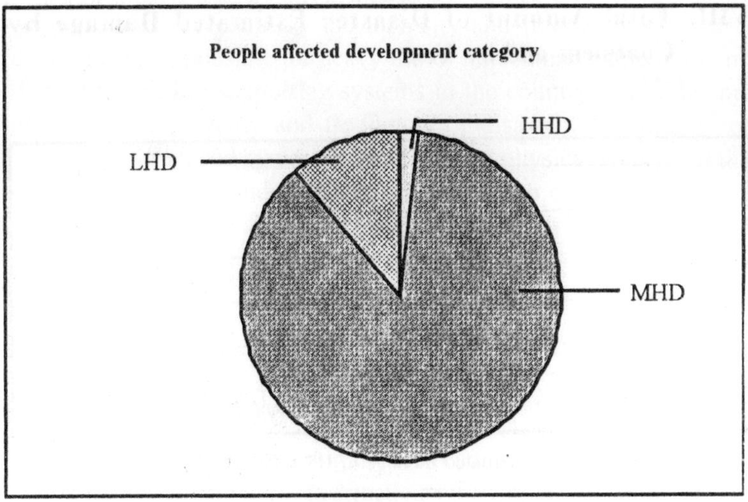

Fig. 2.20 : Number of people affected development-wise.

1. Globally on an average, 200 million people per year were affected by disasters during the decade. Year 1998 was the worst during this decade (Fig. 2.18).
2. During the decade, hydro- meteorological disasters affected the greatest number of the people, (98 per cent of the total affected) people. Flood alone affected around 63 per cent.
3. During the decade, total number of affected people by disasters were more than 2 billion.
4. The maximum number of affected people as reported were during the year 1998 (17.2 per cent).
5. The three consecutive years i.e., 1998, 1999 and 2000 experienced maximum affected people (around 40.7 per cent of total).
6. Among the continents , the people of the Asia were maximum in number to be affected by the disasters during the decade. A total number of 1,774, 841 thousands of people were affected accounting for more than 88.67 per cent of the total world population affected (Fig 2.19).
7. Flood in Asia alone represents 61 per cent of the total number of affected people by disasters.
8. Around 86.5 per cent of the total affected people were from the MHD countries.

VIII. Total Amount of Disaster Estimated Damage by Continent and by Year

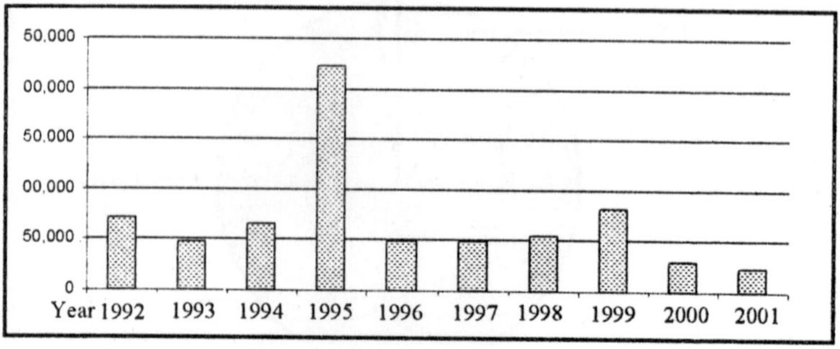

Fig. 2.21 : Estimated damage in US million $, yearwise

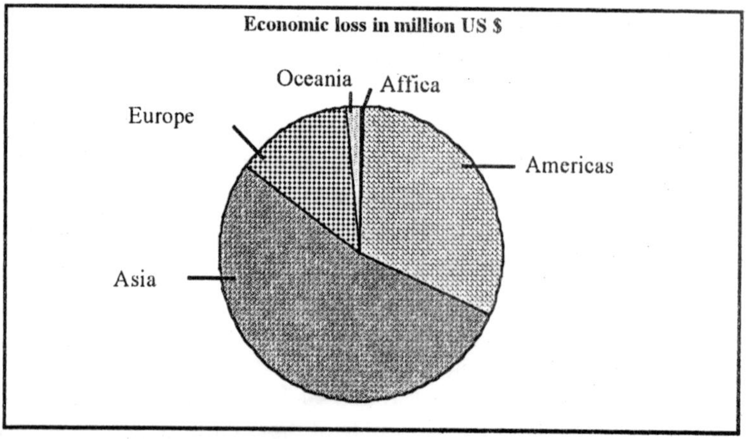

Fig. 2.22 : Economic losses, continent-wise

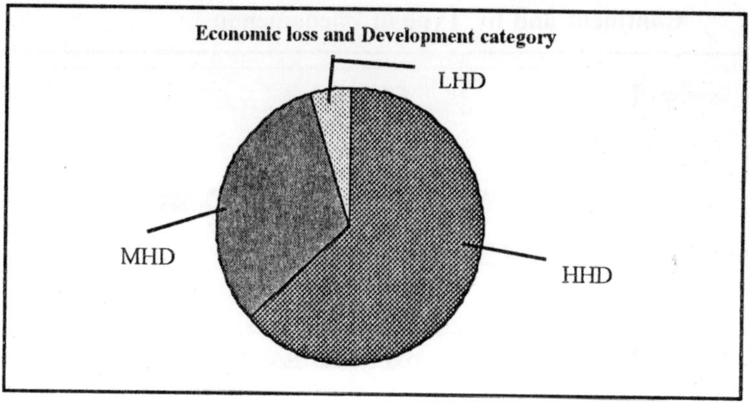

Fig. 2.23 : Economic losses, developmentwise

1. Out of total US $ 694,424 million, the maximum damage was reported from the Asian countries accounting for around 53.5 per cent of the total loss (Fig. 2.22).
2. The countries with HHD were worst affected as far as the economic losses were concerned.
3. The HHD countries accounted for around 63 per cent of the total damage during the decade.
4. The countries with LHD, though accounting for more than 54 per cent of the total death toll, were affected by economic losses of only 5.04 per cent of the total damage (Fig 2.23).
5. The economic loss though did not show any significant trend during the decade, yet two years, i.e., 1995 (32 per cent) and 1999 (11.7 per cent) were economically worst affected by the disasters (Fig. 2.21).
6. After Asia it was the America that observed the maximum loss during the decade, i.e., total US $ 216, 516 millions (Fig. 2.22).
7. Earthquakes and windstorms in HHD countries accounted for 29 per cent and 19 per cent respectively of the total economic loss.

IX. Total Amount of Disaster Estimated Damage, by Continent and by Type of Phenomenon

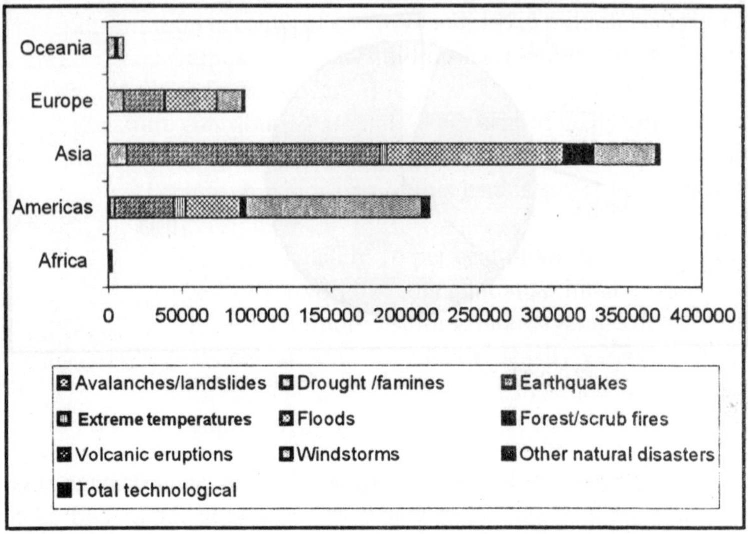

Fig. 2.24 : Total amount of disaster estimated damage continentwise and by phenomenon (in millions of US$ 2001 Prices)

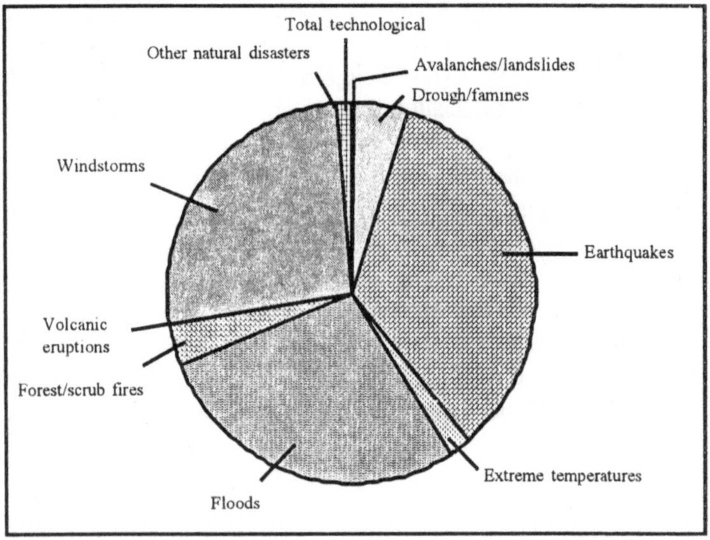

Fig. 2.25 : Estimated damage, phenomenon-wise

1. Economically earthquakes, floods and windstorms caused maximum loss during the decade (Fig. 2.25).
2. Throughout the world maximum loss during the decade was caused by earthquakes, followed by floods and windstorms.
3. Windstorm caused maximum damage in the American continent, whereas earthquakes and floods caused maximum loss in Asia and Europe.
4. Technological disasters resulted more economic loss in America in comparison to other continents.
5. Among the various forms of disasters, floods were responsible for maximum economic loss in Europe, whereas in Oceania it was the drought (Fig. 2.24).

Some Other Facts About Disasters:

1. During the decade 1992-2001. Natural 'Disasters (hydro-meteorological and geo-physical disasters) killed a reported 535.416 people accounting for 86 per cent of all deaths due to disasters. Technological disasters killed 86,947 people during the same period. Although the number of hydro-meteroogical disasters since 1996 has more than doubled. 2001 saw a slight decline in numbers (357 down from the peak of 393 in 2000).
2. During the same decade, 1992-2001, continent-wise Asia was worst affected (no. 2128), followed by America (no. 1071). The number of disasters showed an incresing trend (368 in 1992 to 712 in 2001).
3. For the decade, the hydro-meteorological disasters claimed around 71 per cent of the total death toll.
4. One more significant feature that emerged out of the report is the relation of death toll with the development. Though the Low Human Development (LHD) countries have accounted for just one-fifth of the total number of disasters, yet the death toll in these countries was more than half of the total fatalities. On an average thirteen times more people died per reported disaster in LHD countries.
5. Of the total number of people killed by disasters (during 1992 to 2001), 74.5 per cent were in the Asia. More than half of the fatalities occurred in nations of the LHD, with HHD countries accounting for only 4.4 per cent of deaths.
6. Though the fatality was more in LHD and MHD countries, the economic loss, around 63 per cent of estimated damage is reported in nations of HHD, due to higher valued infrastructure. LHD nations reported just 5 per cent of the estimated damage.
7. There has been very significant increase in technological disasters over the decade, from 147 in 1992 to 323 in 2001.
8. During the decade, hydro-meterological disasters accounted for 64 per cent of the decade's estimated damage from natural and technologocal disasters. compared to 34 per cent from geo-physical disasters and 2 per cent from technological disasters.
9. More than half of the people killed were from during the decade LHD countries.
10. Earthquakes and windstroms in HHD countries accounted for respectively 29 per cent and 19 per cent of total amount of estimated loss. In LHD countries, estimated damage accounts to only 5 per cent of the total. However the fatalities in these countries represent 54 per cent of the global deaths.

Disasters During 2001

During the year 2001, the major observations made in the World Disaster Report are as follows:

1. A total of 39,073 people were reported killed by disasters in 2001. While this was double than the figure of the previous year, it was lower than the decade's annual average of around 62000.
2. Most of the fatalities for the 2001 were reported from the medium human development (MHD) countries.
3. During 2001, earthquake proved to be the deadliest disaster, accounting for more than 50 per cent of the year's toll. During the year more than 13,000 people were reported to be killed alone in Gujarat earthquake.
4. During the year 2001, a total of 170 million people were reported affected by disasters, below the decade's average of 200 million.
5. The total amount of estimated damage inflicted by disasters during the year 2001 was US $ 24 billion (the decade's lowest and well below the annual average of US $ 69 billion.

Disasters in India

Due to its geographical position, climate and geological setting, India is among the top ten countries in terms of life loss due to natural disasters every year. As per the World Disaster Report 2002, during the last two decades (1982-2001), around 10,7813 people were killed due to disasters (on an average of around 5340 people per year) in the couuntry. During the same period, more than 110 crore population of the country was affected by these disasters. The death toll rose more than double. During the decade (1992-2001), the heavy loss of life has been due to large scale disasters i.e. Orissa cyclone of 1999 and Gujarat earthquake in the year 2001.

The country is highly vulnerable to droughts, floods, cyclones, avalanches, forest fire, and landslides. Out of 35 states/union territories in the country, 27 are disaster-prone. This sub-continent is amongst the world's most disaster-prone areas with:

>55 per cent of the total country land vulnerable to earthquake,
Eight per cent area prone to cyclones,
Five per cent vulnerable to floods, and
Fifty per cent forest cover is fire prone.

Out of 27 disaster-prone states / union territories, one state (West Bengal) of the country is prone to four common disasters — flood, drought, cyclone and earthquakes, six face three types of disasters, thirteen face two types fo disasters and seven states face one type of disasters. Thus in brief, almost each and every part of the country is prone to one or the other type of disaster.

Table 2.3 : India's Disaster Vulnerability

State/Union Territory (UT)	Drought	Flood	Cyclone	Earthquake	Total
Andhra Pradesh	Yes	Yes	Yes	No	3
Arunachal Pradesh	No	Yes	No	Yes	2
Assam	No	Yes	No	Yes	2
Bihar	Yes	Yes	No	Yes	3
Chhatishgarh	Yes	No	No	No	1
Gujarat	Yes	No	No	No	1
Haryana	Yes	No	No	No	1
Himachal Pradesh	No	Yes	No	Yes	2
Jammu & Kashmir	Yes	Yes	No	No	2
Jharkhand	Yes	No	No	No	1
Karnataka	Yes	No	No	No	1
Madhya Pradesh	Yes	No	No	No	1
Maharashtra	Yes	Yes	No	Yes	3
Manipur	No	Yes	No	Yes	2
Meghalaya	No	Yes	No	Yes	2
Mizoram	No	Yes	No	Yes	2
Nagaland	No	Yes	No	Yes	2
Orissa	Yes	Yes	Yes	No	3
Punjab	Yes	Yes	No	Yes	3
Rajasthan	Yes	No	No	No	1
Sikkim	No	Yes	No	Yes	2
Tamilnadu	Yes	No	Yes	No	2
Tripura	No	Yes	No	Yes	2
Uttar Pradesh	Yes	Yes	No	Yes	3
Uttaranchal	No	Yes	No	Yes	2
West Bengal	Yes	Yes	Yes	Yes	4
Andaman & Nicobar (UT)	No	Yes	Yes	No	2
Totals:	14	18	5	14	

(Source : Indu Prakash, *Disaster Management)*

In the recent past the frequency of natural disasters in India has increased drastically. Earthquakes of Gujarat, Chamoli, Jabalpur, and Latur; landslides in Garhwal and Kumaon; cyclones of Gujarat, Andhra Pradesh and Orissa; tornadoes of Balasore and Midnapore, etc., are some of the examples of recent catastrophes in India. Natural disasters in the country are resulting into colossal loss to life and property. The Tables 2.4 and 2.5 give an idea about the annual damage caused due to disasters in the country:

Table 2.4 : Annual Damage due to Disasters

Year	Number of people affected (in crores)	Number of houses and building partially or totally damaged	Amount of property damage (Rs. in crore)
1990	3.17	1019930	171.0
1991	3.477	1190109	190.0
1992	1.909	570969	205.0
1993	2.624	1529916	580.0
1994	2.353	1051223	183.0
1995	5.435	2088355	473.0
1996	5.499	2376693	543.0
1997	4.438	1103549	n.a.
1998	5.217	1563405	n.a.
1999	5.017	3104064	n.a.
2000	4.162	2736355	1020.90
2001	7.882	846878	12000

(*Source :* Ministry of Agriculture)

Table 2.5 : Annual Damage due to Heavy Rains, Landslide and Floods

Year	Districts affected	Villages affected (No)	Population affected (Lakh)	Affected Crop Area (Lakh Ha.)	Houses Damaged (No.)	Human life loss (No.)	Cattle loss (no.	Estimated value of loss to houses (Rs. in crore)	Estimated value of Public properties (Rs. in crore)
1999	202	33,158	328.12	8.45	884,823	1,375	3,861	0.72	
2000	200	29.964	416.24	34.79	2,736,355	3,048	102,121	631.25	389.72
2001	122	32,363	210.71	18.72	346,878	834	21,269	195.57	676.05

Source: Annual Reports of the Natural Disaster Management Division, Ministry of Agriculture.

Floods,earthquakes, cyclones, hailstorms, etc., are the most frequently occurring natural disasters in the country. During the year 2000-2001, the country faced the most severe earthquake in the known history claiming around 13,000 lives. In the same year, the loss of the life due to floods was also very high and about 3,000 people were killed by this natural calamity in different parts of the country (Table 2.6).

Table 2.6 : Loss of Human Lives due to various types of Disasters in India (Yearwise)

Year	Flood	Cyclone/ flood	Hailstorm	Earthquake	Total
1990-91	1320	979	—	—	2299
1991-92	1185	304	—	768	2257
1992-93	1193	497	—	—	1690
1993-94	1690	318	—	7938	9946
1994-95	2038	247	59	—	2344
1995-96	2072	361	31	—	2464
1996-97	2069	1719	40	—	3828
1997-98	1560	216	247	39	2062
1998-99	2567	1292	—	106	3965
1999-2000	1896	10589	—	—	12585
2000-2001	3048	—	—	13000	16048

Source: Ministry of Agriculture.

Among common form of disasters, while floods are the annually occurring phenomenon, earthquake is the most damaging. January 26, 2001 earthquake in Gujarat has not only shaken the entire country, the colossal loss due to this natural calamity has been as the worst in the learning history of the country. The impact of this natural hazard is so sudden and unwarned that its prediction and making preparation to save life and property become almost impossible. As already mentioned, 55 per cent area of the country is prone to earthquake. Out of this—

(a) 12 per cent area is prone to severe earthquakes such as of Gujarat;
(b) 18 per cent area is susceptible to earthquakes like in Latur / Uttaranchal; and

Table 2.7 : Major documented earthquakes in the Country

Year	Area	Date	IST time hr. m.s.	Mag-nitude M	Deaths
1819	Gujarat (Kutch)	Jan 16	Midnight	8.0	Several thousand
1833	Bihar	Aug 26	—	7.7	Hundreds
1897	Assam (Shillong)	Jun 12	16:36	8.7	1,600
1900	Kerala (Palghat)	Feb 8	—	6.6	
1905	Himachal Pradesh (Kangra)	Apr 4	6:20	8.0	20,000
1930	Assam (Dhubri)	Jul 3	02:33:34	7.1	Many
1934	Bihar - Nepal	Jan 15	14:13:26	8.3	14,000
1941	Andamans	Jan 26	—	8.0	Many
1943	Assam (NE)	Oct 23	22:53:17	7.2	
1950	Assam (NE)	aug 15	19:39:28	8.6	1,500
1956	Gujarat (Anjar)	Jul 21	21:02:36	7.0	Hundreds
1956	U.P. (Bullandshahar)	Oct 10	—	6.7	Many
1958	U.P.	Dec 28	—	6.3	Many
1960	Delhi	Aug 27	21:28:59	6.0	
1963	Kashmir (Badgam)	Sep 2	07:04:32	5.5	Hundreds
1966	Western Nepal	Jun 27	—	6.3	
1966	U.P. (Moradabad)	Aug 15	—	5.3	
1967	Nicobar	Jul 2	—	6.2	
1967	Maharashtra (Koyna)	Dec 11	04:21:19	6.5	200
1970	Andhra Pradesh (Bhadrachalam)	Apr 13	—	6.5	
1970	Gujarat (Broach)	Mar 23	07:23:03	5.7	
1975	Himachal Pradesh	Jan 19	—	6.5	
1988	Bihar-Nepal	Aug 21	04:39:10	6.6	1,003
1991	Uttar Pradesh (Uttarkashi)	Oct 20	02:53	6.6	715
1993	Maharashtra (Killari)	Sep 30	03:55:47	6.3	7,928
1997	Jabalpur	May 22	04:22:31	6.0	38
1999	Chamoli	March 29	12.35	6.8	103
2001	Gujarat	Jan 26	8.45	7.9	>13,000

(c) 25 per cent area is exposed to relatively less severe erthquakes as in Jabalpur and its adjoining areas.

In India, flood is the second most severe natural hazard, affecting one or the other part of the country every year. The basic main cause of flood in the country is unevenly distributed and period specific rainfall. The country receives an annual rainfall of 1200 mm, 85 per cent of which is concentrated in four months, i.e., June to September. Due to this intense and period specific rain, all rivers of the country are fed with huge quantity of water, much beyond their carrying capacity As a result of deforestation and other unscientific developments in hilly regions, the problem of sedimentation during rain has increased tremendously. The carrying capacity of the rivers is further reduced due to sedimentation and drainage congestion. In all, country's 40 million hectares land is prone to floods and 8 million hectares on an average is annually affected by floods. Every year almost 8 to 10 million hectares area is flooded, which causes great loss to life, crops, property and environment. Floods occur very frequently in Ganges basin in north and north-eastern part and Bramhaputra basin in the eastern part of the country.

Landslide, the down slope movement of earth or surface material due to gravitational forces is very common natural disaster in the country's hill terrain. Whole of the Himalayan region experiences landslide damage. Along with the Himalayan hill ranges, Western Ghats also frequently observe this disaster of varying intensities. The earthquakes in Himalayan region also trigger major landslides. The environmental degradation due to deforestation has further intensified the problem to landslides in the hilly regions. The heavy monsoon rain and cyclones in Western Ghats cause intensive landslide calamities. Landslides along with resulting extensive loss to life and property also create damage to various infrastructures like roads, bridges and other means of communication. In recent years, landslides have become an annual phenomenon during rainy season in Himalayan region.

Cyclone in the coastal area of the country is the most disastrous natural calamity, claiming huge life loss and property damage. These cyclones are created by intense low-pressure areas in the atmosphere, due to which wind blows with a very high speed in circular motion resulting into cyclones. Horizontally this area extends from 500-1,000 km and vertically from surface to 12-14 km above. India with a long coastline of 8,041 km is exposed to on an average 5-6 tropical cyclones annually from the Bay of Bengal and Arabian Sea. Cyclones are very common in pre-monsoon (May-June) and post-monsoon (October - November) seasons in the country. Andhra Pradesh (1996), Gujarat (1998) and Orissa (1999) are the recent cyclones which caused colossal

Table 2.8 : Damage due to Cyclone in Orissa

Date of occur-rence	Total no of districts	Districts affected	Villages affected (No)	Population affected (Lakh)	Crop Area affected (Lakh ha)	Houses Damaged (no.	Human life loss (no.)	Cattle loss (no.)
17-18.10.99	30	4	5,181	37.47	1.58	331,580	199	10,578
29-30.10.99	30	12	14,643	129.22	18.43	1,828,532	9,887	444,531

Table 2.9 : Worst Cyclones documented in India

Year	Death
1737	3 lakhs
1833	50000
1847	75000
1864	50000
1974	80000
1946	750
1971	10000
1973	5000
1977	10000
1979	700
1990	928
1998	1261
1999	10086

loss to life and property (Table 2.8). The other damaging cyclones that hit the country coast are shown in Table 2.9.

Drought, occurred due to less than average rain fall, decreasing water bearing capacity of the land (due to incresed salinity and deforestation), damaged natural drainage pattern, etc. is the most common type of disaster, experienced in the States of Rajasthan, Guajarat, Madhya Pradesh. Chhatisgarh, Bihar, Jharkhand, West Bengal, Orissa, Andhra Pradesh, Tamil Nadu and Karnataka. Around fifty million population of the country is annually affected by the drought. In the country, around 70 per cent of the total sown land is prone to drought, which hit it one or the other time. Though in the past, country has experienced severe drought conditions many times but drought of 1987-88 was one of the worst kind after independence. Recently, during 1999-2000 and 2000-2001 also, many states of the country were affected by this calamity.

The major droughts during the last five decades in the country are as follows (Tables 2.10 and 2.11).

Table 2.10 : Major Droughts in India

Year	% area affected of the country	Category
1951	33.2	Moderate
1952	25.8	Slight
1965	42.9	Moderate
1966	32.3	Moderate
1968	20.6	Slight
1969	19.9	Slight
1971	13.3	Slight
1972	44.4	Severe
1974	29.3	Moderate
1979	39.4	Moderate
1982	33.1	Moderate
1985	30.1	Moderate
1986	19.0	Slight
1987	49.2	Severe

Source : *Yojana* (16-30 June, 1989):8.

Table 2.11 : Losses due to Droughts : 1999-2001

Year	Districts affected	Villages affected (No)	Population affected (Lakh)	Damage to crops area (Lakh Ha)	Estimated value of damaged crops (Rs. crore)	Cattle popula-tion affected (in lakh)
1999	125	—	369.88	134.22	6.44	345.60
2000	10	54,883	378.14	367.00	371.87	541.67
2001	103	22,255	88.19	67.44	NA	34.28
Total	338	77,138	836.21	568.66	378.31	921.55

Source: Annual Reports, Natural Disaster Management Division, Ministry of Agriculture.

Forest or bush fire, though not resulting much loss to human life, is a major hazard for forest cover in the country. As per Forest Survey of India report, 50 per cent of the forest cover of the country is fire prone, out of which 6.17 per cent is prone to severe fire damage causing extensive loss to forest vegetation and environment. Average annual physical loss due to forest fire in the country is estimated to worth Rs. 440 crores. The major loss due to forest fire is caused to the environment, which gets adversely affected by this calamity. The degradation of climate, soil and water quality, loss of wildlife and its habitat, deterioration of human health, depletion of ozone layer, etc. along with direct loss to timber are the major adverse impact of forest fires. The coniferous forests in the Himalayan region are very susceptible to fire and every year there are one or more major fire incidences in these areas. The other parts of the country dominated by deciduous forest are also damaged by fire up to an extent. It is worth mentioning that in India 90 per cent of the forest fires are man-made (intentionally or unintentionally).

3

INDIA AND ITS VULNERABILITY

India is one of the ten worst disaster affected countries of the world. Floods, cyclones, earthquakes, landslides and avalanches are the major natural disasters that repeatedly and increasingly affect the country. Some important facts about the adverse impact of natural disasters in India may be enlisted as:

— Floods and cyclones are the most devastating types of natural hazards in the country, claiming maximum casualties and property loss.

— Earthquakes, though effective in limited zones, in the recent past claimed heavy death toll.

— Droughts, though common in past history, have become less severe, resulting only in loss of livelihood and not much loss to lives.

— Due to heavy deforestation and environmental degradation, especially in hilly regions, landslides have become a common annual phenomenon in Himalayas and Western Ghats.

— Non-scientific development and urbanization has caused a serious threat to human population in metropolitan cities and other towns of the country.

— The data illustrated in preceding chapter clearly depict an increasing trend in life and property loss due to natural catastrophes.

India is prone to natural disasters due to combination of various natural and human induced factors, including adverse climatic conditions, geological structure, topographical features, environmental degradation including deforestation, population growth, urbanisation, industrialisation, non-scientific development and agricultural practices, lack of long term strategies, etc. These factors either in original or by accelerating the intensity and frequency of natural disasters are responsible for heavy toll of human and cattle lives and disrupting the life supporting systems in the country. These factors affecting the intensity and frequency of disasters are directly or indirectly influenced by various political and physical features of the country. To understand disaster situation in the country, it will be quite helpful to have a glimpse of these features in brief.

Political and Physical Features of India

Politically, India is a democratic republic having a federal structure, consisting of 29 states and 6 Union territories. It is the largest democracy where power and responsibilities for governance are shared between the Central and State Governments. It has Union Government and State Governments having different administered states and the Union territories administered directly by the Union Government. The state governments in turn share the responsibilities with districts in India.

At district level Zila Parishad and at local level Panchayats are the forms of self- governments. India exhibits striking contrasts with enormous ethnic and socio-cultural diversities. To cite an instance, some 1,600 languages are spoken in the country and there are people belonging to almost all religions and culture. There is considerable difference in population density between the states, in their pattern of development and other socio-economic and demographic profiles.

Physical Features

The geological regions, broadly following the physical features of the country may be grouped into three parts: the Himalayas and their associated group of mountains, the Indo-Gangetic plain, and the Peninsular shield. In geological recent past, most of the Himalayan region was under sea. About 70 million years ago, in a series of mountain building movements through northward movement of Indian plate, the sediment and the basement rocks rose to great heights of Himalayas.

The Indo-Gangetic plain separate the Himalayas in the north from the peninsula to the south. The peninsular region has a relative stability. Highly metamorphosed rocks of the earliest period, dating as far back as 3800 million years are found here. Lava flows belonging to the

Deccan Trap formation and younger sediments at the places cover these old rocks of peninsula.

As far as soil is concerned, India has a wide range of soils. The two important soil types, from point of view of agriculture production are alluvial and black cotton soils. The alluvial soil, composed of sediments of silt and sand are deposited by rivers constituting the great Indo-Gangetic plains from Punjab to Assam. Alluvial soils are also found in the valleys of Narmada and Tapti in Madhya Pradesh and the Cauvery in Tamil Nadu. These soils are very good for the production of wheat, rice, cereals, pulses, oil seeds, potato, and sugarcane, etc.

Black cotton soil is distributed through Maharashtra, Gujarat, Madhya Pradesh, Karnataka, Andhra Pradesh, Tamil Nadu, Uttar Pradesh and Rajasthan. These soils are very good for cotton, cereals, pulses, oil seeds, citrus fruits and vegetables production. Other soil types are found in central and southern India — Tamil Nadu, Karnataka, Kerala, Mahrashtra, Andhra Pradesh, Madhya Pradesh, Bihar and West Bengal are good for rice, ragi, tobacco and vegetable cultivation. Besides, lateretic and desert soils also occur in some parts of country.

Climatically, India is tropical country but due to great altitudinal variations, almost all climatic conditions from hot desert to cold desert exist in India. The climate of India may be broadly described as being mostly tropical, tropical-monsoon and temperate in the Himalayas.

The monsoon wind, responsible for rain in India passes over the Bay of Bengal. The south-west or summer monsoon provides 80 per cent of the total precipitation. On an average India receives rainfall of 1200 mm/year. The total rainfall over the country comes to 400 million ha. meters. But this rainfall is confined mostly to the, monsoon months. Out of the 400 million ha. meters, around 160 million ha. meters flows in the form of run off. Out of the balance of 240 million ha. meters, around 140 million ha. meters percolates into the soil and 70 million ha. meters evaporates and around 30 million ha. meters are stored in major and minor irrigation projects.

As mentioned above, the distribution of rainfall is not uniform and varies from 300 - 350 mm per annum in Jaisalmer to about 1000 mm per annum in eastern part of the country. A major quantity of rainwater flows in the form of run-off through drainage and gives birth to major river systems of the country. There are fourteen major river systems.

These major river systems of India may be classified into four groups : (a) Himalayan rivers, (b) Peninsular rivers, (c) Coastal rivers and (d) Rivers of the inland drainage basin.

Himalayan rivers are generally snow-fed and perennial. During the monsoon months the Himalayas receive very high rainfall which leads to the discharge of huge quantities of water causing frequent floods and landslides.

The Ganga sub-basin, a part of the larger Ganga-Brahmaputra-Meghana basin is the largest in India. About one-quarter of the country's total area comprises its catchment area. It has its well-defined boundaries by the Himalayas in the north and the Vindhya Mountains in the south. Before entering to Bangladesh, the Ganga and its tributary rivers flow through Uttar Prdesh, Bihar and West Bengal having two main headwaters in the Himalayas, the Bhagirathi and the Alaknanda. The Ganga is joined by a number of Himalayan rivers including the Yamuna, Ghaghra, Gandak and Kosi. The other important rivers flowing north from central India into the Ganga-Yamuna are Chambal, Betwa and Sone. In the eastern Himalayas, the Brahmaputra and the Barak flowing from east to west in the north-east are international rivers and have immense water resource potential.

The peninsular rivers are generally rain fed and therefore fluctuate in volume. A large number of streams are non-perennial. The river Godavari in the southern peninsula has the second largest basin in the country, covering 10 per cent of India's area. The second and the third largest basin in southern peninsula are Krishna basin and the Mahanadi. The basin of Narmada in the Deccan uplands drains in the peninsula.The basin of Narmada in the Deccan uplands drains into the Arabian Sea and those of the Cauvery in the south discharge into the Bay of Bengal. These basins are similar in size but of different character and shape. The coastal streams, particularly on the West Coast are short in length and have limited catchment area in the inland drainage basin. Streams of Rajasthan are characterised by draining into either individual basins or into salt lakes like the Sambhar, or are lost in the sands, having no outlet to the sea. The only river of this category that drains into the Rann of Kutch is Luni.

Economic Situation

A major portion of Indian land is used for agriculture purpose. Out of total 328.7 million hectares of country land, 142.5 million ha. is used for agriculture purpose and 63.7 million ha. (19.39%) of the total land area is under forests cover.

Agriculture contributing around 30 per cent of GDP form major portion of Indian economy. The net sown area in the country is around 140 million- hectare. A major part of this land is suffering form soil degradation and erosion .

India supports approximately 16 per cent of world's population with only 2.5 per cent of the world's geographic area. India's estimated population has crossed 1 billion resulting in an average density of around 278 persons per sq. km. Population density varies between states, e.g. there are about 60 people per sq. km. in Arunachal Pradesh while over 650 people per sq. km. in Kerala.

Bio-diversity

Due to its climatic and physiographic conditions, India is very rich in bio-diversity. On an average around 65,000 species of animals and 45,000 species of plants are found here.

The country is divided into ten bio-geographic zones, namely-

I. Trans- Himalayan,
II. Himalayan,
III. Indian deserts,
IV. Semi-arid areas,
V. Western Ghats,
VI. Deccan peninsula,
VII. Gangetic plain,
VIII. North-East India.,
IX. Islands, and
X. Coasts.

WHY THE COUNTRY IS PRONE TO DISASTERS ?

The quantum of loss due to a disaster, natural or man-made is the result of vulnerability of a society / region, i.e., the extent to which a community, structure, service, or geographic area is likely to be damaged or disrupted by the impact of particular hazard, on account of their nature, construction, and proximity to hazardous terrain.

Due to various natural and human induced activities, the vulnerability of the country to natural hazards is quite high in comparison to other parts of the world. The basic factor for this high vulnerability is country's unique geographical and geological situations, which make the land very unstable, fragile and thus prone to natural hazards. Being the seventh largest country of the world, India is unique in its geographical and geological features. Covering an area of 32, 87, 263 square kilometers, the country is well marked off, from rest of Asia in north by vast Himalayan ranges and in south by extensive sea boundaries. The main land of the country extends between longitudes 68.7' and 97. 25' east and latitudes 8.4' and 37.6' north. The country has vast land frontier of 15,200 km and coastline of 8,000 km. Beside the main land, many islands in the Bay of Bengal and Arabian Sea also make part of the country.

The main land of the country comprises of five major parts as follows:

(i) The Great Himalayan Mountain Zone,
(ii) Alluvial Plain of Ganga, Brahmaputra and Indus rivers,
(iii) The Desert Region,
(iv) The Southern Peninsula, and
(v) The Coastal Plains.

The vast Himalayan zone, bordering in the north of the country consists, mainly of three mountainous belts running almost parallel for about 2,400 km. This highest mountain of the world is also youngest in age and still in the stage of uplifting. Various tectonic activities like faulting, folding and thrusting are still continuing in this region making the area very unstable and fragile. Due to its tectonic features, the zone is very prone to earthquakes, landslides and other associated forms of natural disasters.

The landslides, themselves causing immense loss to property and life, also initiate other type of disasters like floods in rivers. The rock debris generated by movement of land mass in some of the cases may block the river flow for considerable longer periods by constructing natural check dams. If these dams survive for longer duration, sufficient water is stored and breaching of the dam cause tremendous loss in the down stream areas. Historical evidences suggest that in the past, various Himalayan regions have experienced such devastating floods causing immense loss to life and property. Alaknanada river, a tributary of Ganga and originating from Satopant and Bhagirathi Kharak glaciers, in the past have experienced such floods very frequently.

Besides landslides and earthquakes, floods and flash floods are other natural calamities in Himalaya which cause a lot of damage in hills and other down stream plain areas as well. In western and central Himalayas, the causes of floods are associated with landslides, which block the river flow and build natural temporary barriers. The other major cause of floods in Himalayan rivers is due to increase of soil erosion and sediment deposition in river channels, shallowing them and reducing their water carrying capacity. Due to some natural and other human induced activities, the soil erosion by Himalayan rivers is maximum in comparison to other rivers of the world. Annual sediment load of three major Himalayan river systems is given in the Table 3.1.

Table 3.1 : Erosion in Major River Systems

River System	Annual load (mt/ year)			Erosion Rate in catchment
	Dissolved	Suspended	Total	(t/sq.km/yr.)
Ganga	84	329	413	549
Yamuna	17	125	142	392
Brahmaputra	51	597	648	953

Among the various river systems, the Brahmaputra is most prone to floods. Flood is a common hazard in Brahmaputra valley causing large-scale devastation and adverse impact on socio-economic set-up of the region. Due to this river, around 45 per cent of Assam state is prone to floods. The main reason of flood in Brahmaputra river system had been large scale deforestation in the north eastern hill states. The region endowed with rich forest wealth covering 163.799 sq.km. has shown a gradual forest loss during the last few decades. As per the State Forest Report, 1999 of Forest Survey of India, the total forest loss during the period 1991 to 1999 has been of 2012 sq.km. State wise forest cover along with the changes during the past five assessments years is shown in the following table.

Table 3.2 : Changes in forest cover of North- Eastern States
(State of Forest Report, 1999)

States	Forest cover (1999 assessment)	Change during different assessments			
		1991-93	1993-95	1995-1997	1997-99
Arunachal Pradesh	68,847	-96	-40	-19	+245
Assam	23,688	-243	-447	-237	-136
Manipur	17,384	-64	-63	-140	-34
Meghalaya	15,633	-106	-55	-57	-24
Mizoram	18,338	-156	-121	+199	-437
Nagaland	14,164	+27	-57	-70	-57
Tripura	5,745	+3	0	+8	+199
Total	163,799	-635	-783	-316	-278

This immense forest loss and degradation of dense forests has made the north-eastern area very fragile and prone to erosion. The heavy rain in the region has resulted into large-scale soil erosion and its subsequent deposition in river channels causing aggressive floods.

The alluvial plain lying in south of Himalayan belt is formed by basins of three distinct river systems *viz.* the Indus, the Ganga and the Brahmaputra. The region, very young in age, consists of undulating plains, carved by highly developed river systems. The sediments brought by these river systems make this area very fertile and the agricultural production in this region is the highest in the country. Besides making the area fertile, the river systems in this part of the country also causes floods, resulting into vast devastation.

In the west of Alluvial Plains lies the desert part, characterised by low rain fall. The region is clearly delineated in two parts—the Great Desert and the Little Desert. The first one, the Great Desert is running beyond Rann of Kutch to Rajasthan, while the Little Desert extends from Jaisalmer and Jodhpur to Punjab. Due to low rainfall and inadequate moisture content in the soil, the land of this region is very frequently affected by drought and famine.

The fourth division of the country, the Peninsula is a stable mass consisting of older metamorphic rock bodies. Topographically the region is rugged but the mountains are not so sharp and high as in the Himalayan belt. These mountains are denuded and eroded. The area is also characterised by plateaus, high elevated land mass formed of igneous lava flow during the geological past. Though in general the region is very stable but few neo- tectonic movements have caused earthquakes and other associated disasters.

The hilly terrain of peninsular India also faces the trauma of landslides. The Eastern and Western Ghat hills are also equally affected by the natural calamity of floods, landslides and rock falls. Areas near Godawari and its tributaries experience very frequently landslide and rock falls. Besides occasional earthquakes, floods are very common phenomenon in the Godawari valley. The areas nearing the river have observed devastating floods during 1886, 1900, 1907, 1953 and recently in 1986. During the latest flood in 1986 the water level of Godawari rose upto 22 feet high affecting millions of people from more than 700 villages. The floods claimed nearly 80 human lives and killed thousands of cattle.

During May 1990, Vadera area near Visakhapatnam in Andhra Pradesh was affected by heavy landslide and flood due to continuous heavy rain fall for three days. This catastrophic event devastated large chunk of habitation of around 2,000 villages. Nearly sixteen people were killed and 2,500 houses completely and 10,000 partially damaged.

Along with Eastern Ghats, the Western Ghats area is also frequently affected by such catastrophic events. Landslides, flash floods, etc. are very common in Nilgiris of Western Ghats. As the land forming the peninsular India is geologically more stable compared to the Himalayan region, the major reasons for these catastrophic events are man-made or induced due to human interference in exploiting the nature.

During the last few decades a large-scale deforestation has been carried out in these regions. As per an estimate in East Godawari alone, more than 100,000 hectares forest has been cleared for various purposes. Road construction and developmental activities are major causes for environmental degradation and consequent increase in intensity of natural disasters.

The coastal plains surrounding the peninsular part is the fifth division of the country. The region, characterised by continental margin, is made up of very recent sediments, brought by the rivers falling in the ocean. The western and the eastern coastal plains are very much different in geology and structure. While the western coastal plains are very sharp and almost straight, the eastern coastal plains are bit wavy with wider continental shelf. One more characteristics of western coastal plain is the presence of high angle faults running almost parallel to the coastal plains.

As far as natural disasters are concerned, these five distinctive regions of the country have their own specific problems. While on the one hand the Himalayan region is very prone to natural disasters like earthquakes and land slides, on the other hand the plain region is affected by heavy flood almost every year. The desert part of the country is affected by droughts and famine and the coastal zone of the country is severely susceptible to cyclones and wind storms. Thus in brief, the country's disaster problem is very diversified and thus requires area specific management planning for effective results.

Before going into details about disaster and its management in the country, it will be of much help to provide information, about various factors and causes for disasters, which may be subgrouped as nutural and man-made.

Natural Causes

Natural geological setting of the country is the primary basic reason which makes it very susceptible and prone to disasters. This instability of the land can be best understood by "Plate Tectonic Theory". As per the modern thinking, the earth formed about 5 billion years ago from the very hot gases that over time cooled and became denser. While solidifying, the earth divided into three distinct layers. The inner most central part of the earth is of solid nickel and iron (20 per cent of the earth radius), surrounded by a larger part of molten nickel and iron (35 per cent of the earth in radius), Around this metabolic centre lies the mantle (45 per cent of earth in radius), formed of molten rock with a viscous, molasse-like material. This mantle part of the earth is surrounded by "asthenosphere" and "lithosphere" The lithosphere is the outermost layer of the earth and on an average is 100 km thick. The outermost part of the lithosphere is the "crust" that makes "continents" and ocean floors. The thickness of this "crust" is around 30 km in continental parts and about 5 km under the oceans.

The outer most layer of the earth, the lithosphere, is not a single body, instead it is cracked like an "egg shell". These cracked parts of the lithosphere are termed as "tectonic plates", which are floating over the viscous, semi-liquid molasses like structure or mantle. There are seven large and twelve small such plates, which are in continuous motion. The energy for their motion comes from deep hot interior of the earth. The heat energy from the hot core part of the earth is released in the form of convection currents. There currents, continuous in motion gives sufficient energy to make the tectonic plates move. The collision of two plates creates very unstable condition. The movement along the plate boundaries make the region lying nearby unstable and various tectonic movements take place here due to which earthquakes, volcanic activities, etc., become very common and prevalent. The Himalaya characterises a region where two continental plates are colliding against each other. These two plates, the Indo-Australian plate and the European plate are both floating over the asthenosphere. But due to its lightweight, the Indian-Plate could not submerge or shrink into the asthenosphere, instead due to continuous pressure toward north, this plate slided between the asthenosphere and the Asian-Plate. Due to this sliding, the part of Asian-Plate and the sediment lying between these two plates rose high and formed the great mountain range of Himalaya.

The Indo-Asian plate is still in the movement phase and creating pressure on Asian-Plate. Due to this pressure, the Himalayas are still rising at a rate of 5 cm per year. Besides uplifting of the Himalayas, the pressure of plate is creating stress on the rocks forming the mountain. Due to this stress, the rocks are deformed in various patterns, i.e., tilting, breaking and moving away after rupture. These deformations respectively called faulting, folding and thrusting in geological term are basically ways to release the stored energy in the rock bodies, created due to continuous increasing stress, as a result of plate movement. Whenever this energy is released, the rock bodies forming the land here shatter and roll and earthquakes occur.

The earthquakes are very common in the vicinities of large deformation structure, i.e., thrust. As mentioned earlier, thrusts are the rupture planes running miles of distance in the rock bodies along which the broken fragments of rock move apart. Himalaya has many thrusts in it, the most prominent among them are:

(1) Main Boundary Thrust (MBT), which demarcates the

Sivalik Foot Hills from rest of the Himalaya,

(2) Main Central Thrust (MCT), separating the Central and Lesser Himalaya, and

(3) Central Counter Thrust (CCT), demarcating Central Himalaya from the Tibetan Himalaya block.

This is not all about the structural complexity of Himalaya, there are fault planes also present in the rock bodies, which are diagonal to the thrust plane and dip at higher angle.

Seismically whole of the Himalayan region is very active and falls in zone IV and V. In the Himalayan region the largest number of epicentres are located near two major tectonic features—Main Boundary Thrust and Main Central Thrust. Besides these two, other smaller features like transverse faults are also responsible for most of the earthquakes in the region.

All these features in the Himalayan rock bodies are the results of Indo-Australian plate movement towards North. The plate movement is continuously mounting a pressure on the rock bodies forming Himalayas. This pressure creates stress in the rocks and to release the stress, the rock bodies fold, fault and thrust. Whenever there is stress release, the rock bodies along the thrust or fault plane shatter. These tectonic features including faults, thrusts, and folds further crumble, shear and break the rocks and make them very weak and fragile. These weak rocks, forming the Himalaya are susceptible and prone to land slides and soil erosion.

Along with Himalayan region, the plate movement is also affecting other parts of the country. Though peninsular India is considered to be the most stable portion but occasional occurrence of the earthquake in the region shows that geo-tectonic movements are still going on within its depth. The peninsular shield, as it is commonly known among geologists, also has many old major faults and thrusts, which become active due to various unknown factors. Some of these faults and thrusts are shown in Fig. 3.1.

Alluvial Plains of Indus, Ganga and Brahmaputra are formed by alluvial deposition in the basin developed in the southern part of Himalaya. The rivers flowing from the Himalaya into this basin have been continuously depositing sediment in this basin since the origin of Himalaya. With the passage of time, a thick deposit of the eroded

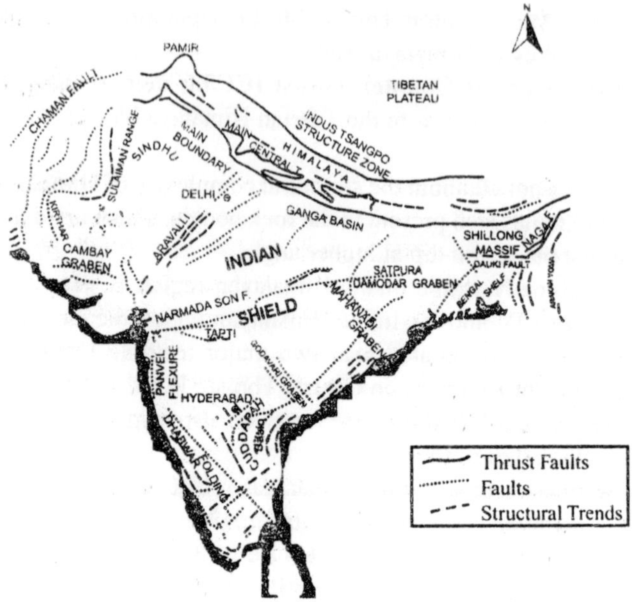

Fig. 3.1 : Tectomic map of India, showing major weak zones

material from Himalayan rock bodies is deposited here in the form of thick alluvium. The rocks lying below the alluvial plane are extension of the Himalayan range only. The tectonic features, characteristics of the Himalaya are prevalent in this region also and that is why this part of the country is also as susceptible to disasters as the Himalayan region itself. Various frequent seismic activities in this part of the country are evidence of this fact.

As a result of various major river systems flowing from Himalaya and huge quantity of sediment brought by them, the area is also suffering from river channel siltation, resulting into frequent floods, especially in the low lying plain areas of Uttar Pradesh and Bihar.

Monsoon plays very crucial role in natural, social and economic conditions of India. It is very important for Indian agriculture system, which is mostly rain fed. While on one hand excess of monsoon rain may result into floods in the country, on other hand the weak monsoon creates drought. Though many causes for the drought are human induced, the failure of monsoon is the major natural cause for this calamity in the country.

Fig. 3.2: A clever or foolish intervention?

The western part of the country including Rajasthan, Gujarat, some parts of Maharashtra are very frequently hit by drought like situation. If monsoon worsen as in the year 2002, the situation may spread to other parts of the country also. The alluvial plain being the most fertile belt of the country is worst affected by the drought situation in India.

The other major natural causes of disasters in India is disturbance in pressure condition over the oceans, resulting into cyclones and windstorms. India having 8,041 km of sea coast is very frequently affected by such conditions on both the western and eastern coasts.

The extreme heat and cold conditions, huge quantity of ice and snow stored in the the glaciers causing snow avalanches, very frequent hail storms, etc. are the other naturally occurring causes, which make the country prone to disasters.

Human Induced Causes

Along with the natural conditions discussed above various human induced activities which include increasing demographic pressure, deteriorating environmental conditions, deforestation, grazing, unscientific development, forest fires, construction of huge dams on river channels, etc., are also responsible for accelerated impact and increased frequency of disasters in the country.

Demographic Pressure

According to the provisional results compiled for the Census of India, 2001, the population of India at 00:00 hours on 1st March 2001, stood at 1,027,015,247, comprising 531,277,078 males and 495,7398,169 females. Thus, as widely believed and expected, India became the only second country in the world after China to officially cross the one billion marks. It is certainly most unlikely that in the history of mankind any country other than India and China would be shaping the lives and future of over a billion people (Annexure XII & XIII).

Population of India: Some Facts and Figures

Some significant facts and figures about Indian population, which influence its vulnerability to natural hazards are discussed below—

1. Population— India and the world:

India accounts for only 2.4 per cent of the world surface area and yet it supports and sustains 16.87 per cent of the world population. In 1950, China with 22 per cent share of the population led the world followed by India, which had a share of 14.2 per cent. It is estimated that by 2050, India will overtake China to become the most populous country on earth with about 17.2 per cent population living here.

2. Population share of states/Union territories

Uttar Pradesh continues to be the most populous state of the country. The next most populous states are Maharashtra and Bihar followed by West Bengal, Andhra Pradesh, Tamil Nadu and Madhya Pradesh. More than 50 per cent of the total population of India lives in these seven states. The smallest state (excluding the Union territories) in terms of population is Sikkim.

3. Growth of population: 1991 - 2001

The results of 2001 census indicate that despite many efforts and expenses, there has been only a minor decline in the growth rate of population in India during 1991-2001, in comparison to the previous decade. Decadal growth rate 21.34 per cent of population between 1991-2001 is lower than 23.86 per cent recorded between 1981-91.

4. Density of population

Results from the Census of India, 2001 show that the average population density of the country is 324 persons per sq km, having risen from 77 persons per sq km in 1901. Among the states, West Bengal has recorded the highest population density (904) followed by Bihar (880) and Kerala (819), and Arunachal Pradesh has the lowest population density (13).

5. Sex ratio

Sex ratio is an important social indicator to measure the extent of prevailing equity between males and females in a society. The worrying factor is that there is a decline in the sex ratio between 1991-2001 in Himachal Pradesh, Punjab, Haryana, Gujarat, Sikkim, Maharashtra and Goa. Defined here as the number of females per thousand males, sex ratio for India as a whole is recorded as 933. Among the states, Kerala has registered the highest sex ratio (1,058) and Haryana the lowest (861).

7. Literacy rate

The total number of literates (who can both read and write with understanding any language) in India are 566 million as per the 2001 Census. The literacy rate for India was 65.38 per cent improving upon 52.21 per cent in 1991. Among the states, Kerala has the highest literacy rate (90.92 %), followed by Mizoram (88.49 %) and Goa (82.32 %). There are fourteen states/Union territories, which have more than 70 per cent literacy rate in 2001. All the states and Union territories without exception have shown improvement in literacy rates during 1991-2001. The major states that registered more than fifteen percentage points increase during the decade are Rajasthan (22), Chhatisgarh (22), Madhya Pradesh (17) and Uttar Pradesh (17). Bihar however, registered an increase of only ten percentage point from 38 per cent in 1991 to 48 per cent in 2001. The female literacy rate as per the Census of India, 2001 is 54.16 per cent which is about fifteen percentage points higher than that recorded in 1991. Thus about half of the female population is now literate.

Table 3.3 : Population data of India showing decadal growth, Sex ratios and Population density

India, States/Union Terriotries	Population	Percentage decadal growth 1991-2001	Sex ratio	Population density
INDIA	1,027,015,247	21.34	933	324
Jammu & Kashmir	10,069,917	29.04	900	99
Himachal Pradesh	6,077,248	17.53	970	109
Punjab	24,289,296	19.76	874	482
Chandigarh	900,914	40.33	773	7,903
Uttaranchal	8,479,562	19.2	964	159
Haryana	21,082,989	28.06	861	477
Delhi	13,782,976	46.31	821	9,294
Rajasthan	56,473,122	28.33	922	165
Uttar Pradesh	166,052,859	25.8	898	686
Bihar	82,878,796	28.43	921	880
Sikkim	540,493	32.98	875	76
Arunachal Pradesh	1,091,117	26.21	901	13
Nagaland	1,988,636	64.41	909	120
Manipur	2,388,634	30.02	978	107
Mizoram	391,058	29.18	938	42
Tripura	3,191,168	15.74	950	304
Meghalaya	2,306,069	29.94	975	103
Assam	26,638,407	18.85	932	340
West Bengal	80,221,171	17.84	934	904
Jharkhand	26,909,428	23.19	941	338
Orissa	36,706,920	15.94	972	236
Chhatisgarh	20,795,956	18.06	990	154
Madhya Pradesh	60,385,118	24.34	920	196
Gujarat	50,596,992	22.48	921	258
Daman & Diu	158,059	55.59	709	1,411
Dadra & Nagar Haveli	220,451	59.2	811	449
Maharashtra	96,752,247	22.57	922	314
Andhra Pradesh	75,727,541	13.86	978	275
Karnataka	52,733,958	17.25	964	275
Goa	1,343,998	14.89	960	363
Lakshadweep	60,595	17.19	947	1,894
Kerala	31,838,619	9.42	1,058	819
Tamil Nadu	62,110,839	11.19	986	478
Pondicherry	973,829	20.56	1,001	2,029
A & N Islands	356,265	26.94	846	43

Source : Ministry of Rural Development (GOI)

9. Population growth trends

The population of India at the turn of the twentieth century was only around 238 million which increased by over four times to reach 1027 million at the dawn of the twenty first century. Interestingly, the population grew up one-and-half times in the first half of the twentieth century. In absolute terms, the population of India during the decade 1991-2001 increased by a whopping 180.6 million, more than the estimated population of Brazil, the fifth most populous country in the world.

The population data mentioned above depict many important factors directly or indirectly affecting the vulnerability of the country to disasters, discussed in chapter IV.

Environmental Degradation and Disasters

Owing to various other factors, the deterioration of the overall environmental condition is the major cause for increase in both physical as well as socio- economic vulnerability of country to disasters. Environmental degradation increases the intensity of natural disaster and is often the factor that transforms a natural hazard or climatic extreme into a disaster. In the recent past due to so called developmental activities, particularly in sensitive or disaster-prone regions, the environment had been very adversely affected resulting into exponential increase in fragility of land mass. Though there had been many factors responsible for the present bad shape of the environment, the deforestation and degradation of the forests during the last 50 years is the most prominent and major one among them.

Deforestation and Disasters

At the time of independence, 22.74 per cent of the total geographical area of the country was covered by forest representing nearly 2 per cent of the world's forest area, which reduced to 19.39 per cent in 1999. The loss to forest has been very high during the mid-1970s to 1980s. Though this degradation of forest has somewhat slowed down after the promulgation of the Forest Conservation Act, 1980, but it still remains a cause of concern and alarm.

Table 3.4 : Status of Forests in India

Category	Area (million hectare)	Percentage of total geographical area	Percentage of forest area
Total geographical area	328.73	100.00	—
Legally classified forest	76.53	13.18	100.00
Actual forest cover[a]	63.73	19.39	83.27
Open forest[b]	25.51	7.76	33.33
Dense forest[c]	37.73	11.48	49.30
Mangroves	0.49	0.15	0.64

Source : State of Forest Report 1999
[a] Forest having at least 10 per cent crown cover
[b] Forest with crown cover betweenm 10 per cent and 40 per cent
[c] Forest with over 40 per cent crown cover

The comparative data of forest cover as estimated by the Forest Survey of India in its publications are given in table below indicating an annual net loss of about 74,000 ha. between 1987 to 1997.

Table 3.5 : Forest cover as estimated by the FSI from 1987 to 1997 (sq. km.)

Cycle	Year of Publication	Forest cover estimate	% of total area of the country
First	1987	640,819	19.49
Second	1989	638,804	19.43
Third	1991	639,364	19.45
Fourth	1993	639,386	19.45
Fifth	1995	638,879	19.43
Sixth	1997	633,397	19.27

Most of the forest areas in the country are ecologically in various stages of retrogression. The forest ecosystems are reeling under acute form of degradation. The direct causes of degradation are poverty, landlessness, and derivation of livelihood from forests, lack of land use planning, uncertainties in land tenure system, biotic interference, inadequate institutional capacity and lack of restrictive covenants and punitive legislation.

The large-scale deforestation in the country along with faulty development and management practices have resulted a serious environmental degradation. Deforestation has increased the frequency and intensity of various cataclysmic disasters like soil-erosion, landslides, floods, droughts , desertification, etc. It has also very adversely affected the eco-balance resulting into various problems, ultimately leading to increase in vulnerability of the society and the land to various forms of natural hazards. In ecologically more sensitive and destabilised areas like Himalaya and other hill regions like Western Ghats, the impact of deforestation has been more severe.

Grazing, mining, shifting cultivation, developmental plans like road , building and dam construction, etc., caused enormous damage to forests of the country. Deforestation and other allied land degradation activities such as water logging, flooding, ravines, shifting cultivation, mining, salinisation, soil erosion, landslides and rock falls and desertification have affected more than half of the total geographical area of the country. The deforestation in the form of mangrove removal has made the coastal region more susceptible to erosion and damage to human settlement.

While on one hand the deforestation lead environmental degradation, has increased the intensity and frequency of natural disasters, on the other hand it has also enhanced the people's

Dependence on forests

- Over two-thirds of rural and half of the urban population uses fuelwood for cooking purposes.
- About a quarter of India's livestock population, which is the largest in the world, is almost totally dependent on forestlands.
- About 70 per cent of India's population uses traditional medicine (mainly forest-based), and many of the rural poor have no access to other systems of medicine.
- Forest-based activities are often an important source of cash income for the poor, especially during lean seasons. A study carried out in 26 villages of Madhya Pradesh, Orissa and Gujarat revealed that forests contribute between 37 per cent and 76 per cent of the total income of the forest-fringe communities.

(*Source* : Ministry of Environment and Forest, Government of India) vulnerability to natural hazards (increasing both the risk and exposure to disasters). The deforestation and destruction of other natural resources have compelled the people from the rural areas to migrate in search of new livelihood in urban areas, resulting into unplanned settlement even in highly risk zones like seismic zones, steep hillsides and flood-prone areas. The mushroom growths of different slums in the various metropolitan cities of the country, as a consequence of this unplanned development, are at maximum risk to natural disasters.

In ecologically fragile and more sensitive or destabilised areas like Himalayas, the impact of deforestation have been more severe which directly or indirectly affect the lower plains of the country. Deforestation in Himalaya has increased the severity of floods during rainy season and reduced stream flows and dried up springs during dry seasons. The increase of soil erosion has reduced the water carrying capacity of the rivers resulting into shallowing of river beds leading to floods in the plains. Ever increasing population pressure and increasing demand for food and fodder with no alternative source of livelihood has forced the people to convert forest land, even in very sensitive zones to agricultural fields causing enormous loss to environment and stability of the region. Rapid deforestation in the Himalaya and resulting degradation of its ecology has posed a potential danger to the greenery of the Indo-Gangetic belt causing sporadic floods in one and drought in other area. About two-third agricultural land of the country is affected by drought and about one- fifth is very frequently exposed to floods. Deforestation and other allied land degradation activities such as water logging, flooding, ravine formation, shifting cultivation, mining, salinisation, water logging, soil erosion, landslides and rock falls, desertification, etc., have affected more than fifty per cent of the total geographical area of the country.

Poverty and vulnerability are inextricably linked and mutually reinforcing each other. The poor for their survival are dependents on natural resources, mainly forests. This dependency of the poor on forests has caused tremendous loss to forest resources. While this dependency leads to environmental degradation and increases the intensity and frequency of natural disasters, simultaneously it enhances the people's vulnerability to natural hazards as well.

The worst impact of deforestation is the manifold increase of soil erosion and landslides. The mountains consisting of fragile rocks either due to mineral composition or due to fractures and shears are worst affected by deforestation. The loss of tree cover loosen the soil and rock material, otherwise bound by the roots of the trees disallowing it to be eroded by water and wind. The problem has become very serious in some parts of Himalaya, where due to deforestation and soil erosion, a major portion of the fertile topsoil is lost and the areas are approaching desertification. The natural appearance of xerophytic plants in some Himalayan areas is certainly a matter of concern for the country.

Climate Change and Disasters

Large scale industrialisation, deforestation and non-sustainable overuse of other natural resources has increased pollution leading to global change in the environment. This human induced climate change has increased the overall global temperature resulting excessive melting of glaciers in the Himalayas, causing water-related disasters. The main reason for this climate change or increase in temperature is the excessive burning of fuels (coal, petrol, diesel), large-scale deforestation and forest fires resulting into substantial increase of carbon dioxide and other harmful gases in the atmosphere. This increased carbon dioxide prevents the heat rays returning back to the atmosphere. Thus a part of the heat energy absorbed by the earth and carbon-dioxide its objects, partially remains in the atmosphere, causing increase of the overall global temperature. This phenomenon called "Green House Effect" along with excessive snow melting also cause many other adverse impacts on the environment and society. The global warming is also up to an extent responsible for the rainfall variation, accelerating desertification and land degradation. Loss in agriculture production (particularly rain-fed), human and cattle health deterioration, scarcity of water resources are other adverse impact of this phenomenon on society. All these factors have a compound effect on the impact and occurrence of natural disasters. Beside escalating the intensity and frequency of various disasters, they also increase the vulnerability of the society, particularly in the sensitive zones, like Himalayas and the coastal areas.

Unscientific Development

Unscientific development practices adopted in the country have been yet another major factor causing immense loss to environment. The fragile and sensitive eco-systems like Himalayas have been most adversely affected by such practices. Developmental projects, i.e., road construction, hydropower, irrigation, railway tracks, etc., have also caused irreparable losses to the environment of the region increasing the risk of human society towards natural hazards.

Road Construction

The construction of roads, especially in hill areas, is one major factor disturbing the ecological balance. Along with the stability of the region, it also causes serious damage to drainage pattern (both underground and surface) increases soil erosion and leads to mass movement of the soil and rocks. The problem accelerates further if the road construction is carried out without taking into consideration the geological, geo-morphological and ecological aspects. Major destruction caused due to road construction is the result of ignoring all these aspects. This leads to excavation of steep and unstable slopes, felling of trees, dumping of debris down the slope neglecting the damage to drainage pattern of the hill area. The construction of roads has adversely affected the eco-balance in all the hill states of Himalayas and also in some southern States of Nilgiri hills. After independence and especially after China War in 1962, the main emphasis of the Central Government was to increase connectivity in Himalayan region through roads. During this period even the interior villages were connected by roads. But the most unfortunate part of this development had been that these roads were constructed without proper scientific investigation. This activity has generated huge amount of debris and other waste, which ultimately deteriorated the environmental conditions and shattered the eco-balance of the region. The blasting carried out to clear mountains for making new roads also results in landslides and rock falls.

In plain areas also the construction of roads has adversely affected the natural drainage system, resulting into floods and stagnation of water during rainy season. The faulty road construction in Gorakhpur and Maharajganj districts of Eastern Uttar Paradesh are examples of this type of development induced vulnerability.

Industrialisation and Urbanisation

Industrialisation and urbanisation are two other major causes for environmental degradation. After independence, availability of natural resources (forest, minerals, raw material, etc.), electricity, communication and cheap labour have encouraged prospective industrialists to establish industries in various towns and cities of the country, resulting into environmental problems like pollution, deforestation, etc., and thus further exposing the region, making it more susceptible to natural hazards.

Urbanisation has also been responsible for increased vulnerability to disasters (Fig. 3.3). With the urbanisation the demand for various natural resources increases, leading to their brutal exploitation and consequently environmental degradation. The impact of this activity has been more prominently observed in the hilly regions of the country. It has been observed that mostly in newly developed / developing towns or cities in hills, the constructed buildings are mere replications of buildings constructed in plain areas without giving due consideration to local seismicity, ecological or environmental aspects. These concrete and brick structures proved very fatal during earthquakes in the past. At the time of Chamoli earthquake the

Fig. 3.3: An unorganised habitat — More vulnerable to disasters

traditional buildings made up of local materials proved to be relatively safer than the newly constructed structures. The concrete structural collapse proved to be very fatal during 1991 and 1999 earthquakes in Uttaranchal. Deforestation, pollution, soil erosion, etc., are other problems associated with urbanisation.

Faulty Agricultural Practices and Grazing

Agriculture constitutes a major portion of Indian economy with 40 per cent geographical area is used for this purpose. However non-scientific agricultural practices, without taking into consideration the local physiological and climatic factors have proved very fatal and disastrous. The intensive use of chemical fertilisers and insecticides for the sake of "Green Revolution" has intensified the problem very seriously. Such faulty practices in hill terrain of the country have very adversely affected these areas making them prone to various forms of disasters. Around 85 per cent of the total sown area of hill states is primarily on terraced slope and is rain-fed. Agriculture in this fragile and difficult terrain is neither economic nor eco-friendly. Despite the constrains and hardships in carrying out agriculture in the hilly terrain, the people are forced to depend on it due to non-availability of other livelihood sources. The increasing population pressure, which has forced the people to move to more sensitive and unstable areas on steeper slopes to make agricultural fields, has further deteriorated the situation. This compulsion has further worsened the condition and made the local population more vulnerale to disasters. Carrying out agriculture on steeper slopes has led to serious problems of landslides and soil erosion.

Along with hill regions, in plains also, the faulty agricultural practices have created havoc. Excessive irrigation and use of chemical fertilisers and pesticides have deteriorated the land quality in Haryana and Punjab and other fertile areas of the country. The excess of irrigation has resulted salt percolation into soil that has reduced its soil permeability, resulting frequent floods in these areas during rainy season. The use of chemical fertilisers and insecticides have resulted into considerably soil and water pollution, affecting the human and cattle population at large scale.

The agricultural cropping practice which do not have enough resilience and capacity for protection has tremendously increased the soil erosion from the fields hundred times more. The unscientific ploughing—parallel to slope without contour terraces and drainage/ ditches—has also been responsible for soil erosion and deterioration of land. Due to scarcity of land and increasing population dependent on agriculture, ignoring the old practice of having marginal levees on terraces and making drainage has further increased the vulnerability of land to soil erosion.

India has around 470 million cattle (19 per cent of the total world cattle population), which is directly or indirectly dependent on (about 1.8 per cent of the World Forest Cover). The situation is much more serious in hilly terrain, where the land is more fragile and susceptible to erosion. The worst part is that most of these cattle are directly or indirectly dependent for their fodder or food on the nearby forest

Throughout the country the incidence of grazing is much higher than the carrying capacity of the forests. This grazing pressure on forests, besides adversely affecting the vegetation, also leads to many other problems like increase in the soil erosion and landslides, reduction in regeneration, retardation in tree/ plant growth, siltation in stream channels and so on. The pounding and troddling by cattle hoofs along with destroying vegetative cover also segregates the soil mantle. The cattle tracks become permanently devoid of grass and vegetation and easily fall prey to gully erosion. This intense grazing ultimately converts the land to desert or initiates desertification.

Dams and Reservoir Construction

Dam construction, obstructing the natural water flow, considerably affects the ecological balance in an area. This disturbance along with creating environmental degradation of the area also increases its vulnerability to many forms of hazards. The normal flow pattern, in equilibrium with the ecosystem is upset, the geological and geo-hydrological conditions are altered and the riverine and geo-hydrological ecosystems are altered due to dam construction in an area. The main adverse impacts of this activity are—

Erosion / landslides increase

Intensity of soil erosion and landslide incidence increases with dam construction. This is due to change in water table in the rocks/soil along the reservoir. This change in water column also increases the intensity of soil erosion. Due to change in water table, the soil or the rocks along reservoir loosens and becomes susceptible to erosion by rainwater and wind. The other reason for this increased rate of erosion is the clearance of vegetation in the upstream side. The rate of erosion is observed increased in down stream area also.

Damage to forest cover and wildlife

The construction of dams causes massive damage to forest and wildlife. A large part of the forest gets drowned under the reservoir. The labour force also cause destruction to forest for its fuel need.

Earthquake frequency increase

Seismicity is induced and increased after the accumulation of water in a reservoir. The induced seimisity has direct correlation with the height of the water column. The degree of seismicity and strength of shock wave increase rapidly if the height of a reservoir is more than 100 metre. The dam construction in Himalayan region, which is very young in age and still active, construction of large dams is very risky.

Loss of agriculture land and uprooting of human communities

Major portion of fertile land is lost due to reservoir construction. The local population is forced to migrate to other places. This migration and shifting of agriculture fields in new areas have adversely affected the local ecology and environment.

All this shows that the overall environmental condition of the country has become very alarming due to increasing population pressure and other related factors and in near future it is going to further aggravate. It is the prime time that necessary preventive and progressive steps are taken to check further deterioration of the environment and consequently the disaster valnerability of society and land.

4
INDIAN RURAL SOCIETY AND ITS VULNERABILITY TO DISASTERS

India, due to its geographical position, climate and geological setting is one of the most disaster-prone countries of the world and has been experiencing natural disasters every year. The country is highly vulnerable to droughts, floods, cyclones, avalanches, forest fires and landslides. Though the whole country is more or less commonly affected by these disasters, the impact of these disasters on rural population due to its physical, poor socio- economic and specific socio-cultural condition is comparatively more and long lasting. The vulnerability, that may be defined as the extent to which individuals, community, sub group, structure, service or geographic area is likely to be damaged or disrupted by the impact of particular disaster is basically a function of human action and behaviour and is determined by the following factors :

(i) The condition of settlement and infrastructure.
(ii) The socio- economic condition of the society referring to :

— the education and awareness,
— the economic condition, and
— basic facilities available with the society.

(iii) The socio-cultural values referring to the cultural and traditional values of the society.
(iv) Public policies and administration.
(v) Organisational set-up, and
(vi) The development pattern the society has undergone through ages.

If the condition of Indian rural society is analysed in context of the above mentioned factors, its vulnerability to disasters is comparatively higher and hence the rural society is at more risk from natural hazards. In the recent past, the changing social and physical conditions have influenced these factors and further increased the vulnerability of the rural society and land to natural disasters. As the risk or loss to a society due to natural hazard is the function of the vulnerability and the nature of the hazard, an effective disaster management should aim to reduce it.

Major Factors Influencing Vulnerability of Rural India

In the root of increased vulnerability of rural India to disasters there are basically four factors i.e. increasing demographic pressure, socio-economic conditions, environmental degradation and changing socio-cultural pattern of the society. These factors ultimately influence the overall condition of rural society, making it more susceptible or prone to adverse impacts of natural hazards.

Demographic Pressure

Increasing demographic pressure in the rural areas has increased the vulnerability of the land and society to natural disasters. Increasing demand for the livelihood and the scarcity of other employment opportunities in rural areas has forced the rural population to exploit the natural resources, specifically the forests for their own survival. The increasing demand for agricultural land (in absence of the other livelihood resources) has compelled the rural population to encroach upon the forest land for agriculture purpose. In most of the cases this encroachment is in very sensitive areas like the hill slopes, which accelerate other disasters like landslides, soil erosion, etc. The increasing dependency of rural poor on forests has escalated the instances of forest fires and also initiated many other disasters.

Population and Vulnerability

India's population recently crossed one billion mark. After China, India is the second most populous country of the world. The country having 2.42 per cent of the total world area is forced to bear the burden of the 16 per cent of the world population. This exponential increase in population is the driving force behind all the perils facing mankind.

According to *State of World Population Report* 1998, the population of India is increasing at a very rapid rate, if this continues, it would overtake the most populous country China by 2050 A. D. The report further states that Indian population growth is contributing one-fifth of total world population growth of 80 million per year. India's population multiplied more than four times during this century (from 23.8 lakh in 1901 of undivided country- India and Pakistan both, to more than one billion in 2002).

Table 4.1 : Population growth of India projected to 2016

(*in millions*)

Year	1901	1911	1921	1931	1941	1951	1961	1971	1981	1991	1996	2001	2006	2011	2016
Population	238	252	251	279	319	361	439	548	683	846	934	1012	1094	1179	1264

Source: Statistical Outline of India, 1997-98.

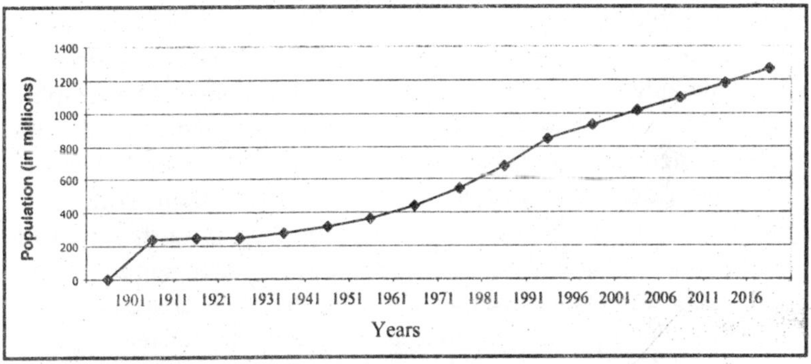

Fig. 4.1 : Graphic presentation of population growth (based on data from Statistical Outline of India 1997-1998).

The basic reason for this exponential population growth of the country has been improvement in life saving system and climate suitable for all living beings (animals and plants both). *It is law of nature that favourable growth condition, primarily involving the link between climate and food, lead to exponential growth of population until all the resources have been used up. During the last few hundred years the conditions both climatic and food availability have been much favourable. In countries with common climate like India, the conditions favoured the population growth very positively.*

During earlier decades the India's population was characterised by high birth rate as well as high death rate. Along with high death rate, high infant mortality rate and low expectancy of life were other major reasons for population control. But after independence, due to introduction of good medical facilities, improvement in hygiene and nutritional status, control over major fatal epidemics like plague, malaria and cholera reduced death or mortality rate to more than half. In comparison to reduction in death rate, there was not much difference noticed in birth rate, resulting into adding of more than 1.5 crore (million) population every year in the country.

Though exponential increase in population escalated people's vulnerability to natural hazards both, in rural and urban areas, the impact has been much higher in rural population due to diminishing livelihood resources, which compelled rural population to migrate to urban areas and further exposing them to various other hazards. The increase in rural population and scarcity of livelihood resources have forced people to expand agriculture activities in very sensitive areas, which accelerated intensity and impact of natural hazards, especially the landslides, soil erosion and floods. Increasing demographic pressure, especially in rural areas is closely correlated with environmental degradation, increased human vulnerability and increase in the intensity of the impact of disasters. Rapid population growth is one of the main factors contributing towards increased vulnerability to natural hazards. More and more population are forced, through lack of choice to expand into disaster prone areas, i.e., steep hillsides, flood plains, landslide prone areas, etc., increasing easy access to adverse impacts of natural hazards.

The favourable condition for population growth, which used to be blessing, is now becoming curse day-by-day. Most of the essential resources for life in the country are getting exhausted. Among such resources, water is on the top. Many rural region of country are in short supply of drinking and irrigation water. Continuous drought in western India is the prime indication of the future explosive situation, which country is going to face. Like water, other resources i.e. forests, fossil fuel, agricultural land, etc., are also falling short to the increasing need of the people.

Thus uncontrolled population growth has posed a serious threat to our socio-economic set-up along with environment (Fig. 4.3). The major consequences of this population growth are reflected in:

- Environmental degradation
- Degradation in socio- cultural values
- Escalation in- unscientific development

Fig. 4.2 : This tree was suppose to protect us....
Timely intervention can make a difference !

- Scarcity of livelihood resources
- Overall degradation in life quality
- Increased vulnerability of land and society to disasters.

As it is the escalating rural population that hampers the achievements of all developmental programmes including disaster management in rural areas, it becomes imperative that to get maximum progress and achievement in the field of disaster management, a check is put on population growth. Thus population or birth control becomes the prime objective of sustainable development in rural areas.

Population Control

The first step in controlling population in the country was started in 1951 with the introduction of Family Planning Programme, which was a purely demographic programme. However, later the elements of public education and extension was included to facilitate outcomes under the programme. The basic objective of family planning, later renamed *family welfare* have been to encourage citizens through information, education and communication to adopt birth control methods voluntarily. However, despite a partial success (fertility rate fall from 6.2 to 4.3 in the period between 1965 to 1987, in comparison to China for which it fell from 6.4 to 2.4), it could not achieve much and still the population explosion remains the major problem faced by the country.

The basic reason for population growth in India, especially in rural India has been the lack of education. The target of education for all is still a distant dream for the country to achieve. Failure to provide basic facilities to rural areas has been the other major factor for partial success of the programme. Religion and cultural values and traditions in rural society have been other factors for escalating population growth. Behind all these issues, the major drawback had been that the family planning or welfare programmes were only a government programme and involvement of local bodies have been very negligible in propagating such programmes. This is why the people's participation in such programmes has not been very encouraging. Taking all these aspects of the problem into consideration it is required that-

- Family planning or welfare becomes an integral part of rural development policy of the country.
- Local elected bodies and NGOs should be involved at all the stages of programme, i.e. policy formulation, implementing and monitoring.
- Family planning facilities and devices should be made available in rural areas easily.
- Religious NGOs should be specially encouraged to take the responsibility for popularising this programme in rural areas.
- Advertisement through various local media means may also help in propagation of this programme up to an extent.
- Educating people through school, adult education and anganwadis, etc., may be very helpful.
- Various government incentives may also yield good results in the field of family planning.

Thus, in brief, the birth control problem in India needs a thorough review and modification so that it becomes people's programme and helps in getting desired results in the field of rural development and allied aspects.

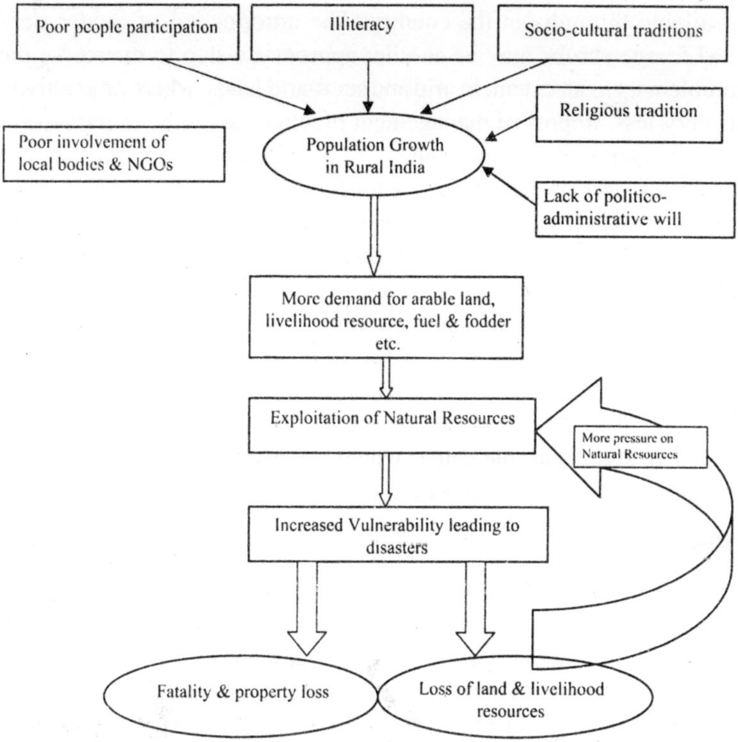

Fig 4.3 : Population Growth - Its causes and impact on vulnerability

Livestock Population

Cattle or livestock are integral part of Indian rural society. India with total livestock population of 4,700 lakh (470 million) is the world's most populous country as far as cattle are concerned. Along with human population, the exponential increase in cattle population has also been a major problem in the way of sustainable rural development. The dependency on forest for fodder of this huge cattle population is creating enormous pressure on our already diminishing forest resources.

To overcome this problem, it is required that appropriate measures are taken for proper cattle management. Scientific researches are to be carried out to evolve new technical package to increase significantly the carrying capacity of arid and semi-arid land, which is extensively available through out the country. The introduction of fodder trees and forage shrubs may be another appropriate step to overcome the problem up to an extent. In arid and semi-arid lands, where productivity is very less, improved management practices are to be introduced to turn this land into pastureland.

Lack of marketing facilities for cattle products is the other major problem with the cattle management. Due to non-availability of this basic facility, the poor cattle holders in villages are forced to sell their products at throwaway prices. In such circumstances it becomes impossible for them to feed their cattle, ultimately compelling them to leave them in forest area for free grazing, leading to forest degradation and soil erosion. Besides creating suitable marketing facilities for cattle products, if efforts are made to develop pasture lands at wasteland, the cattle, which seems to be the burden for the country, may prove as an asset.

Poverty

Poverty, a state of deprivation is the curse in our society. Poverty reflects the inability of an individual to satisfy certain basic minimum needs for a sustained, healthy and a reasonably productive living. There is no standard definition of poverty. Though it is very difficult to define poverty, even then an absolute definition of poverty assumes that it is possible to define a minimum standard of living based on a person's biological needs for food , water, clothing and shelter. Poverty is where people fall below this level -when they cannot own house, clothes or feed themselves (*Poverty: The Face by Oppenheim ,1993*).

Poverty is the curse in our rural society. Despite the high priority for rural poverty alleviation and sustainable development in developing countries, the majority of world's poor (1.3 billion) are still found in these countries and 3/4th of them live in rural areas. In India, the situation is not much different than the other developing countries

In India, a vast majority of rural people depend for their livelihood on farm and non-farm activities. Ensuring opportunities to enable them to cross over poverty on sustainable basis is a formidable challenge. Poverty eradication is one of the major objectives of planned development of Government of India. Though government is spearheading its frontal attack on rural poverty and endured to reach out to the last and the most disadvantaged section of the society, yet the magnitude of the problem of poverty is still quite staggering. It is in the rural areas where poverty and its various manifestations are predominant.

Poverty in Rural India

For identifying the poor one looks at the level of personal expenditure (or income) that enables the individual to satisfy a certain minimum consumption level. The proportion of population not able to attain the specified level of expenditure is then segregated as poor. The Planning Commission, based on such approach, has been estimating the Head Count Ratio of the poor at state level, separately for rural and urban areas for over three decades. At present Planning Commission uses a minimum consumption expenditure, anchored in an average (food) energy adequacy norm of 2400 and 2100 kilo calories per capita per day respectively to define state specific poverty line, separately for rural and urban areas (Annexure XIV to XIX).

In India, poverty is in its worst form, particularly in the rural areas where more than 70 per cent population of country reside. Many of them neither have any source of earning nor access to necessary food, shelter, drinking water, and sanitation, resulting in poverty and sufferings. Rural poverty is inextricably linked with the low rural productivity and unemployment, including under-employment. While the normal process of growth has to play a significant role in improving the living standards of the poor, this by itself cannot ensure growth with equity and social justice.

Though the poverty is widespread in Indian rural sector, it is worse in certain sections or groups of the society, who are forced to live a miserable life. In the rural Indian society there is higher disparity of income between rich and poor. .

The degree of the poverty is worse in rural areas than the urban areas owing to :

- Low wages
- Sluggish agricultural growth
- Unemployment
- Scarcity of other livelihood resource

— Social and cultural traditions which restrict job opportunities (caste system)
— Higher disparity of income between rich and poor.

Some important observations of poverty distribution in the country are :

1. The relatively drier states (in west) harbour lesser poverty proportions than the wetter ones (east). The probable reasons are the impact of *zamindari* regime and ineffective agrarian and land reforms and there after the failure of green revolution in these states.

2. The so-called BIMARU states inhabit 51 per cent of the poor population in the country. These figures are very important and contrasting. These seven states, out of 32 (now 9 out of 35) and Union Territories in general have the agro-climatic condition favourable for potential to high yield in agriculture. This suggests that the basic reason for poverty in these states is human induced rather than natural.

3. The states of Assam, Bihar, Orissa, U.P and West Bengal have 75.7 per cent of total poor in the country.

4. The seven states (Eastern and BIMARU) comprise about 70 per cent of poor people in the country.

5. Along with region specific, one other significant feature about poverty distribution in the country is prevalent caste based structure. The SC/ST and other backward classes make higher proportion of poor people. The literacy rate also up to an extent decides the poverty ratio. The poverty is more prominent in areas with more illeteracy.

6. The occupations of the people also play important role in deciding the poverty. The landless, including the agriculture and non-agriculture labour class is more poor than the real agriculture community with land holding. The casual labourers engaged in agriculture farms are found to be poorest and those working outside were experiencing less poverty.

7. Among the major States, Orissa, Bihar, West Bengal and Tamil Nadu had more than 40 per cent of their population below the poverty line in 1983. By 1999-2000, while Tamil Nadu and West Bengal had reduced their poverty ratios by nearly half, Orissa and Bihar continued to be the two poorest States with poverty ratio of 47 and 43 per cent respectively,

8. Among others, Jammu & Kashmir, Haryana, Gujarat, Punjab,

Andhra Pradesh, Maharashtra and Karnataka have also succeeded in significantly alleviating poverty.

9. Rural Orissa and rural Bihar continued to be the poorest among rural areas both in 1983, as well as in 1999-2000. In urban areas, the poorest three States in 1983 were Madhya Pradesh, Uttar Pradesh and Orissa whereas in 1993 it was Orissa followed by Madhya Pradesh and Bihar.

Statistical data about Poverty in India

As per Planning Commission's latest report of 2001, at the national level, the incidence of poverty on the Head Count Ratio declined from 44.48 per cent in 1983 to 26.10 per cent in 1999-2000. While in the rural areas the proportion of poor declined from 45.65 per cent in 1983 to 27.09 per cent in 1999-2000, the decline in urban areas has been higher i.e., from 40.79 to 23.62 per cent during this period. Thus the problem of poverty in rural India is still much more serious and matter of concern. As per the Planning Commission's special publication- National Human Development Report-2001, the latest figure about the poverty in the country, is given state-wise in Table 4.2.

The Planning Commission has used one more parameter to measure the poverty in the country and that is Human Poverty Index or HPI. It is basically a composite variable capturing deprivation in three dimensions of human development *viz.* economic, education and health. These have been captured by relative proportion of population below poverty line, population ratio without access to safe drinking water/ sanitation/ electricity, medical attention and proportion living in *kutcha* houses; fraction of illiterate population and children not enrolled in schools, and proportion of population not expected to survive beyond age 40.

Poverty and Vulnerability

Poverty and hazard vulnerability are inextricably linked and mutually reinforcing. It is the poor section of the society that is worst affected by the adverse impacts of the natural calamity. The situation further aggravates due to the compulsion of poor to exploit environmental resources for their survival. This exploitation of natural resources increases the risk and exposure of the society to disasters, in particular

Table 4.2 : Poverty in Rural and Urban India

STATE/UTs	RURAL			URBAN			COMBINED	
	No. of Person	% of Person	Poverty Line (Rs)	No. of Person	% of Person	Poverty Line (Rs)	No. of Person	% of Person
Andhra P.	58.13	11.05	262.94	60.88	26.63	457.4	119.01	15.77
Arunachal P.	3.8	40.04	365.43	0.18	7.47	343.99	3.98	33.47
Assam	92.17	40.04	365.43	2.38	7.47	343.99	94.55	36.09
Bihar	376.51	44.3	333.07	49.13	32.91	379.78	425.64	42.6
Goa	0.11	1.35	318.63	0.59	7.52	539.71	0.7	4.4
Gujarat	39.8	13.17	318.94	28.09	15.59	474.41	67.89	14.07
Haryana	11.94	8.27	362.81	5.39	9.99	420.2	17.34	8.74
Himacahl P.	4.84	7.94	367.45	0.29	4.63	420.2	5.12	7.63
Jammu & K.	2.97	3.97	367.45	0.49	1.98	420.2	3.46	3.48
Karnataka	59.91	17.38	309.59	44.49	25.25	511.44	104.4	20.04
Kerala	20.97	9.38	374.79	20.07	20.27	477.06	41.04	12.72
M. P.	217.32	37.06	311.34	81.22	38.44	481.65	298.54	37.43
Maharashtra	125.12	23.72	318.63	102.87	26.82	539.73	227.99	25.02
Manipur	6.53	40.04	365.43	0.66	7.47	343.99	7.19	28.54
Meghalaya	7.89	40.04	365.43	0.34	7.47	343.99	8.23	33.87
Mizoram	1.4	40.04	365.43	0.45	7.47	343.99	1.85	19.47
Nagaland	5.21	40.04	365.43	0.28	7.47	343.99	5.49	32.67
Orissa	143.69	48.01	3323.92	25.4	42.83	473.12	169.09	47.15
Punjab	10.2	6.35	362.68	4.29	5.75	388.15	14.49	6.16
Rajasthan	55.06	13.74	344.03	26.78	19.85	465.92	81.83	15.28
Sikkim	2	40.04	365.43	0.04	7.47	343.99	2.05	36.55
T. N.	80.51	20.55	307.64	49.97	22.11	475.6	130.48	21.22
Tripura	12.53	40.04	365.43	0.49	7.47	343.99	13.02	34.44
U. P.	412.01	31.22	336.88	117.88	30.89	416.29	529.89	31.15
W. Bengal	180.11	31.85	350.17	33.38	14.86	409.22	213.49	27.02
A& Nicobar	0.58	20.55	307.64	0.24	22.11	475.6	0.82	20.99
Chandigarh	0.06	5.75	388.15	0.45	5.75	388.15	0.51	5.75
Dadra & N Hav.	0.3	17.57	318.63	0.03	13.52	539.71	0.33	17.14
Daman & Diu	0.01	1.35	318.63	0.05	7.52	539.71	0.06	4.44
Delhi	0.07	0.4	362.68	11.42	9.42	505.45	11.49	8.23
L. Dweep	0.03	9.38	374.79	0.08	20.27	477.06	0.11	15.6
Pondicherry	0.64	20.55	307.64	1.17	22.11	477.6	2.41	21.67
All India	1,932.43	27.09	327.56	670.07	23.62	454.11	2,602.50	26.1

Source : Planing Commission, 2002.

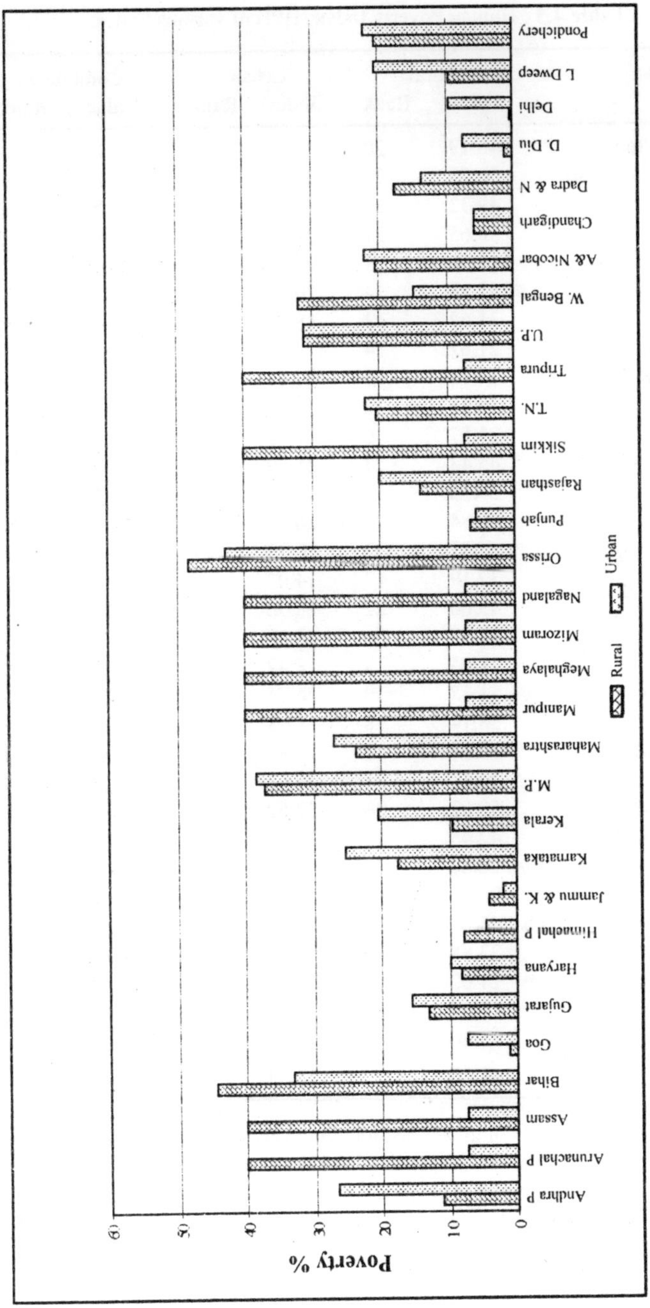

Fig 4.4 : Poverty distribution in Rural and Urban India (based on data of Planning Commission, 2002)

Table 4.3 : Human Poverty Index (HPI) of various States

States/Uts	Rural		Urban		Combined	
	Value	Rank	Value	Rank	Value	Rank
Andhra Pradesh	43.19	20	25.12	25	38.34	19
Arunchal Pradesh	50.75	29	25.65	26	47.40	30
Assam	49.32	27	22.52	22	46.29	28
Bihar	53.65	31	29.70	31	50.48	32
Goa	15.58	1	13.78	3	36.10	17
Gujarat	31.83	14	20.87	18	28.05	13
Haryana	31.64	13	18.57	14	28.41	14
Himachal Pradesh	21.67	4	9.91	1	20.90	5
Jammu & Kashmir	34.94	15	17.67	10	30.95	15
Karntaka	35.28	16	21.59	19	30.99	16
Kerala	24.57	6	17.23	8	22.73	7
Madhya Pradesh	45.43	23	25.69	27	40.79	22
Maharashtra	29.30	11	17.65	9	24.73	8
Manipur	43.84	21	26.51	28	39.82	21
Meghalaya	55.81	32	20.15	17	49.41	31
Mizoram	37.19	17	14.07	4	26.47	12
Nagaland	45.00	22	23.56	24	41.3	23
Orissa	47.97	26	28.29	30	45.22	27
Punjab	28.04	9	18.47	13	25.25	10
Rajasthan	51.17	30	26.73	29	44.73	26
Sikkim	38.14	18	17.8	11	38.59	20
Tamil Nadu	30.31	12	18.61	15	26.45	11
Tripura	46.32	25	21.97	21	42.71	24
Uttar Pradesh	50.02	28	32.62	32	46.65	29
West Bengal	42.43	19	23.22	23	37.35	18
Andaman & Nicobar Is.	28.80	10	16.32	7	25.24	9
Chandigarh	25.07	7	15.07	5	15.96	2
Dadra & Nagar Haveli	45.66	24	21.95	20	43.64	25
Daman & Diu	23.88	5	15.82	6	19.90	4
Delhi	21.02	3	17.99	12	18.23	3
Lakshadweep	15.67	2	12.26	2	13.89	1
Pondicherry	25.86	8	19.57	16	22.52	6
All India	**42.25**		**23.03**		37.42	

Note: For the sake of completeness, for some variables used in estimating the indices, the data for all States/Uts have been estimated/assumed following, in general, principles of physical contiguity or similarity in socio-economic or demographic profile.

Source : Planning Commission, 2002.

those triggered by flood, droughts and landslides. Poverty also compels the poor to migrate and to live in dangerous locations, often on unsafe land and unsafe shelters, which is comparatively lower in cost and is in the reach of poor. This inhabitation of the poor in such locations is either due to the fact that there is no other land available at reasonable cost or it is close to employment opportunities.

The inhabitation of poor people on marginal land is prone to all types of disasters. The type of construction of these houses further deteriorates the condition. These dwellings made up of low cost material without giving much consideration to technical aspect are easy targets of various natural hazards (Fig. 4.5).

This phenomenon is very evident in the rural areas, especially in

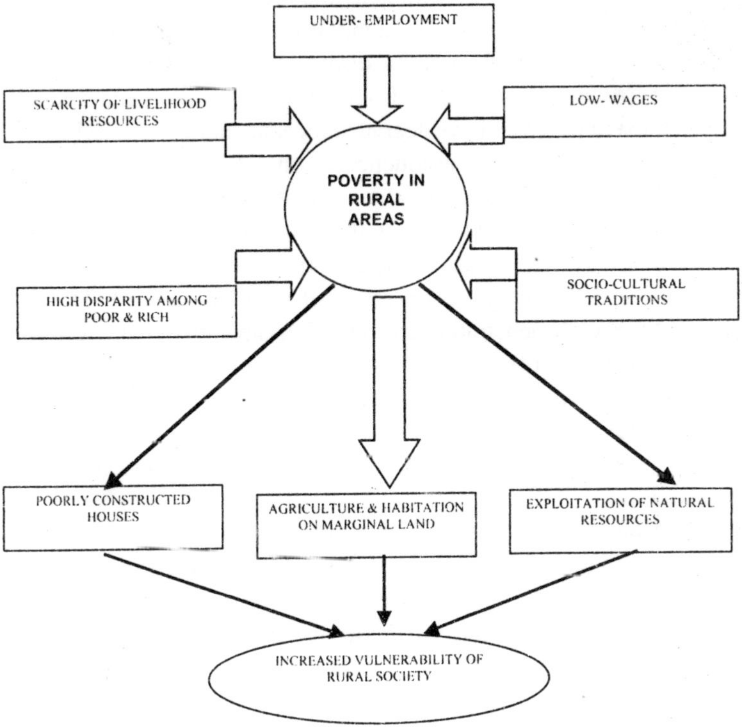

Fig. 4.5 : Rural Poverty and Vulnerability

hills where poor people are forced to live and do agriculture in hazaradous zone, which are mostly on steep slopes and prone to landslides, earthquakes, flash floods, etc. In plain areas also, the situation is not much different and here the poor community are living on marginal land, usually on the periphery of the main village. These lands usually in low-lying regions are themselves very hazardous to human life. The lack of proper drainage system, poor drinking water facilities, etc. are the factors responsible for the break of epidemics and make the area more vulnerable to other forms of disasters.

Land use Pattern

In India, whether it is urban or rural area, the main factor for environmental degradation is unscientific land use pattern. The way land is used, affects the environment and the carrying capacity of the land. Unplanned land use is also a major factor for landslides, floods, soil erosion, and other common disasters in hills and plain areas. Attempts to increase production from land are not always eco- friendly and in most of the cases have degraded the land quality. Desertfication is also up to an extent a consequence of unscientific land use pattern and exploitation of the productive capacity of soil. Degradation of soil in some parts of Haryana is the example of this type of land degradation. Due to excessive irrigation in these areas, the soil has become very rich in salt (as a result of capillary action). This has reduced the water penetration and retention capacity of land, resulting into excessive run off, which is responsible for soil erosion and flood. The use of steep hill slopes for agriculture and housing purpose is another example of land misuse, leading to disasters. Crop pattern without taking into consideration the nature of soil also causes land degradation.

All these examples signify the importance of scientific land use pattern to safeguard environment and prevent disasters up to an extent. Keeping in view the significance of the issue, it becomes necessary that an eco-friendly land use policy be developed, specially for disaster-prone and sensitive areas. The land and other developmental schemes being implemented in these regions have to give due consideration to this aspect.

Land Reforms

Land reforms and land management are two sides of the same coin. Despite legislative measures and other reforms, the most of the country land is still being cultivated by old *zamindari* system. Landlordism, absent landowners and sharecropping still dominate a large portion of the country. In such system both the landowners and the cultivators have their own interests and the land management remains no one's agenda. Lack of security for land holding discourages the cultivators to adopt and implement the appropriate land management practices.

All this leads to over exploitation of land and other associated resources, ultimately degrading the land and the soil. The long-term impacts of land mismanagement results into desertification, drought, excessive soil erosion and flood. Thus the implementation of land reforms should be the first priority of the Central and State governments, which may ensure security to the cultivators, who may in turn take proper care for land management and prevent disasters in the area. The rural development policies should give priority to land reform programme with dual objectives of reducing disparity among the rural society and conserving land and other natural resources.

Environmental Degradation

In general the environmental degradation has been the major factor for increased vulnerability of the society and land to disasters (Fig. 4.6). Due to rural area's specific socio-cultural, socio-economic conditions and its physical position, the environmental degradation has affected the rural society worst. There have been many factors responsible for the present deplorable state of environment, among them deforestation and degradation of the forests during the last 50 years being the most prominent. The tremendous population pressure and its increasing need and greed have diminished our most valuable natural resource up to threshold value.

The major factors responsible for shrinking of the forest cover of the country are :

— Human and cattle population explosion around forestland and overgrazing.

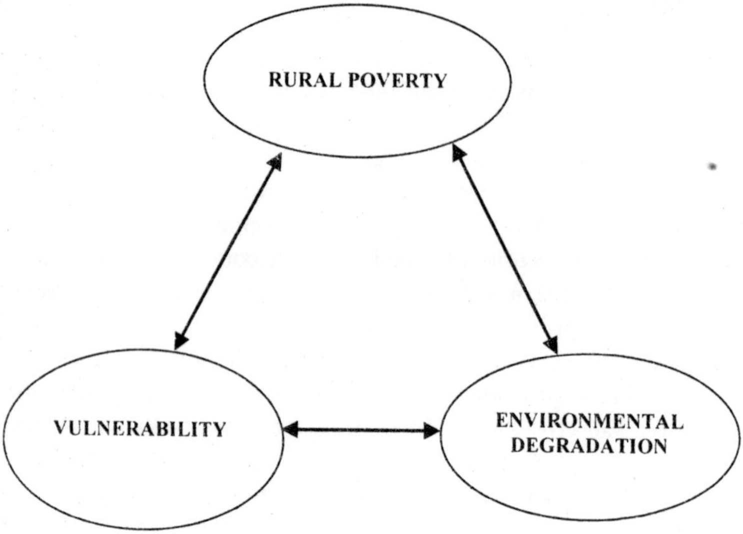

Fig. 4.6 : Poverty, Environmental Degradaton and Vulnerability are inextricably linked

— Agriculture (including shifting cultivation), multipurpose projects, irrigation, industries, mining/quarrying for minerals, construction of roads, erection of transmission lines, and clearing for encroachments (industrialisation, urbanisation and human settlements), illicit felling, over-felling, forest litter removal, lopping for fodder and fuel-wood, etc.

— Forest fires, etc.

The ill-effects of deforestation and forest degradation are enormous, affecting the overall welfare of the people, and causing heavy social cost. In brief these negative impacts fall in two categories:

* *Environmental impacts*: Loss of ecological stability, damage to the ecological foundations of agriculture; loss of bio-diversity; reduction in carbon sink capability; effects of climate change; floods, drought and related losses; damage to watershed; silting up of reservoirs; soil erosion; desertification; and changes in hydrological regime.

* *Economic impacts*: Fall in agricultural productivity and crop yields; scarcity for forest products; closure/unused capacity of forest industries; and continuous and cumulative disinvestment of forest capital.

Grazing, mining, shifting cultivation, developmental plans like road , building , dam construction, etc. particularly in the rural areas have caused a great damage to forest of the country. About two-third agricultural land of the country is affected by drought and about one-fifth by frequent floods. Deforestation and other allied land degradation activities such as water logging, flooding, ravines, shifting cultivation, mining, salinisation, water logging, soil erosion, landslides and rock falls, desertification, etc., have affected more than half of the total geographical area of the country. The deforestation in the form of mangrove removal has made the coastal region more susceptible to erosion and damage to human settlement.

Table 4.4 : Status of Forest in India

Category	Area (mh)	%age of total geographic area	%age of forest area
Total geographical area	328.73	100	—
Legally classified forest	76.53	23.28	100
Actual forest cover (>10% crown area)	63.73	19.23	83.27
Open forest (crown area 10-40%)	25.51	7.76	33.33
Dense forest (crown area >40%)	37.73	11.48	49.30
Mangrove forest	0.49	0.15	0.64

(*Source* : Ministry of Environment and Forest, Government of India).

To some extent, global warming is also responsible for the rain-fall variation, accelerating desertification and land degradation. Loss in agriculture production (particularly rainfed), human and cattle health deterioration, scarcity of water resources are the other adverse impacts of this phenomenon on the society. All these factors have a compound effect on the impact and occurrence of natural disasters. Besides escalating the intensity and frequency of various disasters, they also increase the vulnerability of the society. Though environmental degradation affect the whole society in general, the rural poor due to their settlement are worst affected by it. The floods, landslides, soil erosion and land degradation are the common form of disasters that more adversely affect the rural society in comparison to their urban counterpart.

Changing Socio-Cultutral Pattern of Society

With change of time, the rural community has also gone under a tremendous change in its life-style. Among other factors, the change in housing pattern has more adversely affected the vulnerability of the rural community to natural hazards. In most of the rural constructions the bricks, stones and the cement have replaced the indigenous material and techniques. These new constructions, carried out without giving much thought to the ill effects of natural calamities, have proved very fatal and disastrous during many natural calamities. The Uttarkashi and Chamoli Earthquakes of Uttaranchal are the recent examples, where the maximum lives lost were due to collapse of newly constructed concrete and brick buildings. The buildings constructed with indigenous technique and material were less damaged during these calamities in comparison to other new buildings.

The changing socio-economic condition of the rural society has also affected its vulnerability to disasters. The mechanisation of agriculture practices, excessive use of chemical fertilizers and insecticides, irrigation and various other factors have affected the vulnerability of rural society in many ways.

Since independence the country has achieved quadruple increase in agriculture production. But this achievement has been at the cost of natural forest and environment degradation. After independence a major portion of the forest has been cleared to capture agricultural land. The increase in agriculture production has also increased the disparity between rich and poor farmers. While on one hand the intensive irrigation and use of chemical fertilisers and pesticides has deteriorated the soil and water condition in intensive irrigated areas, the agriculture in rain-fed regions, specially in hill areas has resulted in enormous soil loss and deterioration of the natural water drainage system.

The mechanisation of agriculture has led to rural unemployment also. The mechanisation has deprived many sections of the society like rural artisans, agriculture labourers, carpenter, blacksmith, cobbler and other rural population of their livelihood resources making them poorer, and thus more vulnerable to adverse impacts of natural hazards.

One more obvious change in the present village community is the lack of cooperation amongst people. In the earlier days people used to do *Shram Daan* for the social welfare activities like sanitation, clearing of natural drainage pattern, environmental conservation, etc., which no more exists. This is also an important factor responsible for the increased vulnerability of the rural community to disasters.

Government Policies and Institutions

After discussing most of the factors affecting rural community's economy and its vulnerability to natural disasters, it is the turn of government policies and programmes affecting rural society of the country in its economical, social, political and environmental aspects. Ministry of Rural Development, Ministry of Agriculture, Department of Women and Child Welfare, Ministry of Tribal Affairs, KVIC, Ministry of Environment and Forests are the various Central ministries and departments which are directly or indirectly involved with the rural development and provide funds for it. Among these, Rural Development is the main body which spends a substantial fund for the rural sector. Ministry's annual budget is around Rs. ten thousand crore, which is allocated for various schemes/programmes to be executed in rural areas.

The government policies since its initiation and planning towards rural development have not been uniform. In the early years of planning, about one-fifth of the total allocations were made towards all agricultural and rural programmes, including flood, irrigation and related areas. But this has undergone changes since Fourth-Five Year Plan. In the later 1990s the combined State and Central expenses on agriculture and allied activities, irrigation and rural development did not exceed 12 per cent. In most of the five years plans, the main emphasis of government in rural sector development had been on irrigation and flood control and social services, followed by agriculture and allied services and rural development. All the infrastructural and general technical services and village industries have very small share. The other significant sectors, services, technology and environment conservation had negligible share.

It not only indicates government's lack of initiatives in the field of science and technology, environment and communication (Fig. 4.7) for rural development but also in development of small scale industry. In most of the rural development and allied sectors, conservation of resources is rarely given priority. It is observed that in most of government policies / programmes negligible attempt is made in this regard. Lack of long-term perspectives in government policies has adversely affected rural economy and environment and turned many regions into disaster-prone areas. Clear felling of densely forested area for agricultural purpose to make "green revolution" a success, introduction of polythene bags etc. are some of the major government policy decisions, which affected the economy and environment disastrously. Before introduction of polythene bags, many poor families were involved in making of paper bags, using old news papers and other waste papers. These families were getting additional income from this small scale industry and there was no adverse impact on environment. But introduction of polythene industry reversed all equations. Besides depriving them of additional source of income, this very adversely affected the environment and has become a serious problem for the present administration. All this happened due to lack of foresightedness of the policy-makers and implementers. An other disaster of similar nature which is going to show its disastrous impact in near future is introduction of plastic/synthetic glass and plates, very popular in catering services by railways, hotels, cold drink stalls, etc. This industry is slowly encroaching upon livelihood resource of the village potters and also causing environment degradation, as most of the material used is non-degradable. Clear felling of forest in Tarai belt of Uttaranchal is another example of such disastrous policy. The deforestation in the area for agricultural purposes had very adverse impact on downstream plain areas. The increase in soil erosion, landslides and consequent floods in these areas have really damaged much more than the benefits. These are few of the long list of examples about the government policies which have disastrous impact on rural economy as well as environment. In such circumstances, it becomes inevitable that the policies and programmes of rural development be reviewed keeping in view its impact on society and environment. Necessary modifications, if required, can be made taking into consideration local conditions for desired results.

Fig. 4.7 : Why papa insists to become an engineer or doctor?

One other major drawback with government policies is lack of provision of coordination among various departments working at field level. This lack of coordination among various institutions and between the government and poor beneficiaries generally create unfavourable policy climate for environmental conservation.

Inadequate Scientific and Technological Support in Rural Sector

During the last few decades, new technical and other scientific researches have been carried out for production increase, ignoring the environmental aspect. This has led to serious environmental and land degradation problem in most of the rural areas of the country. The traditional tools and techniques of rural artisans are of no more use for rural market, causing adverse impact on this section of the society and making them poor to poorer. Research and technical institutes of the country are engaged in very sophisticated hi-fi research, which is of negligible use to our rural society. The real requirement of the rural society, especially the landless artisan community has till now been ignored by our researchers and technocrats. Rural eco-friendly technologies have not been of much interest to our scientists and research institutes. If some research has been carried out in this regard that has not been of much practical use and its extension and publicity has been very limited. Publicity, extension and incentives by administration for new researches have not been very enthusiastic either. All this has forced the rural poor artisans to still depend on their traditional technology, small old tools, which are of not much use in changing scenario. Very few attempts have been made to improve and develop indigenous technologies in the field of rural energy production, dry land farming, small gobar gas plants, weaving charkhas and khadi manufacturing khaddis, rural pottery, furniture and other wooden and iron/steel agricultural implement manufacturing techniques, small scale irrigation facilities, *gur* and *khandsari* manufacturing units, portable pottery manufacturing etc. at village level. The ignorance of these sectors has put big shot back to rural economy, adversely affecting almost each and every component of rural economy. The most adverse impact of this had been the attraction of rural society to urban market to fulfill its demand. The Indian rural society for almost all its basic needs like clothes, shoes, agricultural implements, household things, etc., is now dependent on urban market and the products by rural artisans are in no more demand as they could not be updated along with changing scenario.

This backwardness in the rural technology has been the major cause for poor rural economy and the cramped rural economy is forced to open its door for outside products. But unfortunately this change or flow of economy has been one-sided and the rural money is being spent on products being produced by heavy industries but the product of rural sectors have not been able to penetrate into urban market. This lop-sided flow of money from rural sector to urban sector has turned rural poor to poorer, adversely affecting the rural economy. Publicity, extension and incentives by administration for new researches have not been very encouraging to adopt such researches which may encourage the village—rural based cottage industry to improve rural economy. The execution and implemention of such policies has compelled rural poor to migrate to urban areas, inviting disasters in both rural and urban areas. Along with this, population pressure on agricultural land has forced on the poor farming class to look for alternative livelihood resources, but unfortunately government and other sectors responsible to evolve and invent alternative resources have not taken much initiatives in this regard.

Along with the lack of scientific research and technological development in rural sectors, the other basic major problem had been poor marketing of rural products. It can be proudly proclaimed that if given proper marketing facilities, our rural artisons have good capabilities to produce the products of international standard. But the handicraft sectors of most of tribal belts and other areas are unable to prosper without proper marketing facilities.

Along with artisans, the cattle industry has also good scope. But unfortunately, the traditional cow-dwellers neither have proper facility to transport milk and its products to cities, nor the proper facilities for marketing. The milk and the other cattle oriented industries, due to lack of these basic facilities, are dying their own death. In such circumstances, these traditional cow-dwellers are forced to shift to other petty livelihood resources. If under rural development sectors basic facilities like marketing, making raw material available at fair prices, proper transportation and research and development etc., are given proper care, a major portion of the problem of unemployment, environmental degradation, poverty, etc., will automatically diminish, making rural society economically more sound and resilient to natural hazards.

Disaster Management in Rural Areas : Problems and Shortcomings of the Existing System

The preceding discussion about the vulnerability of the rural areas clearly shows that the rural population of the country, comprising more than 70 per cent of the total population is at maximum risk due to natural hazards. Despite many sincere efforts at Central and State levels during the last few decades, the results are not satisfactory and the rural community of the country is still suffering from various ill effects of disasters. The major ones are human life loss and injury, livestock loss, house and property damage, land damage, water and food scarcity, livelihood loss, diseases, loss of educational and other social systems, psychological shock and damage of communication system.

Detail analysis of the primary and secondary data regarding disaster management reveals that the results of present practices are not upto the mark. The main problems being faced during disaster management operations in rural areas are:

Delay in relief and rescue: It has been a common observation that in most of the cases the rescue and relief operation is usually delayed after an area is hit by disaster (Fig. 4.8). In remote areas due to bad communication, sometimes it takes weeks to reach the first aid help. Beside this, the damage to infrastructure like road, telephone lines, etc., also make it difficult to approach the affected area in time. This delay in relief and rescue results into considerable loss to life and property in disaster affected areas.

Discrimination in survey: While assessing for loss by the district authorities or any other organisation, various allegations have been made about the integrity of the agency involved in survey. The primary data reveals that survey to assess the loss of property or livestock in most of the cases is not fair.

Mis-utilisation of relief money: For the persons who lost their houses, land or livestock during disaster, the compensations is given in cash. This money in some of the cases is not properly utilised and used for some other purposes.

The unsuitability of the constructed houses Ignorance of local needs: In most of the places, it has been a common observation that the houses constructed by the donor agencies or the administration are not as per the need or requirement of the local community and hence after some time the houses are vacated by the occupants, as they are not fulfilling their basic needs and are not getting with their local ethos.

The training of locals: During implementation of the disaster management programmes, the training and awareness programme are either very few or mostly ignored. Revenue, medical, university and other staff, locally available can also handle training programmes very effectively. But generally these local resources are not utilised at all.

Fig. 4.8 : A delayed response has got no meaning

Lack of technology: The housing construction or reconstruction of damaged houses by various organisations are not technically suitable or earthquake-resistant. Except few, the administration and other agencies involved in the construction activities, usually do not have simple technical know-how about the construction of disaster resistant houses, due to lack of the proper awareness and training about such technology (Fig. 4.9).

No provision for creating employment: In effective disaster management strategy, the agenda for generating employment opportunity is very critical and important. During disasters most of the villagers lose their productive land, shops or other livelihood resources. In such cases, the generation of employment for such population is very essential and crucial. While implementing disaster management plans, this aspect of disaster management is not given due consideration.

Rehabilitation or shifting of people from very sensitive areas: In most of the disaster-prone areas of the country, the experts from various fields, especially environmentalists and earth-scientists have carried out extensive research work about the hazard sensitivity of these areas. Hazard zonation maps have also been prepared for some

Fig. 4.9 : Always consult a qualified person to design and supervise the disaster resistant shelter

of the areas. Selected villages, falling in these areas have been declared very sensitive and are under continuous threat from one or another type of natural calamities. But no sincere effort seems to have been made in this regard by the concerned authorities. Thus the people residing here are under continuous threat from calamity, which can strike any day.

Faulty development schemes: In disaster-prone and affected areas along with relief and rescue operations, assistance is being provided from Central and State governments and other agencies for employment generation and other developmental activities. The common practice is to use these funds without giving much thought to local conditions or needs. In most of the cases, this fund is used for such developmental activities, which are very hazardous to the environment and stability of the fragile zones. The improper construction of roads and community buildings, etc. is common example for such activities. These activities further accelerate disasters.

Poor monitoring and evaluation: The most sensitive issue in the disaster management programmes is the lack of proper monitoring and evaluation, which leads to corruption, inferior construction and many other irregularities.

False promises and assurances by politicians and administrators: In most of the cases after disasters, it is felt that the expectations of the affected population from the government are usually very high. The reason for this is that the politicians and senior bureaucrats make impractical promises, which are not feasible with the limited resources. This creates a disbelief and unrest among the people and they refuse to cooperate with the administration.

Representation of NGOs: During disasters the representation of NGOs and other public and private sectors is usually not very encouraging. Though some of the NGOs have worked exceptionally good in some of the disaster affected areas but in some cases it is also learnt that few NGOs mark their presence only for the sake of name and no concrete work is carried out by them. Some articles have cited that some of the NGOs make their presence to take political mileage and monetary benefits.

Lack of co-ordination among various departments: Proper co-ordination among various departments is absolutely essential in handling emergency situation like disasters, which in most of the cases is seen lacking. This hampers the rescue, relief and rehabilitation work badly. The lack of cooperation also causes delay in relief and rescue and also results in overlapping or duplication of work in some of the activities.

No efforts for psychological recovery: During disasters, psychological or emotional injuries are very significant and causes various disorders. In general, no mechanism is applied to handle this widespread malaise.

No link between need and relief: The relief material that come in from various agencies is not based on any feedback from the area affected. Most of the material supplied is of no use for the affected population. The material, which is needed most, is not supplied in time. Thus, this communication gap between the donor agencies and the administration cause a lot of confusion and wastage of energy and resources.

5
SUSTAINABLE RURAL DEVELOPMENT FOR DISASTER MITIGATION

Rural Development Perspective

Despite fast urabanisation, majority of Indian population still lives in rural areas and is mainly dependent on agriculture for its livelihood. In comparison to urban counterpart, the rural India is much backward and undeveloped. The very popular word in Hindi belt of the country *Ganwar* meaning villager and used as synonym for the backward and illiterate person, in real sense describes the condition of rural population of the country.

The most common standard in the country to distinguish rural and urban is based on the Census record. During 1991 Census some standards were adopted to distinguish rural and urban area. According to this definition, urban areas are to be distinguished as : (a) all places with a municipality, corporation, cantonment board or notified town area committee, etc.; and (b) all other places which satisfied the following criteria: (i) a minimum population of 5,000 (ii) at least 75 per cent of male working population engaged in non-agricultural pursuits; and (iii) a density of population of at least 400 persons per sq.km.

Thus, all places, which were found to satisfy the prescribed conditions were considered as urban, and the remaining were treated as rural.

The Indian Rural Society

The Indian rural society is quite different and distinguished from its urban counterpart in many ways. The most prominent and the visible difference between the two societies is the contrast in their socio-economic conditions. The rural economy in most of the cases is closed-circuit economy, where different segments are inter-woven and inter-dependent in term of the economic and social context. Though with the passage time there have been a lot of changes, yet the rural society is still more inter-dependent and inter-linked. Most of the needs and requirements of Indian rural society are fulfilled from the village production itself and for very little it is dependent on outside. In such closely inter-linked and inter-woven society, the people are much more dependent on each other and thus are more attached and affiliated to their socio-cultural and traditional values. However, in recent past, due to so called modernisation and fast growing urbanisation, the socio-cultural and socio-economic pattern of the Indian rural society are showing significant changes which unfortunately have more negative impact. Due to this changing socio- cultural pattern and various other factors, the overall condition of the Indian rural society has become more pitiable. Poverty, illiteracy, inadequate basic facilities and infrastructures, unemployment, diseases, etc., are the common features, the Indian rural society is suffering from. Despite sincere efforts at government and non-governmental levels, these curses are still prevailing in our rural society.

Rural Development Approach

The development of the Indian rural society has been a matter of concern for the government since independence. The development does not mean merely the development of physical infrastructures, instead it covers quantitative and qualitative changes in various aspects of human life like social, economic, cultural, technical and natural. This development means desired positive change in the society. This positive change refers to socio-economic and socio- cultural pattern of the society. The rural development means desired positive change in rural society in its totality. In other words it is the improvement in economic and the social life of villages and its inhabitants. In developing countries like India, the main concern of the government in the field of rural development has been to fulfill basic needs of food, clothes, health care and education.

Though the concept of rural development was initiated well before the independence, however in concrete form it was launched only during 1950s. The abolition of the *zamindari* system was the first attempt in this regard after independence. "Land to Tillers" was the slogan of rural development during this period of 1950s.

But unfortunately the land reform failed to achieve its target in terms of growth or social justice. The two major reasons being—

- Land was distributed among the kith and kin of the erstwhile owners and later dispersed among different dominant caste groups and not to the tilling cultivators.
- The Land Reform Act understood the land mere as an independent means of production, rather than it being intricately linked to other markers and social institutions like caste.

Side by side to land reform, the government initiated various other rural development programmes also to uplift the status of rural society. The plan-wise list of such programmes is as follows:

Five Year Plan	Rural Development Programmes
First	Community Development(1952) and National Extension Scheme (1953)
Second	Khadi and Village Industries (1957), Tribal Development Blocks (1959), Package Programme (1960) and Intensive Agriculture District Development Programme (1960).
Third	Applied Nutrition Programme (1962), Intensive Agricultural Area Development Programme (1964), High Yield Variety Programme (1966), Rural Works Programme (1967), Rural Man- power Programme (1969) and Composite Programme for Women and Pre School Going Children (1969)
Fourth	Drought Prone Area Programme, Crash Scheme for Rural Employment (1971), Small Farmers Development Programme (1971), Tribal Area Development Programme (1972), Minimum Needs Programme (1972), Pilot Intensive Rural Employment Programme (1972) and Command Area Development Programme. (1974).
Fifth	Hill Area Development Programme (1975), Desert Development Programme (1977), Whole Village Development Programme (1979), Training of Rural Youth for Self Employment (1979) and Integrated Rural Development Programme (1979).
Sixth	National Rural Employment Programme (1980), Devlopment of Women and Children in Rural Areas (1983), and Rural Land Less Employment Guarantee Programme (1983).
Seventh	Jawahar Rojgar Yojana (1988).

Eighth	Pradhan Mantri Gram Sadak Yojana, Rural Water Supply Programme, Central Rural Sanitation Programme, Jawahar Gram Samridhi Yojana, National Social Assistance Prorgramme, Swarnajayanti Gram Swarojgar Yojana, Integrated Wasteland Development Programme etc.

Green Revolution and Rural Development

Among the programmes mentioned, the Green Revolution has brought revolutionary change in the field of agriculture production. The acute shortage of foodgrain during 1960s in the country was the initiation of the programme. The "technology school" headed by the agricultural scientists and the Ford Foundation were the two main agencies behind this. This school of thought made following suggestions to enhance the agricultural production up to desired level:

1. Use of chemical fertilizers and its production.
2. Multiplication and distribution of improved hybrid seed varieties.
3. Appropriate measures for plant protection, soil and water conservation, livestock breed improvement, agricultural extension, more emphasis on research and technology improvement, improve marketing and credit facilities.

On the basis of the report, the Intensive Agricultural District Programme (IADP) was started in various districts. The Programme later renamed as Intensive Agricultural Area Programme (IAAP) was very successful in enhancing the agriculture production, leading to the very renowned success of the Green Revolution in the country. The main characteristics of the Programme were to: supply of credit and fertilizers, pesticides, agriculture implements, etc., through the cooperatives; provide good facilities for the marketing, etc.; disseminate the scientific knowledge among the farmers in very effective manner; provide adequate storage facilities in the village and nearby town for the seeds and other farming materials; strengthening of cooperatives at village level; timely monitor and evaluation of the programme.

These programmes gained a big success in increasing the food production of the country. However it remained a fact that the success of these programme was mainly restricted to the big farmers and the condition of poor and middle class farmers with low land holding were left at lurch.

As a result of these rural development programmes along with Green Revolution, though the percentage of people living below poverty line slightly decreased and country became self sucificient in food production, yet the condition of real rural peasantry had not shown much change. The basic cause for this partial failure had been that most of the government programmes and policies in the field of rural development, were formulated ignoring the basic ground realities in the rural sector of the country, and that is why the benefits of these programmes could not reach to the needed ones.

The Shortcomings

On account of partial success of Green Revolution and limited gains to the poor section of rural society, the government was forced to rethink and redesign its basic programmes and a second phase of rural development was started with the launch of new "Area Specific" and "Target Group" programmes. The main among them were the Desert Development Programme (DDP), Drought Prone Area Programme (DPAP) and the Integrated Rural Development Programme (IRDP), which basically aimed at providing income earning assets to the below poverty line families in the villages. The Public Distribution Programme (PDP), National Rural Employment Programme (NREP), Rural Landless Employment Guarantee Programme (RLEGP), Jawahar Rojgar Yojana (JRY), Employment Assurance Scheme (EAS), etc., were the later additions in the series of these rural development programmes. However, the evaluation and monitoring of these programmes revealed some major flaws and on the basis of these flaws, necessary modifications were made in them. Later some target-oriented programmes were also launched by the Ministry of Rural Development.

The evaluation studies of these programmes have pointed out many shortcomings. The implementation mechanism of these programmes have led to large scale corruption in the system, depriving the rural poor of the benefits of the schemes. In the words of our late Prime Minister Sh. Rajiv Gandhi, only ten per cent of the allocation of our developmental schemes reaches to the real poor and is utilised for the implementation of such programmes and the rest of the ninety per cent is percolated at various levels. If this is true, whatever schemes of programmes we make the result is going to be zero.

The major drawback in the rural development programmes lies in their execution and implementation at the field level. On the basis of field visits, discussion with various stake holders — bureaucracy (State and Central both), people's representatives, academicians, NGOs, and last but not the least the common people, it may be concluded that the main reasons for the partial failure of the rural development schemes and also other development programmes in the country have been:

- Corruption,
- Lack of interest and enthusiasm in the State and Central bureaucracy,
- Lack of synchronisation in the work.
- Lack of willpower at political and as well as bureaucratic levels,
- Lack of proper monitoring and evaluation,
- No accountability to the people,
- Lack of awareness among the beneficiaries,
- Politicisation of the rural development programmes,
- No involvement of the beneficiaries.

One more important thing the authors feel, is the impracticality of many programmes, being implemented by the Rural Development Ministry. Most of these programmes have been formulated ignoring the real ground situation of the rural society. The socio- cultural and socio- economic reality of the society have either been ignored or not given due weightage while formulating programmes policies at ministry level. In many programmes the flexibility (that is must for successful implementation of the programmes) is totally lacking, which makes it very difficult to implement the programme in its real sense. All this lead to partial failure in achieving the desired results of the programmes.

In brief, these and many other drawbacks in the programmes/ policies and their implementation have denied the poor to get fair benefits out of government programmes. If analysed in detail, we find that the basic reason for most of the drawbacks in the rural development programmes seems to be the denial of the beneficiaries from participation. It is very unfortunate to say that the real poor, for whom these programmes and policies are being formulated and designed are totally unaware about them. If somehow they are able to get a glimpse of the scheme and tries to get some benefit out of it, the red-tapism and demand of commission compel them to rethink and probably forego it. In some areas it came as a revealation that there exists a scheme mediator in each district and even in block, who works as a middleman between the government department or bank and the beneficiaries. It is really very harassing and also impossible to get benefits of the schemes without these touts, even for educated youths.

If we peep further deep into the disaster management and administrative set-up of the rural development and other developmental programmes, we find same level corruption everywhere. The system seems to be totally rotten and suffering from some incurable disease. In this darkness all around, if some ray of hope is visible that is strengthening of the will of rural poor to ask for his right. This can be made possible only through implementation of local self-government system, having good representation of rural poor class.

Taking all the aspects discussed into consideration, the Government of India tried to overcome the shortcomings by renovating or wrapping up a number of non-viable programmes. In the new programmes launched, it is ensured that the beneficiaries and the PRIs have good role to play during the programme implementation. Most of these programmes have been redesigned during 1999-2000 and it will take some more time to review and analyse their impact on the rural society. The various newly modified programmes being implemented by the Ministry of Rural Development are discussed here in brief:

Pradhan Mantri Gram Sadak Yojana

One of the major reasons for partial failure of rural development programmes has been the lack of connectivity between rural and urban areas. This mainly makes the rural society devoid of marketing its products at appropriate prizes. There is a close link between rural connectivity and growth, be it in the area of trade, employment, education or healthcare. States with poor connectivity are also states that reflect poor socio-economic indices. Various studies reveal that a nationwide network of all-weather roads in our rural areas is a critical link for progress.

As per an estimate, there are more than 40 per cent of India's villages, numbering over 2.5 lakh remain unconnected by all weather roads. Keeping this in view a programme has been launched, that is dedicated solely to the construction of rural roads—Pradhan Mantri Gram Sadak Yojana (PMGSY). The Programme envisages connecting every habitation with a population of over 1000 persons through good, all-weather roads, by the year 2003; and those with a population of more than 500 persons by the year 2007. Besides providing connectivity to about one lakh habitations, the programme also aims to upgrade to specifications, about 5 lakh km of existing rural roads.

Rural Housing

The major programme in rural areas has been of rural housing for poorer classes. Efforts are being made to end the shelterlessness by the end of the Ninth Plan period. All unserviceable *kutcha* houses will be turned to semi-*puccu/pucca* by the year 2007. There are two separate schemes for poor and other classes.

For poor class, two schemes, namely the Indira Awas Yojana (IAY) and the Pradhan Mantri Gramodaya Yojana; Gramin Awas (PMGY:GA) are in operation. Under the scheme, each beneficiary is granted Rs. 20,000 as assistance for construction of a house and Rs.22,000 to those in the hill/difficult areas. Selection of beneficiaries is done by the Gram Sabha. Houses are to be constructed by the beneficiary and contractors are discouraged. Ownership is given to female member of the household or in the joint name of the husband and wife. A sanitary latrine and the smokeless *Chullah* are an integral part of houses under these programmes.

Rural Water Supply Programme

Water is the basic necessity of life. The importance of safe drinking water cannot be underestimated. Poor quality of water causes many problems related to health and environment . Though providing safe drinking water is a State subject, yet the Government of India assists the State governments in this regard by providing funds under the Accelerated Rural Water Supply Programme (ARWSP). As on January 31, 2001, out of a total number of 14,22,664 rural habitations in the country, 12,12,243 are fully covered, 1,87,139 are partially covered and 23,282 are yet to be provided with drinking water supply facilities.

Under the Rural Water Supply Programme, Government has so far installed more than 3.50 million hand-pumps and over 1.5 lakh piped water supply schemes. The quality maintenance of drinking water is also taken care of under the programmes.

In the rural areas almost 85 per cent of the rural drinking water supply is dependent on ground water. Therefore sustainability of drinking water sources is very important in order to ensure long-term sustainability of the ground water sources. The Government has introduced reforms in the rural water supply sector with a view to institutionalise community participation in the implementation of rural drinking water supply schemes, wherein the beneficiaries will have to bear partial capital cost and full operation and maintenance responsibility. It is envisaged that gradually the rural water supply schemes will be implemented by the Panchayati Raj Institutions, once the sector reform concept is institutionalised.

Central Rural Sanitation Programme

The sanitation problem in India is very serious. The total sanitation coverage stands 16-20 per cent, of the total rural households in the country, which is lower than some of the least developed countries. To widen the sanitation coverage, Central Rural Sanitation Programme has been restructured and launched since April 1, 1999 in a project mode in 150 pilot districts throughout the country. The objectives of the restructured programme are to accelerate coverage of rural population by 25 per cent by 2002; generate felt need through awareness creation and health education; cover schools in rural areas with sanitation facilities; encourage suitable cost effective and appropriate technologies; bring about a reduction in the instances of water and sanitation related diseases.

To achieve these objectives under Central Rural Sanitation Programme, "Total Sanitation Campaign" has been implemented in the identified 150 districts. The major components are construction of individual household latrines, sanitary complexes for women, school sanitation and awareness generation.

Jawahar Gram Samridhi Yojana

The programme launched in 1999 is implemented by the gram panchayats with the approval of the Gram Sabha. Government of India release funds to the DRDAs/ ZPs, who in turn release the funds directly to the gram panchayat. The gram panchayats are required to prepare an action plan regarding works relating to infrastructures required in the village and to get it approved from the Gram Sabha. The approval of Gram Sabha is to ensure that the assets created under the scheme conform to the felt needs of whole village community. Preference under the scheme is given to SC/ST families living below poverty line (BPL) and to physically handicapped persons. Women are also given due representation in employment opportunity.

The Gram Sabha can choose any work of their choice. It should however result in a durable asset. Preference may be given to works in the areas inhabited by poor and the SC/STs with 22.5 per cent of the expenditure to be incurred exclusively for their benefit. With the approval of the Gram Sabha, gram panchayats can themselves take up works involving expenditure upto Rs. 50,000 without approaching any other agency. However, technical/administrative management approval of appropriate authorities is required only for works costing more than Rs. 50,000.

National Social Assistance Programmes

The programme aims to help for the most vulnerable section of rural society. In order to take care of the old and destitute as well as families that lose their primary bread-winner, the Government has instituted the National Social Assistance Programme covering the National Old Age Pension Scheme and the National Family Benefit Scheme.

National Old Age Pension Scheme

Under this programme, if a rural poor (a person who figures in the BPL list) is more than 65 years and has no regular source of income or financial support from family members, he is given a pension from the Government . The beneficiaries under the programme are identified by the gram panchayat the Gram Sabha level. Government of India gives pension under the National Old Age Pension Scheme to such persons at the rate of Rs. 75 per month, which is distributed in two or more instalments. Some states add more money to this and raise the amount of pension. The pension in such cases is preferably distributed in public meetings, and is given in cash. Otherwise, pension has to be paid through the bank account of the beneficiary in a commercial bank or a post office savings account or through a money order.

National Family Benefit Scheme

Government of India has launched the National Family Benefit Scheme (NFBS) to provide financial security to the bereaved families at the premature death of the bread-winner . A lumpsum grant of Rs. 10,000 is given to the family in the event of death of its primary bread-winner. A primary bread-winner is a person- male or female - who was contributing substantially to the total household income. He or she should have been more than 18 years and less than 65 years of age. The bereaved family should be in the BPL list. It is paid to such surviving member of the household of the deceased family after having local enquiry, who is determined the head of the household.

Annapurna

Food is the basic necessity for life. The government is very much concerned about the food requirements of rural poor. Keeping this in view, the Ministry of Rural Development launched the scheme under the Targeted Public Distribution System. Foodgrains are given to persons below the poverty line at the BPL price. However, there are always old people who do not have income of their own and are obliged to depend on pension from the Government. In order to provide food security to such persons, Government of India has introduced the Annapurna Scheme, under which 10 kg of foodgrains are given free of cost every month to the persons covered under BPL and who are above 65 years. The beneficiaries under the Annapurna Scheme are identified by the Gram Sabha. Each beneficiary gets a card, which entitles him to receive the foodgrains, rice or wheat, depending on the local staple diet.

Swarnjayanti Gram Swarozgar Yojana

To create self-employment opportunities in rural areas, government has introduced an effective self-employment programme— 'Swarnjayanti Gram Swarozgar Yojana', (SGSY)— to provide assistance to the families covered under BPL in rural areas for taking up self-employment. The persons taking up self-employment are called *swarozgaris*. They may take up the activity either individually or in groups, called the Self-Help Groups. For successful self-employment, it is necessary to take up the right activity and for this purpose, four to five activities are selected in each block with the help of officials, non- officials and the bankers. These are called 'key activities', and should be such that they give the swarozgaris an income of at least Rs. 2,000 per month.

SGSY is a credit-cum-subsidy programme. Subsidy is given to make it easy for the poor people to start their own self-employment activity. Loans up to Rs. 50,000 for individuals and Rs. three lakh for self-help groups do not require any collateral. Subsidy is given @ 30 per cent of the project cost subject to a maximum of Rs. 7,500. It is 50 per cent of the project cost with a limit of Rs. 10,000 for SCs/STs. For SHGs too, the subsidy is 50 per cent of the project or Rs. 1.25 lakh, whichever is less.

Integrated Wasteland Development Programme

In the country a large portion of the land is degraded but can be brought under plough with some efforts. Such lands are known as wastelands. Redressing these lands is regarded as a powerful tool of tackling the issues of poverty and backwardness. The Government has launched the Integrated Wastelands Development Programme (IWDP) throughout the country to improve the productivity of these lands and thereby improve the living standards of the rural poor, who own these lands. This Centrally-sponsored scheme has been taken up on watershed basis.

The basic objectives of the programme is to control soil erosion which is usually caused by rainwater-run-off. Water and soil conservation also leads to improved green cover in the project areas leading to improved productivity of land. Under this programme, wastelands are sought to be developed in an integrated manner based on village micro-watershed plans. These plans are prepared after taking into consideration the land capability and site conditions and also in consultation with the local people, in regard to their needs. The projects are executed by the local people.

Zilla Parishad/DRDA assigns project areas to Project Implementing Agencies (PIA) which may be either from government sector including Panchayati Raj Institutions or the non-government sector. The PIA facilitates the actual implementation of the projects by the watershed committees through watershed associations. Besides, for planning and execution of the watershed projects, the local people are also responsible to maintain and manage these projects through a special provision in the form of watershed development fund, created through people's contributions.

The project has been very successful in improving the land quality in many areas. The people participation is the most important aspect of this programme at all levels.

Drought-prone Areas Programme and Desert Development Programme

Drought-prone and desert areas form a major part of the country's area. These areas are poor because of the poor natural resource base-unproductive lands, non-availability of water and poor and erratic rainfall. All these factors lead to frequent droughts and process of desertification over a lapse of time. In order to develop the natural resources of these areas thereby improving the standards of living of the people, the Government has launched two special area development programmes, namely, Drought Prone Areas Programme and Desert Development Programme.

The watershed projects have been proved very successful in mitigating the adverse effects of drought and desertification and to restore ecological balance of the affected areas to promote economic development. The DRDA/zilla prishad identifies the priority areas and watersheds for development and assigns them to PIAs to form Watershed Associations at the village level, which have the responsibility of actually implementing the projects through a watershed committee with technical support from the implementing agencies.

The projects mainly concentrate on the rejuvenation of the natural resource base through soil and moisture conservation, water harvesting and improving green cover of the area by afforestation, pasture development, horticulture, silivipasture, etc.

The watershed associations are also responsible to maintain and manage the complete watershed project after the expiry project period for which a separate provision in the form of a Watershed Development Fund is created through people's contribution.

The projects have resulted in the improvement of land productivity, the rise in water table, enhancing employment opportunity and thus overall socio-economic upliftment of drought-prone and desert area.

Employment Assurance Scheme

In an attempt to provide employment opportunity to the rural masses, Government of India has launched the Employment Assurance Scheme. The basic objective of the scheme is to provide employment to persons below poverty line (BPL) during periods of acute shortage of employment such as a lean agriculture season or drought, etc. The scheme provides additional wage employment opportunities in the form of manual work to the rural poor, living below the poverty line. In the process, durable community assets are created to provide sustained employment. The PRIs play important role in scheme implementation. Seventy per cent of the funds are earmarked to the intermediate (block) panchayats, while 30 per cent is intended to be used by the zilla parishad. The intermediate panchayat proposes the works to be taken up for its segment and the zilla parishad decides the selection of works.

Since the programme is self-targeting in nature and only the minimum wages are paid, it is expected that only persons below poverty line would be seeking work under this programme. While providing employment, preference is given to Scheduled Castes / Scheduled Tribes and parents of child labour, who are below the poverty line.

The Missing Link — Sustainable Development

Though in the recently evolved Rural Development Programmes attempts have been made to overcome the shortcomings and drawbacks with PRIs representation, yet if analysed critically, taking an holistic view, it becomes clear that the approach of sustainable development is still missing from them. The existing development pattern has become more need based, ignoring the nature and humanity. The aspect regarding need of the future generation is totally missing and negligible importance is given to long-term strategy. In the present society, whether it is rural or urban, the development has become production-oriented and not people-oriented. The motive of sustainable development of material and spiritual well being of the society is missing from the present development pattern.

Sustainable development is the development that meets the need of the present without comprising the availability of future generations to meet their own needs. It is a process of change in which the exploitation of resources, the direction of the investment, the orientation of the technological development and institutional changes are all in harmony and enhance both current and future potential to meet human needs and aspirations. Strategy for sustainable development aims to promote harmony among human beings and between humanity and nature (Fig. 5.1). The analysis of existing development programmes in this context gives a very shady picture. The present approach of development has multifarious adverse impact on the society and land, loosing the base on which they stand. Though this has affected both rural and urban society, the impact is much more visible in rural scenario because of its susceptibility to change.

Disaster and Development

Natural hazards are not themselves damaging to a society or region instead it is the vulnerability of that society or region that results into

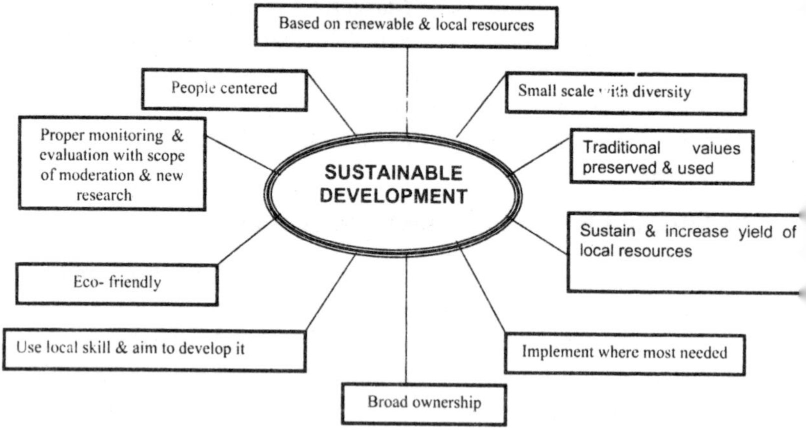

Fig. 5.1 : Ten characteristics of sustainable development

loss to them. The quantum of loss due to a disaster, natural or man-made is the result of vulnerability of a society / region to disaster. The capacity of a society to resist the impact of these forces finally decides the degree of loss to it by hazard and this depends on the precautions, the society has taken, during various stages of development. Thus the disasters are inextricably linked to the development and it is the development pattern of the society which decides its susceptibility / vulnerability to disasters. Taking this aspect into consideration, it is of utmost importance that development pattern of a region/society is to be tailored in such a way, so that the development along with decreasing its vulnerability to natural hazards also makes the society strong and resistant enough to withstand their adverse impacts.

In general, development is treated as the causative factor for disasters. But it is true for unplanned and non-scientific developments. A planned and systematic development in a region certainly helps in reducing the susceptibility of a region and society to losses. Development is an inextricable component of disaster management which is universally applicable but it is more relevant in the areas with continuous threat and frequencies of disasters. In such areas disaster management activities are to be considered as developmental activities and *vice-versa*. The approach of the developmental programmes in the areas should be positive one, with stress on building strong and resistant socio-economic and physical structures, capable to resist the impact of a natural hazard. It is also necessary to view disaster management activities as developmental activities, while revising structural as well as non-structural vulnerability reduction strategies and recognise and integrate the positive elements of indigenous technology.

Thus the main emphasis of a disaster management system should be on reducing the vulnerability, which will automatically take care of post-disaster stages, i.e., emergency and rehabilitation up to an extent. As development pattern and vulnerability are two aspects of a single problem and are inter-dependent, the approach of an appropriate disaster management should be to tailor development of the region in such a manner, so that susceptibility of a society to disaster is minimised. Conventional development is not able to take care of vulnerability and this is why the areas with high disaster frequency needs specialised development planning.

According to Kofi Annan (2000), U.N. Secretary General, there is a wide variety of ways in which disaster risk can be reduced as part of development policies. These involves gender-sensitive regulatory and legal measures, institutional reforms, improved analytical and methodological capabilities, educational awareness, financial planning and political commitment.

The ultimate objective of involving development with disaster management is to motivate society at risk to become engaged in the conscious management of risk and reduction of vulnerability. The process is to expand traditional disaster management beyond practices and defending against the impact of natural hazards. In real sense, it is an on-going process that does not focus on singular disaster event. It is gender sensitive multi-sectoral and inter-disciplinary in nature and comprises of a wide variety of inter-related activities at the local, national, regional and international level.

The basic aim of rural development programe is rural poverty alleviation. The poverty in rural areas is inextricably linked to rapid degradation of the natural resource base. Indeed, rural poverty and degradation of the environment are mutually inter-linked and reinforcing, it is the degradation of natural resources, which is worsening the poverty of rural community. Though environmental degradation is a global phenomenon, it has damaged the natural resources of developing countries more adversely which has most immediate impact on rural poverty in these countries. It is the lack of proper management of natural resource (particularly water and soil) that has enhanced the rural poverty and also the vulnerability of land and society to natural hazards.

If visualised with an holistic approach, the basic factors responsible for poverty leading to environmental degradation and consequently the increased vulnerability of rural society are common. Population growth (both human and cattle), lack of political will, lack of awareness and public participation, unscientific land use pattern, faulty land reform system, lack of proper national policy and inadequate budgeting, less priority to rural technology development are the basic common factors resulting into enhancement of rural poverty, environmental degradation and consequently increase in vulnerability to natural hazards. Thus, these prominent problems like poverty, environmental upgradation and increased vulnerability are also inter-linked and reinforcing. It is required that to achieve the ultimate aim of sustainable development, the existing policies or programmes are to be moulded or tailored to take care of these three aspects of the problem with an integrated approach. This approach in development, with due consideration to poverty alleviation, environmental conservation and vulnerability reduction may lead to sustainable rural development. For this, the development programmes in rural areas should be formuluted to take care of all the factors mentioned above along with the development of the physical assets.

The separation of disaster management from development and environmental conservation will certainly increase vulnerability of the society and subsequently the risk to natural hazards. But the question arises is what type of development makes things worse and what may make things better? The answer to this question is that the development should take due care of four essential aspects of socio-economic system of a society—politico-administrative, economic, social and environmental issues.

(i) There should be politico-administrative will for such type of development. The development should be acceptable to political/ administrative elites and all other sections of the society. For this the involvement of the people from the beginning is a must.

(ii) While considering the social aspect, the development should be acceptable to the people and in tune to their local needs. It should cover all the social obligations i.e. education, health facilities, to take proper care of vulnerable groups of the society etc.

(iii) To take care of the economic aspects, the development should take care of all the economic requirements of each and every section of the society and should not be heterogeneous. The uneven or heterogeneous development helps in accelerating the vulnerability of all the sections of the society to natural hazards.

(iv) The most important aspect for appropriate development, specially in disaster prone area is the environmental consideration. This means the development should be eco-friendly and in such a way so that environment is least disturbed.

Thus in nutshell, a sustainable development refers that it should take proper care of all these four aspects. Sustainable development basically makes us to work with and within the natural system, so that along with reaping benefit from the system, the integrity of the system be protected. These natural systems are under control by a complex mechanism. If this control mechanism is disrupted, the eco-system is damaged which costs innumerably to human society. In other words the hazards are converted to disasters only due to the exceeding limits of a system. It is usually far less expensive to prevent damage to an eco-system through proper management than to repair that damage, once it occurred. In most of the cases, environmental management operation starts once the environment damage has been done. It often operates through hindsight, rather than through foresight or prior planning. This approach costs much more and in most of the cases makes it impossible to restore the degradation to environment. The introduction of polythene bags in Indian market is the recent example of such type of unsustainable development. The people have become so much used to them that for administration it has really become difficult to ban them. This makes it essential that any planning or policy formulation should be chalked out keeping in view, the long-term consequences for its real success and achieve its objective.

As far as development is concerned, it in itself is not a deciding factor about the environment quality or vulnerability decrease or increase in a society. Instead it is the people or society, who make a system eco-friendly or disastrous. Environmental degradation problem does not occur exclusively where people are rich or where people are poor. In reality they can occur every where. The poor are forced to deteriorate environment due to their total dependence on nearby sources. They are forced to cut forest for fuel and fodder, cultivate hillside due to scarcity of agricultural land in the safe area and so on. The rich or industrialised on other hand adversely affect environment to overcome their undue higher demand for earth's resources. *(The 25 per cent of the world's people live in Western developed countries and consume about 80 per cent of the earth's resources.*)

The development in itself is not totally responsible for environmental problem. Instead, if development is carried out with proper care, taking into consideration all aspects of society, land and long-term perspective, it can turn the situation in reverse manner. Economic development, if carried out with due care to all these factors discussed, can prove to be very helpful in environmental restoration and reducing vulnerability of region and society to natural hazards. There are plenty of global instances where environmentally very destructive economic activities like road and dam construction have been carried out without having any adverse impact on environment. But this needs a great dedication, perseverence and foresightedness at all levels (policy makers, implementers, and beneficiaries), which unfortunately are lacking in our existing politico- administrative system.

The sustainable development in real is based on thorough intense knowledge of and respect for the people, the eco-system and the indigenous natural resources. The programmes for sustainable development are evolved involving people at each and every stage of its formulation and implementation. These programmes use expertise to take care of local problem and situation for better and long-lasting results.

The ideal development programme/ project has following characteristics :

- It is to be based on renewable and local resources.
- The project should be undertaken on small scale so that it permits diversity, flexibility, and resilience against mechanical or social break-down.
- While formulating the project, the traditional values and knowledge should be preserved, respected and utilised to the full extent to use them to learn and implement the same in the project for sustainable development.
- Projects should be formulated in such a way so that they sustain and increase the yield of natural resources, and they use them efficiently with long term perspective in mind.
- Project must be implemented where it is most required. It must be planned and implemented keeping in view the needs of local people. For this the involvement of local people and elected bodies is necessary at each and every stage of its formulation and implementation.
- The project is to be formulated keeping in view its objectives of broad ownership rather than concentrated. It is to be ensured that the owners are local and directly involved.
- While using the strength and already present skills, the projects should aim to encourage the development of realistically attainable and useful new skills by permitting growth of individual and society.
- The most significant feature of sustainable development projects/

programmes is that they respect and enhance the variety and productivity of local eco-system and do not create many disturbances for it. It aims at sustainable use of local resources and not exploits them for its short-term benefits.

- Monitoring and evaluation must be integral part of such projects with appropriate scope for changes and moderation.
- The last and the most significant feature of such projects is that they are people-oriented and not production-oriented. It must have appropriate scope for local cultural, social and traditional values.

Thus, in brief, the development, if carried out giving due consideration to the above mentioned objectives, is sustainable and makes society and people self-sufficient and motivates them to become engaged in conscious management of risk and reduction of vulnerability.

To achieve these multifarious objectives of sustainable development in the rural sector, it is a pre-requisite that the original rural development schemes are modified within the above parametrical boundaries so that they can have very positive impact on our rural society.

As far as disaster management is concerned, in the area with continuous threat and frequencies of disasters, the disaster mitigation activities are to be considered as developmental activities and *vice-versa*. In the case of our country, with a major part lying in rural areas and more than 70 per cent population still living in villages, various rural development schemes/programmes run by Ministry of Rural Development, may be incorporated for disaster management with slight modifications and changes at a minimal cost.

The basic approach in linking rural development with rehabilitation is that disaster management planning is to be viewed basically as a developmental activity to be taken in extreme and demanding conditions. The approach to such programmes should be positive with stress on building new socio-economic and physical structures. It is necessary to view disaster management activities as developmental activities, while devising structures as well as non-structural mitigation strategies and to recognise and integrate the positive elements of indigenous technology.

This integrated approach of combining rural development with disaster management will also help in reducing vulnerability of the people to disasters in sensitive areas and thus strengthen them against temporary disruption of economic activities caused by natural calamities. In the succeeding paragraphs, broad outlines of the various rural development schemes of Government of India and how they can be used for disaster reduction has been discussed. These practices will also help in reducing the environmental degradation and thus mitigating the disasters.

Methodology

As risk to disasters is the function of natural hazard and vulnerability of the society and land, the ultimate aim of Disaster Management would be to motivate societies at risk to get involved in conscious management of risk and reduction of vulnerability. The appropriate disaster management aims to reduce the vulnerability which depending upon its nature can be categorised as physical, socio-economical and ecological or environmental. Based on the lessons learnt from IDNDR-1990-99, the best approach for disaster management is risk reduction, which refers to activities to reduce both vulnerable conditions and, when possible, the source for the hazards (especially for drought, flood and landslides).

To reduce the vulnerability of all types, mentioned earlier, it is more economic and sustainable to tailor the developmental policies so that it ultimately reduces the vulnerability of society at risk. The policies or programmes to be designed in such a way so that they, along with routine development, take care of various factors discussed earlier. By proper implementations of such modified policies or programmes, the rural society will become resilient to natural hazards and related environmental and technological disasters. This approach, basically covered under sustainable development, will take care of preparedness, mitigation, emergency and post-disaster rehabilitation parts of disaster management.

For Indian rural society which comprises more than 70 per cent of Indian population, disaster management may be carried out through already on going programmes by modifying or redesigning them in such a way so that they lead to sustainable development taking due care of all factors responsible for increased vulnerability of the society and land.

Jawahar Gram Samridhi Yojana, Swaranjayanti Gram Swarojgar Yojana, Employment Assurance Scheme, Rajiv Gandhi Drinking Water Mission, Rural Housing, Drought Prone Area Programmes, Desert Development Programme, Wastelands Development, Land Reforms, etc., are the major rural development schemes, which along with poverty alleviation and rural development, can also play an important role in disaster mitigation. The schemes broadly, depending upon the objectives, may be sub-grouped into three main types—employment generation, area development and miscellaneous ones. These schemes/programmes with slight modification / adjustment can be used for disaster mitigation to check environmental degradation and rehabilitation in the disaster prone areas. This integrated approach of combining rural development with disaster management will also help in reducing vulnerability of the people to disasters in sensitive areas and thus strengthen them against temporary disruption of economic activities caused by natural calamities. How these schemes can be managed for disaster mitigation is elaborated in the succeeding text.

Employment Generation Programmes

Owing to various factors like demographic pressure, lack of alternative livlihood resource etc., the unemployment has become a serious problem in the rural India. Besides increasing poverty, the lack of employment directly or indirectly affect the vulnerability of the society to disasters also. Thus the employment generation programmes, if moulded and utilised giving due consideration to the object of vulnerability reduction, may prove very effective in making area and society quite resilient to various forms of disasters.

Among the various programmes being implemented, Employment Assurance Scheme (EAS) is the basic employment generation scheme of the Ministry of Rural Development. The scheme is to provide gainful employment during the lean agricultural season by way of manual work to all able bodied adults in rural areas, who are in need and desire to work, but are unable to find the same. The secondary objective is to create social and economic assets for sustainable employment and development.

Employment Assurance Scheme may be the major scheme of employment generation for the people residing in disaster-prone areas.

Works to be carried out under the scheme are to be selected in such a way so that they are as per the requirement of the land and the people. Afforestation, soil conservation, revival of drainage pattern, construction of check-dams, watershed management, etc., should be the major works, which can be carried out under the scheme. These types of works will definitely help in disaster mitigation in the area.

The other schemes like Jawahar Gram Samridhi Yojana (JGSY) and Swaran Jayanti Gram Swarojgar Yojana (SGSY) may also be good source for employment generation in disaster-prone rural areas. The basic objective of JGSY is the creation of demand driven village infrastructure, including durable assets, to enable the rural poor to increase the opportunities for employment. The second objective is generation of supplementary employment for the unemployed poor in the rural areas. In the disaster-affected areas, the scheme may be slightly modified, keeping its broad objectives intact. The development works, which are to be carried out in such areas, should be oriented in such a way that they help in mitigation of disaster in the region. Revival of drainage pattern, afforestation, plantation in landslides-prone areas to check further erosion and degradation, construction of check-dams, mechanical work to check soil erosion and landslides etc. are the major works, that can be carried out under the scheme. These types of works in disaster-prone areas, along with generating employment opportunities for the disaster affected population, will also help in reducing the environmental degradation and thus reduce the chances of disasters.

In the similar way SGSY that aims at establishing a large number of micro-enterprises in the rural areas, building upon the potential of rural poor may also prove very effective in vulnerability reduction. The programme is conceived as a holistic programme of micro-enterprises covering all aspects of self-employment, *viz*. organisation of rural poor into self-help groups and their capacity building, planning of cluster, activities, infrastructure building, technology, credit and marketing. In the disaster-prone areas, the programme may be slightly modified, so that along with overall development of rural poor it may help in environmental conservation and disaster mitigation. Under the modified scheme, various eco-friendly activities listed below may be carried out:

- Plantation of fast growing species which have market value.
- Installation of small forest-based industries, which will create interest of people in afforestation.
- Horticulture activities, which will also check soil erosion and environmental degradation along with giving livlihood to the disaster affected population.
- Installation of small horticulture-based industries, i.e., fruit juice, jam, pickles, etc.

These type of activities under the scheme will certainly help in poverty alleviation and employment generation in the disaster-prone areas along with disaster mitigation.

Area Development Programmes

The programmes related to rural housing, rural connectivity, sanitation, water supply, wasteland development, etc. come under this category. The rural connectivity scheme has been designed with the sole objective of connecting all rural habitations and upgrading of all existing roads. In hilly terrain, construction of road is very sensitive issue and in most of the cases lead to environmental degradation and other related disasters like soil erosion, landslides, etc. It is utmost important that due care should be given to geology, ecology and other aspects while carrying out road construction work in such terrain. In plain areas also the river and other water channels are to be taken care of during road consturction work, so that they do not create obstruction in natural water flow system of the area.

In disaster affected areas, the scarcity of water becomes a major problem. The Accelerated Rural Water Supply Programme can help in providing water to the affected population. In rural areas, people are dependent for drinking water on natural resources like water springs, ponds, lakes, etc. During disaster, these resources are damaged and the people tend to face the problem of water scarcity. Under the scheme, these natural sources of water may be revived and thus the problem of water scarcity may be solved up to a large extent.

The Rural Housing scheme of Ministry of Rural Development aims at providing houses to the rural poor along with improving the quality of life as well as overall habitat in the rural areas. For disaster prone areas, necessary amendments may be made to suit the local needs and environment. In such areas, the houses to be constructed

1. Horticulture not only provides good economic support to rural farmers but also helps in making land and soil more stable.

2. Soil conservation through afforestation and water harvesting.

3. Construction of small check-dams are very useful in water conservation and check soil erosion.

4. Rural connectivity–the key for development.

5. Proper conservation and utilization of water–revolutionary change in rural development.

6. Financial and technological support along with proper marketing facility– must for improving deteriorating conditions of rural artisans.

7. Along with improving rural economy, proper cattle management practices also help in reducing grazing pressure on forest.

8. Training and education of women make whole rural society strong and resilient to adverse impact of disasters.

9. Low cost technological support in rural sector is of utmost significance in improving rural economy and mitigating disasters.

10. Poverty and hazard vulnerability are inextricably linked and mutually reinforcing.

11. Temporary shelters are important aspect of disaster management.

12. It is the week building, not the earthquake that kills people.

13. Removal of debris is huge task after devastating earthquake, like in Gujarat.

14. Not even the home of God is spared of nature's fury. Damaged temple after Bhuj earthquake, 2001.

15. Proper counselling is required to overcome the trauma of disasters.

16. Damage assessment is a professional task–only trained persons can do it properly.

must be made earthquake-resistant with slight modifications and changes. These houses should be constructed in such a way so that they fulfill the local needs of the people and the material used for these houses is locally available. In such areas, the scheme may be implemented with these amendments and modifications to solve the housing problem.

The schemes of Ministry of Rural Development related to waste land development may prove very helpful in improving the degrading environmental condition of the villages and the surrounding areas. The basic objective of all these schemes is to develop wastelands, check land degradation, increase bio-mass availability and thus put such wastelands into sustainable use. In disaster-prone region, where the bio-mass is decreasing due to increasing biotic pressure, the scheme may be very appropriate and useful. Special amendments may be made in the scheme to suit the local needs. In the disaster affected areas, where the land is turned into wasteland, the implementation of these schemes may be of immense utility. A special task force may be formed recruiting local persons from the Gram Sabha, which may work for soil and moisture conservation, plantation and its protection, revival of drainage pattern, checking soil erosion, etc.

Besides the above mentioned schemes, the Ministry of Rural Development is running few schemes for drought-prone and desert areas. Drought Prone Areas Programmes (DPAP) and Desert Development Programme (DDP) are the examples of sustainable rural development schemes. It is advised that a new programme i.e. Disaster Prone Areas Programme may also be induced in the schemes of Ministry of Rural Development, which may target the fragile areas, which are under continuous threat of severe natural hazards.

Miscellaneous Group

National Social Assistance Programme (NSAP), Annapurna and CAPART are other programmes of Ministry of Rural Development , which along with their original development objective may also help in disaster mitigation up to an extent. The NSAP programme is to extend financial assistance to old persons having little or no regular means of subsistence or household living below the poverty line in case of death of the primary breadwinner or to pregnant women of household below the poverty line up to the first two live births. In disaster-prone areas this scheme may be very useful to give relief to the affected population. As the old persons, women and children are most vulnerable to disasters, provisions can be made under the scheme to give financial support to such persons under the scheme. Special funds may be created for these relief activities in disaster affected areas.

One of the basic drawbacks of the Disaster Management System in the country is the poor training and lack of awareness among various stakeholders. The Ministry of Rural Development has a good network of various training institutes across the country. The basic aim of these institutes is to impart training to the rural development functionaries about the various schemes of the Ministry. In the country, new centres may be opened under the scheme, which along with giving training pertaining to rural development schemes, may also include disaster management as special subject in its syllabi. The institutes may provide training to various departmental officials, the village representatives and the villagers about the disaster management. These institutes may also organise the off campus training programmes in disaster-prone areas to create knowledge base and awareness amongst the people about disasters and thus help in reducing their vulnerability to natural/man-made hazards.

As discussed earlier, the voluntary sectors play an important role in disaster management, particularly with reference to the programmes in rural areas. Council for Advancement of People's Action and Rural Technology (CAPART) is the scheme under which financial assistance is provided to the non-government organisations (NGOs). In disaster-prone areas, the scheme can play very significent role. There are a large number of NGOs in the country who are really working in good capacity for various development activities in the area. Some of the NGOs with good track records have been recognised by the High Power Committee on Disaster Management and enlisted in its report. Such NGOs may be encouraged to do work in the field of disaster management and mitigation. The Ministry may decide about the fields in which these NGOs may be given financial support. It is also advised that a new cell be created in CAPART which exclusively may look after the disaster management projects in the country.

Thus it may be envisaged that various rural developmental schemes mentioned above with slight modification and amendments may prove very useful in disaster affected/prone areas. If these integrated rural development programmes are adopted with area-specific modifications, they will certainly revitalise the rural life in the country. Along with directly influencing the factors responsible for the disasters, they will help in making the society strong enough to resist the adverse impact of natural and man-made hazards. These on-going schemes, with suggested modifications will certainly help in disaster mitigation with minimal expenditure. The suggestions may be given a serious thought by the planners and policy- makers and after thorough research and study of the disaster-prone areas, various amendments along with the suggested one may be made in these schemes to get the maximum output of the expenditure incurred on such programmes.

6

PANCHAYAT AND DISASTER MITIGATION

The discussion in the preceeding chapters clarifies that the disaster management in rural areas is suffering from various problems. If analysed in detail to look into the root cause of these problems, one glaring instance is lack of emergence of any effective local agency. It is this agency which can look after the problems in context to local conditions and provide solutions within the existing circumstances. Analysis of response to past disasters has supported the view that communities play a major role in response. Local communities are the first responders and they also have contextual familiarity. Knowledge of local resources, traditions, culturess, etc. helps them in planning and executing immediate rescue and relief actions. More often local bodies get more acceptance than outsiders when they offer help. Thus, the socio-political equations also accept the interventions of local communities than outsiders. Lack of an effective agency creates communication gap among various stakeholders of disaster management system in the rural community, resulting into various problems and shortcomings. In such circumstances it is required that some local agency with good organisastional set-up and understanding of the local physical and social conditions is given this responsibility to look after the disaster management in the rural areas. In the existing scenario, the panchayats or local self-governments may be the best choice. The vital strength of PRIs lies in their working at grassroots level and providing ideal forum for decentralised planning and implementation of programmes in accordance with the people's need and aspirations and this is what in reality required for long- term sustainable disaster management in the rural areas. If slightly reoriented and given proper facilities and strength, panchayats may work very effectively in managing the disasters in rural areas. Over three million elected representatives of panchayati raj bodies may prove to be a good and effective human resource to tackle the problem in more scientific and effective manner at minimal cost.

Why PRIs for Disaster Management

Within rural communities there is a lack of organised capacity to mobilise resources to identify and solve their problems and to act as pressure groups and make claims upon the government concerning developmental needs (Bajpai, 1997). Due to lack of local body, which understands the local needs, resources and problems in a better way, the disaster management becomes ineffective. Thus, it is the local institution, which can play a pivotal role in the field of disaster management, especially in a developing country like India, where democratic set-up is very deeply rooted. The rural institutions like panchayats can be very effective in performing major functions in the field of disaster management, i.e., planning, resource mobilisation, provision of services, integration of services, control of administration and making claims. All these points are detailed and discussed below:

Planning

The local body, like panchayat is very well versed with the local needs, local resources and local problems. All these factors play very strategic role in the success or failure of a programme. As the local body is at ease to collect these information, it can be very good and effective in planning and goal setting in a particular region.

Resource mobilisation (material and HRD)

For the long-term success of a programme or project, the primary requirement would be to see that local resources are utilised in sustainable and economic manner. This is possible only when the resource mobilisation is carried out by a local body for the developmental work. Along with the materials, the same is true for the human resource as well.

Efficiency in providing services

As the local institutions are quite familiar with the services required in the rural areas, they will be able to moblilise necessary services in time and in an efficient manner.

Control and Monitoring

The local institutes may be in better condition in monitoring and evaluation of rural development progrmmes in more effective manner.

The major drawback of the disaster management planning in rural India is the lack of people's participation. The development and disaster management plans in most of the cases have remained as exclusive government programme and in general people's involvement has been very negligible. This is true at both the stages of programme formulation and implementation. To overcome this problem, the only way is to involve panchayat at each stage of the development and other planning including disaster management planning. The developmental programme discussed earlier and their utility for disaster management can only be possible with the strengthening of PRIs and their involvement in the formulation and implementation of these programmes. However, in practicality it is not so easy and for strengthening of the PRIs, a number of decisions are to be taken at political and administrative levels. The functions of the PRI bodies are confined to rural development and the entrustment of PRIs functions is governed by Article 243 G of the Constitution. The eleventh schedule of the Constitution gives the list of the 29 items, mainly related to development activities. These activities may be entrusted to PRIs for the implementation.

As discussed earlier, the tailoring of the rural development programmes will have a long-term impact on the disaster mitigation. However, for practical purpose and for proper supervision at modification and implementation level, some responsible separate body may be entrusted for this job. Disaster Management Panachayat Committees may be constituted in disaster-prone areas at all the three levels—the village, the block and the district levels. The committee members may be invited from other working committees at village and intermediate level. For the district level, a separate body is to be formulated to look after the disaster management programmes. District planning committee may be entrusted with the preparation of a disaster management draft plan. Experts from the other fields may also help in this planning.

Decentralisation of planning and implementation of disaster management programmes at local level have to be compatible with the national objectives, regional requirements, local needs and people's aspirations.

Good NGOs working in the field of disaster management may be encouraged to initiate innovative and experimental programmes in the field of disaster management.

Zila panchayats should assume all the planning and implementation functions at the district level. The District Disaster Management Committee should be the single authority at district level to implement these plans and various departments of a district should work together as per the instructions set by this Committee. However, the technical and administrative control over the officials of various departments at the district level may continue to be with the concerned department at the state and regional level. The process of disaster management planning has to start from the village level.

Panchayat System in India

The concept of local self-government in India is not new, the historical evidences suggest that in olden days the system was much more strong and effective. During ancient time, the village was the basic unit of social and economic life and there existed the autonomy of village in itself. The rulers at that time were aware of the strength of the panchayats and used it for their own and other interests. The village panchayats with substantial power and resources used to solve both civil and criminal cases at local level in a very simple and acceptable manner. We read in the stories also that the members of the panchayats were very much respected by the whole community and by the rulers as well. Panchayat members were treated as the gods by general public and were called as *Panch Parmeshwar*.

However, during British period the autonomy of panchayats gradually started declining due to various vested interests of the rulers. The establishment of civil and criminal courts, police department and many other departments made the panchayat system redundant in the country. In few exceptional cases, some British administrators made attempts to establish a new local self-government in the country. Under such attempts, the name of Lord Ripon comes on the top. Lord Ripon in 1882 took the policy initiative and tried to establish elected institutions at local levels to look after various functions. Different bodies, like village panchayats, district boards, city corporations and town municipalities came into existence as a result of attempts made by Lord Ripon. But due to internal politics and various other factors, the system did not last long, and after independence also the old system continued without any significant change.

Though the PRI system got major setback during the British rule and later for a long period, after independence, the policy-makers and the leaders recognising its strength and significance in the Indian democratic set-up, tried to revive it again. The first sincere attempt in this regard was made in 1957, when a committee was appointed under the leadership of Shri Balwant Rai Mehta to review the panchayat system in the country and give recommendations to improve and modify the system, as per the need of the changed political and social set-up of the country. The committee recommended a three-tier system of local rural self-government. On the basis of these recommendations some state governments took initiatives in this regard and tried to establish the three-tier panchayat system. However due to various political and bureaucratic reasons, the attempts could not be much successful. It was realised that in most of the states, the PRIs could not gain the status and dignity of viable and responsive elected bodies. The major reasons for this failure had been-

- Insufficient devolution of power,
- Undue delay and absence of elections,
- Poor representation of weaker sections, and
- Lack of fund.

To overcome these shortcomings and make the PRIs system a success in the country, the Central Government made the seventy third amendment in the Constitution, 1992 mainly to strengthen the PRIs (Annexure XX). According to this Act, provisions have been made in the Constitution to provide essential power and strength to the panchayat to overcome the shortcomings, which it was facing earlier. The essential provisions made under this act are-

- Constitution of panchayat at three-tier pattern, i.e., village level, intermediate level and district level.
- Reservation of seats for weaker sections, i.e., Scheduled Castes and Scheduled Tribes.
- Reservation for the women.
- Regular elections on the pattern of Assembly elections and essential guidelines for selection of various officials of the panchayat at different levels.
- Constitution of state finance commission to review financial

condition of the state and recommend devolution of the financial power to the panchayat.
- Essential power and authority devolution to the panchayat.
- These amendments of the Constitution revived and added more effectiveness in PRI functioning.
- Augmentation of the consolidated fund for and to supplement the resources of the panchayats.
- Establishment of the district planning committee to consolidate the plan preparation by the panchayats and the municipalities and prepare a draft development plan for the whole district.

Along with these provisions, the Act also provided some discretionary power to the state governments to decide about -

(i) The nomenclature of the panchayats and the chairpersons to be used at different levels.

(ii) The norms in terms of population and area for constituting panchayat at the village and intermediate level.

(iii) The powers and functioning of gram sabha.

(iv) Number of seats in the panchayat at different levels.

(v) The repersentation of the lower level persons at higher level panachayat.

(vi) Representation of the people's representatives, MLAs and MLCs, in the panchayat.

(vii) The mode of election of the chairperson of the panchayat at the village level.

(viii) The reservation of seats for SCs, STs and women in the panachayats at different levels.

(ix) Reservation of seats in any panchayat for the offices of chairpersons in the panchayats at any level in favour of backward classes of citizens.

(x) To endow the panchayats at various levels with such powers and authority as may be necessary to enable them to function as institution of self-government and to make provisions for the devolution of powers and responsibility upon panchayats at the appropriate level.

(xi) The taxes, duties and tolls for which the panchayat will be authorised to levy and realise them.

(xii) The amount and grant-in-aid which shall be provided to the panchayat from the consolidated fund of the state.

(xiii) The composition, qualification and the manner of selection of members of the Finance Commission.

(xiv) Procedure and manner in which the accounts by panchayats are to be maintained.

(xv) The condition and service of the office of the State Election Commissioner and make provision with respect to all matters relating to or in connection with the election of the panchayats at different level in the state.

(xvi) The provisions in respect to all matters relating to election of the panchayats at different levels.

(xvii) To make provisions regarding the composition of district planning committee and procedure of election of its chairperson.

PRI in India—The Scenario after 73rd Amendment

After the 73rd Amendment in the Constitution, the state legislatures were required to amend their relevant acts/ laws. All the states accordingly made the essential amendments in their laws or made new laws. The amendment provides establishment of a three-tier panchayati raj structure (village panchayat, intermediate panchayat and district panchayat) and for giving constitutional status to the gram sabha- the general assembly of the villagers. There are at present 496 district panchayats, 5905 panchayat samitis (intermediate panchayats) and 2,30,762 gram panchayats in the country (Annexures XXI & XXII). The various aspects of the existing panchayat raj system in India are discussed under different heads as follows:

The Composition

The Constitutional Amendment Act- 1992 has prescribed a three-tier system of panchayat in the country. The district level, the block, taluka, anchalik or mandal level. However it is not uniform in all the states, some of the states do not have one or the other level.

Gram sabha is a body comprising all the members of the village or group of villages, whose names are registered in the village electoral list. The main functions of the gram sabha are: to make suggestions to the gram panchayat about the annual statement of the account, audit, development programme, identification of the beneficiaries, and to promote various welfare and other developmental programmes.

The number of members of panchayats differs from state to state at all levels. The Act- 1992 stipulates direct elections for all levels on the basis of territorial constituencies.

As far as reservation of the weaker section and the women are concerned, all the states have made essential provisions in this regard; however for the backward classes there is no uniformity in the reservation and it differs from state to state.

Resources

Before 73rd Amendment, the financial position of the panchayats in most of the states was very pitiable. The fund generation capacity of the panchayats was very restrictive and that too was not utilised further to generate more funds. Thus the overall condition of the panchayats in term of finance was very miserable.

After the 73rd Amendment, necessary provisions were made with regard to the financial viability of the panchayati -raj bodies. The financial resources for the PRIs, as laid down in Article 243 H of the Constitution, which may be enforced by the concerned state are:

(a) to authorise a panchayat to levy, collect and appropriate such taxes, duties, tolls and fees in accordance with such procedure and subject to such limits;
(b) to assign to a panchayat such taxes, duties, tolls and fees levied and collected by the state government for such purposes and subject to such conditions and limits;
(c) to provide such grants-in-aid to the panchayats from the consolidated fund of the state; and
(d) to provide constitution of such funds for generation of money received by or on behalf of the panchayats and also the withdrawal of such money there from different sources, as may be specified in the law.

As mentioned earlier, there is sufficient provision in the Constitution and law to authorise the panchayats for collecting its own resources, however it is not generally in practice and in most of the states this power and authority are rarely used by the PRIs. The main reason behind this is the lack of political will and clash of interests.

State Finance Commission

As per the constitutional amendment, every state has to constitute a finance commission with an objective to review the financial position of the panchayats and to make suggestions to augment their resources. The Article 243 of the Constitution provides that the governor of the state shall constitute a finance commission to review the financial position of the panchayats and make recommendations regarding-

(i) The distribution of the net procedures of the taxes, duties, tolls and fees between the state and the panchayats, leviable by the state.
(ii) The determination of the taxes, duties, tolls and fees may be assigned to, or appropriated by the panchayats.
(iii) The measures needed to improve the financial position of the panchayats.
(iv) Any other matter referred to the Finance Commission by the Governor in the interest of sound financial position of the panchayats.

District Planning Committee

For the purpose of consolidating the plans prepared by the panchayats and the municipalities and preparing a district draft development plan for the district as a whole, the state legislature has been empowered to constitute a district planning committee. The state legislature has full power to decide about the —

- Composition of the committee and elections for its various members and chairperson,
- The manner to fill the seats of the committee, and
- The functions and duties of the committee.

District, Intermediate and Panchayat Level Committee

The panchayats are entitled to perform various functions at village, block and district levels. To carry out these wide range of functions smoothly and without any hurdle, the state governments have provided the standing or the functional committees at the three levels. The number and function of these committees varies from state to state. These committees usually vary from two to eight in number, mainly perform two types of functions, i.e., related to production and sectoral development programmes, and social welfare of the weaker sections of the society. The number of members and election are at the discretion of the concerned state government.

Functions of Panchayats

Under the new amendment act, the state governments have been entrusted to endow the panchayats with such powers and authorities as might be necessary to enable them to function as institution of the self-government. Under the eleventh schedule of the Constitution, 29 subjects have been enlisted for which the state government is required to take decision about the specific nature and type of activities to be carried out by different tiers of the panachayats. But in practice there is no uniformity in this regard among the states and the states have made some modifications in the list of functions to be carried out by the panchayats. Despite this listing, negligible sincere efforts are made in real allocation of the work to panchayat level. During 1999-2000, the Ministry of Rural Development, Government of India modified and introduced some new schemes in which provisions are made in the development programme to be carried out at panchayat level. But inspite of the fact, the status of panchayat in most of the states is unsatisfactory and hence necessary steps are called for both by the central as well as the state governments (Table 6.1).

The Government of India aims to decentralise the power right up to village level. Devolution of responsibilities and powers upon PRIs has to be carried out by the state governments in term of—

— to transfer the function,
— to transfer the functionaries, and
— to transfer the funds.

Along with the above mentioned functions and powers and responsibilities and duties of the state governments, the states have been entrusted with some control on the functioning of the panchayats at each and every level. Under these provisions, the state governments have power in respect of inspection, power to dissolution, power to suspension and the execution of resolution/works of the panchayat, suspension and removal of the chairperson, etc. All these provide sufficient strength to run the functioning of the panchayat in a smooth and controlled manner.

Table 6.1 : Performance of Panchayats — All Tiers

(Percentage)

States/UTs	Own Tax/ own Rev.	1990-1991 Own Tax/ own Rev.	CS Exp./ Total Exp.	Own Tax/ own Rev.	1997-1998 Own Rev./ Total Rev.	CS Exp./ Total Exp.
Andhra Pradesh	72.96	6.27	7.57	57.98	5.49	16.11
Arunachal Pradesh*	—	—	—	—	—	—
Assam	99.10	100.00	0.00	99.10	22.32	26.67
Bihar	—	0.00	—	0.00	0.00	0.00
Goa	71.67	28.55	22.66	73.53	37.47	29.15
Gujarat	63.78	2.7	0.82	76.64	1.81	0.73
Haryana	3.33	63.49	0.00	8.49	62.20	0.00
Himachal Pradesh	100.00	0.50	0.00	100	2.68	0.00
Jammu & Kashmir	—	—	—	—	—	—
Karnataka	85.08	1.32	8.77	86.02	0.8	9.77
Kerala	90.54	32.41	32.01	88.35	10.08	11.94
Madhya Pradesh*	24.64	5.11	3.51	36.43	1.8	3.16
Maharashtra	70.92	3.27	7.04	66.50	3.39	7.45
Manipur	—	0.00	0.00	—	0.00	0.00
Meghalaya	0.00	24.73	0.00	1.52	18.03	0.00
Mizoram	—	—	0.00	100	1.43	0.00
Nagaland	—	0.00	0.00	—	0.00	0.00
Orissa	60.2	3.31	5.55	66.11	1.09	1.24
Punjab	3.02	22.12	39.46	1.3	39.78	24.54
Rajasthan	—	3.22	0.48	—	2.02	0.76
Sikkim	—	—	—	—	0.00	0.00
Tamil Nadu	94.16	5.62	30.25	96.77	8.06	33.4
Tripura	0.00	1.14	0.00	0.00	0.09	0.00
Uttar Pradesh	27.34	5.3	0.54	18.55	5.28	5.58
West Bengal	38.41	19.71	1.59	40.05	4.02	0.35
All India	64.40	5.60	5.83	55.67	3.50	7.43

Note: 1. * Panchayati Raj Institutions not in existence.
2. CS: Core services include water supply, street lighting, sanitation and roads.

Source: Planning Commission.

Objectives of PRIs

The basic objectives of the Panchayati Raj system are:

(i) to ensure people participation in local level administration,
(ii) to provide innovative methods for enhancing the people's involvement in the local development issues;
(iii) to create sense of responsibility among the rural population in the country so that they become more responsible and give more concentration to the developmental activities in the village; and
(iv) to ensure that the development reaches to all components of the rural society and more to the persons for whom the benefits of these programmes are intended.

Disaster Management Through Panchayats

The Constitution recommends for an important role to the PRIs in respect of 29 important subjects such as education, health, agriculture, housing, land reforms, social and farm forestry, drinking water, poverty alleviation programmes, social welfare, etc., which play very important and strategic role in the field of disaster management. These subjects, if dealt effectively at local level taking into consideration the local needs and conditions (physical and social both), may be very effective in reducing the vulnerability of the land and the society and make it resilient to the adverse impact of the natural hazards.

Panchayats can play effective role to enhance people's capacities through organising community, forming village level disaster response committees, developing early warning systems, organising rescue team and diversifing livlihood sources. Such community based disaster preparedness solutions also focus on special efforts to ensure livelihood security. The essential requirements for effective involvement of panchayats in preparedness are :

- Mitigation strategy (some of it would include plans to reduce vulnerability);
- Risk assessment;
- Vulnerability analysis, including identification of vulnerable groups;

- Early warning systems (modern as well as traditional); and
- Response plan that reflects actions to be taken, including an evacuation plan after receiving the warning.

PRIs, working in harmony with the state government can be effective instrument to tackle the disaster through early warning systems. The land owned by local bodies can be used for shelter and running relief camps. With the reinforcement of 73rd amendment, PRIs are regarded as central agencies to implement various rural development schemes/programmes. So PRIs can play a major role in integrating disaster mitigation features with on-going developmental activities undertaken at local level.

Why PRIs More Effective

If viewed in a wider perspective, the PRI system in the country has two important functions—it encompasses the development needs of the micro unit and is based on the local felt needs of the people. The need is that while implementing the developmental programmes in a region, the socio-economic, socio-cultural, politico-administrative and environmental aspects are given due weightage and consideration.

The important factors that make the PRIs' role more effective in dealing disasters are:

- In a country like ours with so much diversity, disaster management through PRIs may be a right proposition because of its ability to contrive greater autonomy and resources effectively.
- PRIs may be very effective in using local tradition and wisdom supported with scientific application.
- Ability to effectively manage the programmes which need large scale people participation i.e. land reforms, revival of drainage pattern, sanitation, etc.
- NGOs and other grass roots organisations may be more comfortable while working with PRIs.
- More effective for better resource allocation and more public service in rural areas and effective in mobilising local resources.
- Can help poor more effectively to organise them through grass- roots organisations.

- Being a local body, they will be liable and responsible for long- term impacts of development or other activities being carried out in disaster-prone areas and also able to effectively manage the environmental impact assessment in comparison to other outsider agencies.
- They can provide leadership in the entire process of community participation in disaster management process.
- They can undertake rescue, relief, restoration and rehabilitation activities effectively.
- They can assist building community-based response structure for effective disaster management. It refers to both structural and non-structural measures, i.e., developing and updating database and emergency infrastructure.
- They are able to build consensus on pertinent issues in order to ensure community participation and lay down principles and best practices for community *vis-a-vis* individuals.
- Ability to establish interface and maintain coordination with administration and outer agencies.
- Proper utilization of financial authorities to bring down peoples vulnerabilities towards-life, livelihood, health, property and security.
- Develop community contingency plans and a helping hand in disaster preparedness activities at village level. Ensure participation of community in planning and decision making process.
- Sensitize and promote awareness through meetings, campaigns, competitions etc.
- New researches and investigations in the field of disaster management may be more effectively propagated through panchayats.
- While preparing disaster management plan for the village or the community, local factors may be given more importance and nothing important or strategic will be left without giving due consideration. This will certainly increase the quality of the plan and its practicality.
- The vulnerable group of the society will be given more importance during the disaster management.
- The relief may be more appropriate and as per the need

and the chances of mis -utilisastion will certainly decline.

- Can be more effective in organising the training programmes for the people as per their need and requriement.
- Can be helpful in organising a task force of the able bodied persons of the village, who can be trained for rescue and relief work during disaster.
- Panchayats could create their own relief fund by imposing taxes, rents etc. This fund can be used for emergency and long term disaster management practices.
- The most advantageous thing with the panchayat working for disaster mitigation is that it can provide services without delay and wasting time and waiting outside help. The immediate initial time after a disaster is very precious for rescue and saving life. But it is observed that this time is wasted in waiting outside help, which multiplies the life loss during disaster. If this help is locally available from the panchayat, many precious lives may be saved.
- Their ability to monitor and control the environmental degradation, the most prominent cause for increasing the intensity and frequency of natural disasters. They can make the people aware about the adverse impact of environmental degradation in more effective manner. The Joint Forest Management (JFM) Committees may be formed by Panchayats to look after the natural forest near the villages. It can also persuade people to grow more trees under the social and agro- forestry programmes. The awareness programmes by panchayat may be very helpful in reducing the forest fire incidences also.
- Persuade people residing in dangerous and sensitive zones to shift from. By providing alternative livelihood resources to such people, panchayats can persuade to shift from such locations to safer positions and thus reducing their vulnerability to disasters.
- Provide employment opportunities locally- through various development programmes like EAS, JGSY, etc. thus make them economically more sound and strong. Panchayats may develop and implement such projects without adversely affecting the environment. The local employment

generation may also make a check on the migration of rural population to urban areas in search of livlihood.

- Monitoring and evaluation- One other basic draw back with the existing disaster management practice is the lack of any effective monitoring and evaluation system to make the appropriate check and modify the programmes. Social audit by the gram sabha may fill this gap. The Panchayati Raj Act has given power to gram sabha to perform as a watch dog to supervise and monitor the functioning of the panchayat and other organisations. This check can be more effective in the case of disaster management programmes, because the gram sabha being a local body can monitor and supervise the programmes at micro and meso levels both, which is not possible for an outsider agency.
- Psychological treatment- The psychological injuries due to disasters can be very harmful causing various disorders. Mutual support of the community in the form of panchayat may be very consoling to the affected people.

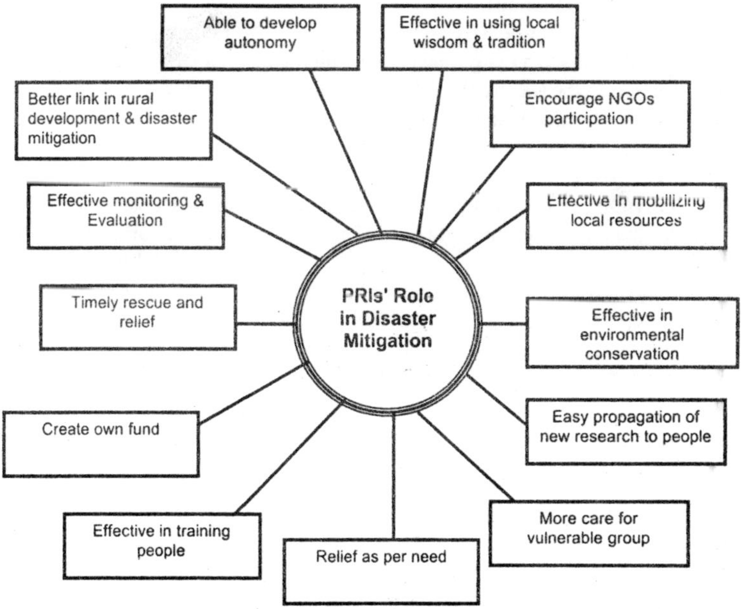

Fig. 6.1 : Role of Panchayati Raj Institution in Disaster Management

As mentioned earlier also, the 29 developmental activities enlisted in the XI schedule of the Indian Constitution may be successfully utilised for disaster mitigation in the rural areas of the country. Broadly, these activities can be grouped into seven categorie. taking care of almost all types of vulnerabilities as shown here.

S.N.	Category of Developmental Activities (XI Schedule)	Types of Vulnerability that is Taken Care of
1.	Conservation and development of natural resources such as forest, land, soil and water resources and take steps to check the environmental degradation.	Ecological vulnerability
2.	Necessary steps to increase the production of agriculture, horticulture , livestock, fuel, food, fodder and raw material for small cottage industries.	Economical vulnerability
3.	Development of physical structures such as rural housing, roads, school buildings, place of weekly market or haats, school and dispensary buildings, etc.	Physical and economical vulnerability
4.	Programmes for poverty alleviation and social justice covering weaker and vulnerable section of the society like BPL families, Scheduled Castes and Scheduled Tribes, women, children and senior citizens of the society.	Economical and social vulnerability
5.	Providing education awareness and training for the human resource of the rural society.	Educational, motivational and cultural vulnerability
6.	Providing various social services like power supply, drinking water and medical facilities.	Social vulnerability
7.	Providing strong leadership to the rural people specially the rural poor.	Organisational vulnerability

Thus it is clear from the table that if the developmental activities to be handled by the PRIs are slightly modified and tailored as per the need of the society, PRIs may be effective tool to reduce various types of vulnerabilities. The reduction in vulnerability will automatically take care of the risk or the loss due to adverse impacts of the disasters - the ultimate aim of the disaster management.

Panchayat as Implementing Agency

As we have discussed earlier, the development and disaster management are inter-linked and inter-dependent. For effective results, appropriate and sustainable development is to be designed to meet the basic need of vulnerability reduction, survival and recovery. For this, the best approach would be to manage the development and the disaster management by the same authority. Development and disaster management handled by two different authorities are like a bicycle, cycle run by two different persons in the opposite direction, leading nowhere.

Taking this view into consideration, the administrative set-up at state, district and other levels is also to be tailored or modified to run the disaster management and development harmoniously.

State Level

At present, the state level relief measures are observed and supervised by relief commissioner or chief secretary of the state. He or she controls the relief operations with the assistance of district collectors. State governments have their contingency plans which are updated from time to time, based on the experience. This contingency plan basically has to follow a framework as laid down nationally, comprising type of preparedness and the relief material required that need to work together, and provide an efficient feedback and monitoring system. A contingency plan of the district, for different disasters shall be drawn up by the collector / deputy commissioner and get approved by the state government. The collector / deputy commissioner also coordinates and gathers inputs from the local defence forces unit for preparing the contingency plans. These plans lay down specific action points, key personnel and contact points in relation to all aspects.

The relief measures are reviewed by the district level relief committee, consisting of official and non-official members, including the local legislators and the Members of Parliament.

In the wake of natural calamities, a control room is set up at the district headquarters for day-to-day monitoring of the rescue and relief operations on a continuing basis.

The collector maintains close liaison with the Central Govternment authorities in the districts, namely, Army, Air Force and Navy, Ministry of Water Resources, etc., who could supplement the effort of the district administration in the rescue and relief operations. He takes all steps for enlistment of voluntary efforts and channeling the NGOs response to natural calamities and interact with different implementation agencies and furnish information on daily basis to the State Relief Commissioner on the implementation of rescue and relief measures.

The district level contingency plans and the state action plans are reviewed annually and updated in the light of lessons learnt in dealing with natural calamities from time to time.

The other departments at district level—Revenue, Home, Civil Supplies, Power, Irrigation, Water Supply, Gram and Zila Panchayat (local self-government), Agriculture, Forests, Rural Development, Health, Planning, Public Works and Finance—are also required to provide all types of technical and physical support during the event of a disaster. Whenever there is a disaster, a control room is set up at state level also.

The modifications that are required at the state level

- The chief secretary or an officer of equivalent post should be designated as Development or Disaster Management Commissioner (DMC) of the state. (The term " relief" should no more be used as it indicates that relief is the only issue in disaster management to be dealt with.)
- DMC should have full responsibility for planning, monitoring and concurrent evaluation of all the developmental and disaster management plans. He will also ensure that all developmental plans give due consideration to the vulnerability of the region and the society and are sustainable in nature. While formulating and implementing a development plan, due attention is to be paid to disaster management aspect. This becomes of strategic importance while dealing with the ecological sensitive areas.
- One State Development and Disaster Management Council is to be established at the state level under the chairman ship of the Chief Minister. The existing State Crisis Management Group may be merged with this council. The chief secretary or development commissioner should be appointed its secretary. To ensure panchayat representation, the chairman

of zila panchayat should also be made its members.

- The Council is entrusted with the approval of the district and the state development and disaster management plans. It will also approve the state annual and five years plan.

District Level

At present the district magistrate or deputy commissioner (DC) or collector is the focal point at the district level for directing, supervising and monitoring disaster management and development activities. The district administration is the focal point for directing, supervising and monitoring field level contingency plans and relief measures. The DC works together with the sub-division officers / tehsildars of various sub division/ tehsils and 'patwaris' of villages along with the entire machinery of the district, which includes the technical officers of other departments also.

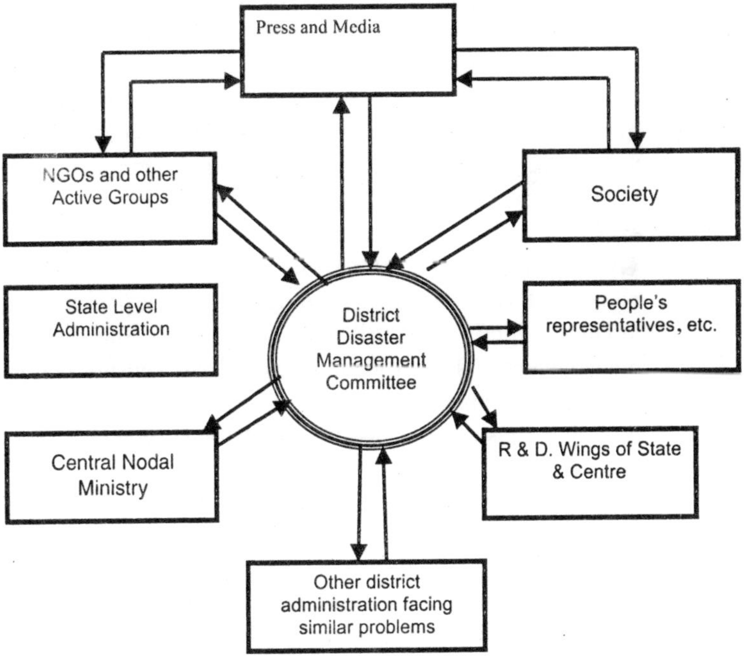

Fig. 6.2 : Linkage and information flow among District Disaster Management Committee and other stakeholders of Disaster Management.

However, due to overburden of the law and order matters and other activities related to land revenue, land records, election matter, public distribution system, etc, he or she is unable to devote much time for the developmental and disaster management activities. In such conditions it is required that a senior officer in the rank of DC or above should be appointed as District Development-cum-District Disaster Management Commissioner (DDC-cum-DDMC), to work as the chief or the executive officer of the zila panchayat. DRDA and district relief commissioner office should be merged with this office. The technical heads of the various developmental departments engaged in the developmental activities shall also work under him or her.

In the districts, ecologically very sensitive or with large forest cover, it will be very appropriate to appoint an officer with both technical and administrative knowledge, preferably a forest officer of Indian Forest Service as DDC or DDMC. Such appointment will be very effective to ensure eco- friendly development of the districts. With following objectives, the district level administration can be made more efficient and effective:

- In the DDC office, a separate committee may be constituted to look after the disaster management under the leadership of DDC. The chairman of the district level panchayat will be executive director of the committee.
- The technical heads of various departments should be nominated as its members who besides looking after other developmental work will also take care of the disaster management at district level. They will also ensure that all development programmes of their respective departments give due consideration to the disaster management aspect also.
- The DDMC will also be responsible to review and approve the district disaster management plan, formally prepared by the experts in the field.
- The Committee will also help in formulating the guidelines for village level disaster management plans and review and approve the same before implementation.
- The actual execution of the development and disaster management plans will be carried out by the PRIs.

- District level panchayats should assume all the planning and implementation at district level.
- The PRI should be activised as an organisation for planning and implementation of the programmes related to development and disaster management.
- Technical control and supervision of the officials of the technical departments at district level may continue to remain with the concerned department. These officials however will be under the control of zila panchayat.
- The DDMC will also look after the other disaster management functions along with the activities mentioned above, which are at present being looked after by the district administration.
- To strengthen district level administration and make it more efficient and effective, following arrangements may further be made—

  (i) Preparation of the disaster contingency plan, laying down specific action points, key personnel and contact points in relation to all aspects.
  (ii) Coordination with the local defence forces and NGOs.
  (iii) Coordination with local people representatives and other organisations like public sectors, educational institutes, etc.
  (iv) Establishment of the control room in the district.
  (v) Close liaison with the Central Government authorities, i.e., Army, Air force, Navy, Central Ground Water Board, Ministries of Rural Development, Agriculture and Water Resources.

A district is sub-divided into sub-divisions, tehsils or talukas and tehsil into blocks and blocks into village. The head of the sub-division is called the Sub-Division Officer (SDO), head of the tehsil is generally known as Tehsildar or Talukdar or Mamlatdar, while the head of a block is called Block Development Officer (BDO), the head of the village or panchayat is recognised as Gram Pradhan or Sarpanch. The disaster management committees may be constituted at these lower levels also as per the guidelines of the disaster management committee of the district. The panchayat members must be given due representation in these committees.

Preparedness and Mitigation Measures by PRIs

Some specific preparedness and mitigation measures for some major natural disasters that can be undertaken by the PRIs:

Disaster	Preparedness Activities by PRIs	Mitigation Activities by PRIs
Earthquake	* Preparation of do's and don'ts for community. * Conducting mock drills and infra-structures and rehearsals * Preparing and materialising preparedness and response plan. * Training of volunteers for search and rescue. * Preparing hospitals for emergency response.	* Ensuring quality construction, dissemination of information to practices while constructing community facilities and see that meets earthquake-resistant codes and regulations. * Retrofitting of weak structures and housing units. * Networking with local NGOs and government agencies.
Cyclone	* Pre-cyclone season rehearsal. * Logistic management * Drainage clearance * Alternative communication and power arrangements. * Stalking of foodstuffs and medicines, etc. * Warning dissemination and evacuation	* Construction of cyclone-resistant houses and cyclone shelter. * Afforestation and restoration of mangrove plantations.
Flood	* Regular maintenance of embankments of river, canal, distributaries, etc. * Pre-monsoon inspection of river, canal * Clearance of drains from slit and weeds * Internalise response plan. * Co-ordination with NGOs/CBOs * Warning dissemination * Evacuation	* Construction of embankments. * Training of volunteers and officials on disaster management.

Involvement of PRIs in disaster preparedness and mitigation: Some Case studies

A study on Role of PRIs in Disaster Management, undertaken by HPC in the states of Andhra Pradesh and Maharashtra reveals that the involvement of PRIs is limited in disaster preparedness and mitigation process. In Andhra Pradesh, PRIs are effective in relief distribution, evacuation and rescue operation. The gram panchayat and zila parishad are very active in awareness generation, warning dissemination, evacuation, and response measure that recommend more attention should be given on strengthening panchayat samitis at block level. However, PRIs have no role in formulation and implementation of disaster management plan. In Maharashtra also the involvement of panchayat is restricted to relief distribution and rehabilitation works, especially in selection of beneficiaries and site of reconstruction. However in Orissa and Gujarat, the role of PRIs has proved more effective in ushering in optimism that the goal of disaster reduction can be achieved at community level through active participation of panchayat.

Community Based Rehabilitation in Patanka, Gujarat

Patanka, a village of about 250 families, suffered extensive damage during the quake, with about 170 houses collapsed and the rest being badly damaged. Since it lies in Patan, outside the focus of most relief teams that had headed for Kutch, somehow it received less attention from aid givers. Even the government compensation, as everywhere, was taking time to reach them.

Kheemabhai, village from Patanka, came across representatives of the Delhi based disaster management organisation, SEEDS, and expressed the village's desire to work themselves to rebuild their lives, and requested for logistics support. SEEDS had been working in the area through its Ahmedabad office, but for the first time came across a community that was wanting to work for itself and was not looking for charity. Things moved fast and never stopped since then.

District Administration and Panchayat Support

A meeting was organised with the Additional District Collector, to ensure speedy disbursal of compensation so that the villagers could start rebuilding their homes. The collector visited the village, and on seeing the enthusiasm there, extended full support to their initiative. The village panchayat took the lead in organising the activities at local level, and most of these activities happened at the instance of the panchayat, with active involvement of all members and community representatives in the planning process, and all community members in the implementation process.

Rebuilding : for the people, by the people

Patanka became a scene of hectic activity. Farmers, who would otherwise be sitting idle in the village square, started scurrying all over the village; everyone become busy in building his house, getting material from the specially set-up material depot, and interacted with engineers on technical details of earthquake-resistant counstruction. Villagers got their construction steel made at the village steel workshop, and their roof timber at the wood workshop. Whole families got involved, with women and children helped in the masonry work with water, or ferrying material to their sites.

The partnership approach : everyone contributes

The initiative was truly community led. Helping hands of course had come from all directions. The SEEDS team helped the villagers to procure building material, with limited amounts of cement and steel, with a ceiling of Rs. 10,000. The villages got their own stone, bricks, wood, rooftiles and labour. Architects and engineers from SEEDS trained the masons, labourers and the villagers themselves on earthquake-resistant technology through on-hands training, and through periodic training workshops.

International cooperation at grassroots level

Patanka became an international centre of good practice in community led rehabilitation and local imbibement of state-of the art technology on earthquake resistant construction. Two expert masons had come all the way from NSET (National Society of Earthquake Technology), Nepal to teach their Gujarati brethren how to build safe houses, under the grassroots cooperation programme between SEEDS and NSET. They commanded a very good rapport with all the villagers, and respect of local masons for their intelligence).

Many supporters, but decision-making by community itself

Each family decided its own house designing and the material it wanted to use. Aid came in for incorporating earthquake-resistant engineering features, which they learned very fast. On completion in the village, there was a pool of trained masons who played an important role in the rebuilding of the rest of Gujarat. Recognising the strength of this community-led rehabilitation model, organisations including the United Nations Center of Regional Development, Earthquake Disaster Mitigation Research Centre, Japan and NGOs Kobe, a consortium of NGOs working for post-earthquake reconstruction of Kobe, Japan, had shown propensity to support and promote it. A wider dissemination campaign was planned to promote such work and create awareness on do-it-yourself, low cost earthquake-resistant construction.

Initiatives in Orissa

In Orissa, an attempt has been made to involve PRIs in the disaster mitigation and preparedness process.

In view of recurrent disasters, the priority of the administration in Orissa has been, formulate and execute effective strategies in disaster mitigation in the community contingency plan to make it sustainable process for regular upgradation.

During the aftermath of super cyclone in Orissa, Orissa Disaster Management Programme has been launched by OSDMA with the assistance from DFID and UNDP with the following objectives:

- Preparation of multi-hazard plans at district, block, gram panchayat and village levels;
- Formation of different groups to respond to hazards;
- Vulnerability reduction through linkages with existing development programmes; and
- Capacity building of all the stakeholders.

The focus of the programme was to build the capacity of the PRIs to enable them to carry forward the community-based disaster management in building the commnity resislience to disasters. The major preparedness and mitigation initiatives taken in Orissa at district, block, panchayat levels are described below:

- The trained volunteers along with local medical officers, and engineers to act as main resource persons for the community level training.
- Village sensitisation meetings and awareness campaigns are also being organised in order to make people realise their role and responsibilities.
- Different awareness generation programmes through distributing leaflets posters, wall paintings, street plays are developed and adopted for the people at all levels.
- Orientation programmes are also organised to sensitise the nodal officers of the line departments at district level.
- District disaster information centres have been established with all infrastructure facilities. District functionaries are also given training on how to use equipments.
- Orientation of newly elected representatives of panchayat samitis and BDOs of CBDP blocks on disaster management are organised in order to enhance the involvement of chairpersons and PRIs to sustain the programme with GPs with local resource persons.

(a) At District Level

- An attempt has been made to upgrade the existing district contingency plans for disaster preparedness and emergency response to make people use it as a reference manual in disasters.
- District level workshops were held to finalise the framework of District Disaster Risk Management Plans (DDRMP). In these workshops appropriate local solutions, based on experience gathered and a framework of DDRMP containing the following aspects have been finalised.

    - Hazard and vulnerability profile of the district
    - Hazard-wise response structure for different levels.
    - Development of SOPs for different hazards
    - Establishment of inter-departmental coordination along with civil society groups
    - Action plan to operationalise the District Disaster Management Plan (DDMP)

(b) At Block level

- The Block Disaster Management Committees (BDMC) have been formed in Block Disaster Management Plan (BDMP) blocks which is headed by the chairperson of panchayat samiti and the BDO works as its convenor. The committees have developed block disaster preparedness plans and guides GPs and villagers for preparedness at their levels.
- Training programmes are organised to orient BDMC members along with representatives of all line departments, CBOs, NGOs, etc.
- Block disaster risk management plan is prepared as per the ground reality with existing resources to combat hazards.
- Block disaster information centres have been set up with equipments' resource inventory, address list, important telephone numbers along with vulnerability maps. Site operational camp and route maps of the block are prepared which will be useful in emergency situation. It will also help in warning, dissemination and establish linkage with district information centre and GP information centres.
- PRI members are being trained on setting up control rooms, emergency responcse, and mobilisation of resources and developing DMPs. The trainers of PRIs are helping village volunteers in organising meeting and motivating the community for preparedness, formation of village task force, organising mock drills, etc.

(c) At Gram Panchayat and Village Level

- GP Disaster Management Committees are formed to facilitate the DM activities and DP at village levels. It consists of following members:
    - Ward member of village
    - Elderly person/opinion leaders
    - School teacher
    - Anganwadi worker
    - Member of women group and youth club.

- Most of the GPs have also developed the emergency preparedness plan for their areas to provide required support to village groups.
- Villagers are mobilised to form community contingency fund to meet emergency needs.
- Formation of village task force by village disaster management committees include the following activities:

  (i) warning dissemination,
  (ii) rescue and evauation,
  (iii) shelter management,
  (iv) first aid and medical services,
  (v) water & sanitation,
  (vi) psychological counseling,
  (vii) damage assessment
  (viii) carcass disposal, etc.

- Training of volunteers : Two volunteers from each village selected by GP are being provided training to develop community contingency plans at village level. They are also given the basic skills of using PRA techniques in social, resource, vulnerable and hazard mapping, etc. The aim of such process is to ensure villagers' participation in Patti sabha for decision-making.

7
DISASTER MANAGEMENT PLANNING AT VILLAGE LEVEL

Disaster, when it strikes, are at first a personal, family and community event and only then a social, national and regional event. Thus the suffering in the case of a disaster is individual and local and then only national. Therefore, it is most appropriate and effective if the resources, both human and material, to manage the disasters and reduce the vulnerability and subsequently the risk are local. It is important for the community, panchayats and the NGOs to play very significant and strategic role in this regard. As a result of increasing frequency and magnitude of disasters, there is a growing realisation among rural communities to be better prepared to face them. Local communities can plan and practice simple preparedness and mitigation measures. However, it is important to note that the process is most effective when the local community assesses its own risk. If a multi-hazard approach is followed, then the community can develop protection against potential hazards, and relate problems together to achieve a tactical primary list of what concerns people most. Community should prepare a contingency plan to safeguard lives, livelihoods and property. This plan is basically a list of activities, a village decides in case of an emergency to follow to prevent loss of life, livelihoods and property. It aslo defines well in advance, actions to be taken by individuals in the community so that each one is aware of his/her responsibilities, when an emergency warning is received. The existence of a disaster preparedness plan not only helps in speeding up the rescue and relief operations, but also serves as guidance to officials and saves precious time, which might otherwise be lost in consultation with senior officers and getting formal approval from authorities. The PRIs can play a major role in preparing such plans at community level and in building up resilient local communities.

In the rural areas, where the society is more cohesive and

integrated, this aspect becomes more significant. Thus the village level, local disaster management plan, which plays very important role in managing disasters in the rural part of the country, must be formulated and implemented with much more sincerity. An ideal village level disaster management plan, along with safeguarding lives, livelihood and property, must give due consideration to disaster mitigation aspect as well (Fig. 7.1). The role and responsibilities of the entire community, i.e., the individuals, families, community leaders, village authorities, panchayats, NGOs, etc., are to be well defined in the plan for effective implementation and better results.

The Plan

Disaster management plan of a village is a list of activities, the village decides to follow, to prevent loss of life, livelihood and property in case of an emergency and also mitigation measures to reduce the vulnerability of the society and make it more resilient to resist the adverse impact of natural hazards. It also identifies, well in advance, actions to be taken by individuals of the village so that each one is aware of his/her responsibilities during emergency. Such disaster management plan has to be made by the inhabitants of the village itself, representing all sections and groups of the village community.

Fig. 7.1 : A User-friendly approach is required

To fulfil this purpose, the village disaster management committee is to be formed, preferably under the leadership of one of the panchayat members.

To carry forward the process of discussions and to guide the community towards drawing a workable plan, the involvement of people's representatives, NGOs and government officials may prove to be beneficial as they possess the necessary authority and skill to motivate the community to come over with a decisive plan.

The preparation of the disaster management plan of the village basically involves long term and short term planning. While the long-term disaster management planning covers the mitigation and prevention aspects, the short-term planning takes care to safe guard village society against the loss of life, property and livelihood in case of emergency. Though the activities to be carried out in both types of plannings are similar yet they are slightly different with no clear-cut demarcation line between the two.

Fig. 7.2 : Human Resource Development in Disaster Management needs proper training by experts.

Steps for Long-term Planning

The major steps of long-term planning are as follows:

1. Analysis of the experience of the last disaster, the village faced.
2. Situational analysis of the village.
3. Hazard and risk mapping.
4. Identifying the factors responsible for increasing vulnerability of the society and the land to natural disasters.
5. Planning and implementation of activities to reduce both vulnerable conditions and, when possible, the source of hazard (flood, soil erosion and landslide, etc.).

For short-term planning, the first three steps are common to long-term planning. In addition to this, the other steps involved are-

- Warning
- Shelter management
- Evacuation and rescue
- Providing medical, food, water and other necessities
- Damage assessment
- Relief and coordination.

Analysis of the experience of the last disaster, the village faced

The first and the foremost step in disaster management planning is the review and analysis of the earlier disasters experienced by the village in the past. On the basis of review of the situation, a critical analysis is to be carried out by the villagers involving other groups as well.

The discussion is mainly focussed on the experience of the last disaster that hit the village. The content of the discussion should be what happened before, during and after the disaster in terms of warning and precautions, effects of warning, extent of severity of disaster and damage, the nature and extent of self-help, etc. The review and analysis also emphasise the drawbacks and the shortcomings that were experienced during the management of earlier disaster. Based on this exercise, the village decides about the different ways through which it can be better prepared to respond to any emergency situation.

Situational Analysis

The participants including, youth volunteers, people's representatives and other government and non-government officials draw a map of the village identifying the following characteristics.

- Physical location and demographic details of village and its surroundings (updated revenue map of village can be used as a reference during the exercise) .
- Number of houses - thatched, tiled, *pucca* RCC houses
- Mark on the map the natural resources in the village: e.g. lands and fields, forests/trees, tanks and ponds/ tube- wells / wells, etc.
- Shelters if any,
- Safe areas and buildings
- Temples, mosque or any community building like panchayat ghar, etc.that can be used as a cyclone/flood shelter
- Schools and education facilities
- Drinking water facilities
- Dispensaries or primary health care units
- Village roads, cart tracks
- Risk-prone embankments and safe embankments.
- Power installations
- Communication means
- Post office and other such structures
- Safe houses and buildings for shelter
- Shelters, concrete buildings and other strong structures that cannot easily be damaged by earthquake, flood, landslides, etc.
- Elevated and up-lands, and other natural barriers for livestock protection.
- Safe evacuation routes that will not be disrupted in case of an emergency.
- Existing health, medical and sanitation facilities that can be used and strengthened in the event of disaster
- Sources of funds to carry on contingency and preparedness activities, for example, family contribution for relief.
- Funds for repairs and construction of shelters, plantation of wind barriers, etc.
- Identification of motivated and responsible volunteers and their training.
- Precautions to safeguard identified people and property.

Along with map preparation, the situational analysis also involves listing of following documents:

- Number of families - men -women -children, castes, the disabled, the terminally ill, pregnant women, mothers, etc.
- Various livelihood assets of the community, i.e., boats, fishing crafts, irrigation facilities of farmers, implements, food grain stores and other inventories, looms and potters' wheels, instruments of artisans and other livelihoods practices in the village, e.g. fishing, farming, weaving, wage labour work and so on.

Hazard and Risk Mapping

Based on the experiences of the earlier disaster and other different hazards faced, the villagers identify the most vulnerable areas as regard to destruction to life, property, infrastructure and economic activities. These are marked on a separate map.

The risk mapping involves identifying vulnerable population and property /assets in the village. The community based on the experience of the previous disaster identifies the groups and people, who are most vulnerable in the village. A vulnerability list is made to be marked on the hazard map. This involves both vulnerable population and the vulnerable property or assets, i.e., elderly and disabled people, children and pregnant women, sick and ailing people, widows and single women, families living near dangerous zones. Besides these, family's valuable documents, houses and weak structures, livelihood assets such as boats, pumps sets and other installations, agricultural implements, looms and such properties, standing crops, horticulture trees and plantation, village water sources, cattle and livestock, etc., are also marked on the map.

The community decides how those at risk can be safeguarded and what should be done as precautionary measures.

Identifying the factors responsible for increasing vulnerability of the society and the land to natural disasters and planning and implementation of activities to reduce both vulnerable conditions and when possible the source of hazard (flood, soil erosion and landslide, etc.): The village action committee identifies the factors responsible for vulnerability to natural hazards. In this regard, suggestions and recommendations of some expert groups may also be sought. The identification of these factors must be carried out by keeping in view the nature of disasters and the area prone to such disasters. The major common factors to be identified under this category are:

- the deforestation and exploitation of other natural resources,
- deteriorated drainage pattern,
- unscientific development and agricultural practices,
- grazing,
- forest fire,
- housing pattern,
- occupancy of steep hill slopes and other dangerous areas for agriculture and residential purposes,
- unemployment,
- education and awareness etc.

All these factors are directly or indirectly responsible for intensification of risk factors in rural society. To overcome and safeguard village from the adverse impact of hazards, various preventive measures, discussed earlier in Chapter 5, are to be carried out by village action committee and panchayat. Most of the activities mentioned can be covered under developmental programmes being carried out in the region. The village developmental agencies i.e. panchayats may be the most suitable body to carry out these functions more effectively. As mentioned in the Chapter 5, the developmental activities may be tailored to meet the requirement for disaster mitigation. The people's involvement is very important to carry out these activities more successfully and effectively. The role of gram sabha in this regard may be quite strategic and important. A long-term planning may be carried out to meet the requirement of the region so that the disasters are mitigated up to certain extent.

Various factors responsible for increased vulnerability, its causes, adverse impact on society and land and action to overcome these factors are tabulated below in Table 7.1.

Table 7.1: Action Plan for Long-term Strategy

Factors responsible for increased vulnerability	Causes	Adverse impacts	Reviving actions	The Implementing agency
Deforestation	Poverty, lack of awareness, demographic pressure, lack of other livelihood resources	Increase in soil erosion leading to accelerated floods, landslides, etc. Scarcity of fuel and fodder and other livelihood resources	Plantation of indigenous species, protection and conservation of forests	Joint forest management committees, village panchayats
Deteriorated drainage pattern and other water resources	Lack of awareness, Mismanagement, over-exploitation of watershed area, unscientific check dams and embankment construction	Increase in soil erosion, high runoff, reduced water bearing capacity of water bodies etc. resulting into floods and decrease in water penetration	Cleaning and de-siltation of drainage pattern and water bodies, construction of small check dams at proper sites. Development of watershed area.	Through panchayats, under various developmental schemes of Rural Development and Agriculture
Unscientific development and agriculture	Lack of awareness and prevailing contract system in which local scientific aspects are neglected.	Disturbing eco-balance in sensitive zones accelerating disaster intensity and frequency	Training and awareness creation about Eco-friendly development causing negligible	Through panchayats and NGOs

Table 7.1 (*Contd.*)

			impact on natural eco-balance of region.	
Grazing and cattle management	Ignorance of optimum utilisation of cattle products and lack of proper marketing facilities, Lack of pasture land	Grazing in forest, increase soil erosion and deforestation leading to increase in hazard both in intensity and frequency.	Providing training and marketing facilities to the cattle breeders. Development of pasture land.	Administration and panchayats.

Joint Forest Management

JFM is a forest management strategy, under which the government (represented by the Forest Department) and the village community enter into an agreement to jointly protect and manage forestland adjoining villages and to share responsibilities and benefits. The village community is represented through an institution specifically formed for the purpose. This institution is known by different names in different states but is most commonly referred to as the Forest Protection Committee (FPC). In some states, panchayats also enter into a JFM agreement with the Forest Department.

Under JFM, an FPC takes the responsibility of protecting a forest patch from fire, grazing and illegal harvesting. In return, it gets great access to forest produce and a share in income earned from that forest patch.

Table 7.2 : Status of JFM (as on March 1, 2002)

Sl. No.	States	Area under JFM (sq km)	No of FPCs
1.	Andhra Pradesh	17,675.70	6,816
2.	Arunachal Pradesh	58.10	13
3.	Assam	69.70	245
4.	Bihar	741.40	296
5.	Chhattisgarh	28,382.55	6,412
6.	Goa	130.00	26
7.	Gujarat	1,380.15	1,237
8.	Haryana	658.52	471
9.	Himachal Pradesh	1,112.47	914
10.	Jammu & Kashmir	795.46	1,895
11.	Jharkhand	4,304.63	1,379
12.	Karnataka	1,850.00	2,620
13.	Kerala	49.95	32
14.	Madhya Pradesh*	43,000.00	10,443
15.	Maharashtra	6,866.88	2,153
16.	Manipur	5,072.92	82
17.	Mizoram	127.40	129
18.	Nagaland	1,500.00	55
19.	Orissa	7,834.67	12,317
20.	Punjab	735.60	184
21.	Rajasthan	3.093.36	3,042
22.	Sikkim	6.00	158
23.	Tamil Nadu	3,733.89	999
24.	Tripura	319.89	180
25.	Uttar Pradesh	507.03	540
26.	Uttaranchal	6,066.08	7,435
27.	West Bengal	4,880.95	3,545
	Total	**140,953.60**	**63.618**

* Based on a recent JFM status paper by Madhya Pradesh Forest Department.

The Action Plan for Short-term Planning

The short-term disaster management planning is designed to meet the emergency situation during the disaster. Warning, shelter, evacuation and rescue, medical assistance to the affected, providing water and sanitation facilities, distribution of relief, damage assessment, etc. are the major activities that are carried out during this phase. Disaster management committee at the village level may appoint separate groups to tackle all these activities as per the capability of the persons. These groups are to be reorganised regularly every year. The constitution and functions and duties of these groups are discussed in the successive paragraphs.

Warning Group

Except earthquake, forecasting in other natural disasters is possible up to some extent. Timely forecasting and warning may save life and property both. The warning group on the basis of information gathered warns other groups and the people in general, to get prepared to face the hazard. Headed by one panchayat member, this group consists of some young boys and girls, most preferably the educated ones. These youths are well acquainted with the geography of the region may also be trained to understand the radio and other warning messages.

Shelter Management Group

The group arranges the shelters for the affected population during disaster. Some lady panchayat or anganwadi member may head the group. The group is responsible for the shelters and other essential requirements like food, medicines, clothing etc., required by the affected people.

Rescue Group

This group, headed by some retired but physically strong army personnel or the village chowkidar should consists of young, physically strong (both men and women) members. The members of this group neea special training for rescuing the entangled persons during the disaster. The members of this group may be trained at some training centre or some *insitu* training may be provided to them to carry out their duties more effectively.

First Aid Group

This group is to be headed by some village doctor or *Vaidya or anganwadi* worker or any other person having some knowledge of first aid. Some young persons (both men and women) may also be trained in first aid. Some expert persons may provide intensive training to this group in first aid activities. The village panchayat may arrange such training at village level also.

Relief Group

Relief group may be headed by some senior level village panchayat member, who can interact with the relief distribution agencies and as well as other action groups of the village. Women should also be given sufficient representation in this group, so that the special requirements of the women may also be taken care. While making selection for the group, the integrity and the honesty of the members is to be given due consideration.

The members of the group collect and distribute relief materials such as food supply, utensils, clothes, kerosene, diesel, etc. and coordinate all the relief requirements of other action groups. Both the men and women members have to be capable of interacting with the local authorities to ensure adequate supplies reach the village in time. They also keep track of all government provisions related to gratuitous relief, relief works to prevent starvation, deterioration, migration, health and sanitation measures for both people and livestock, etc.

Damage Assessment Group

The members of this group (both men and women) have to be literate. As a preparedness measure, this group would collect information about individual families, their income, property and assets, etc. before the disaster and maintain this record, against which compensation claims are verified. The group members can be trained in collecting information on all the above issues/matters.

Reconstruction and Rehabilitation Group

This group would supervise activities needed to help the village to recover from the disaster losses. Members of self-help groups, and other similar groups, who have the experience of planning, might become members of this group. The main aim of the group should be to get government help to carry on reconstruction activities in the village.

Miscellaneous Groups

Beside these, some miscellaneous groups may also be formed as per the need in disaster affected areas. In flood affected areas, the sanitation and drinking water becomes very serious problem. In such circumstances, a separate group may be formed to look after this aspect of the problem. The carcass disposal and counseling group may be other such miscellaneous groups, who if required can be formulated in the village. Their duties and functions may be decided by the village disaster management committee as per the requirement of the conditions.

There is no hard and fast rule for these group formation and necessary amendments may be done as per the situation demands. However, in the case of major groups, the duties and functions may be tabulated for before, during and after disaster categories as shown in Table 7.3.

Management Tools for Disaster Management Planning in Rural Areas

Preparing an appropriate disaster management plan is the prerequisite for dealing disaster effectively in an area. As the proposed action for various stages of disaster management, i.e., mitigation, preparedness, emergency and rehabilitation are governed by the plan prepared, its formulation needs very systematic and strategic approach. For successful disaster management planning it is required that each and every aspect of the problem is given due consideration and all the stakeholders are given due representation. Disaster management plans in general are prepared for country, state and district level. But in country, with so much diversity in geo- agro- climatic, social, cultural, and economical conditions, it becomes essential that this planning be carried out at lower levels also, so that various factors that directly or indirectly affect the disaster management planning may be given due care and response. The second most important thing, that is to be taken care of, while preparing a disaster management plan, is to give due and fair representation of the locals in it. As it is the local family or individual that face the trauma of the natural disasters, the role of this group of stakeholder in disaster management planning cannot be

Table 7.3 : Disaster Management Groups, their duties and functions

Before Disaster (1)	During Disaster (2)	Post Disaster (3)
	Warning Group	
• Monitoring of weather forecasts through radio bulletins and TV throughout the day without fail. And if possible through wireless.	• Cross checking of the warnings received on radio with the nearest tehasildar / BDO/ police station .	
• Transportation and communication aids are needed to pass on warnings to the entire village. Cycles, carts, boats and other transport and megaphones, drums and other communication aids should be obtained and keep ready.	• Dissemination of warning through out the village as quickly as possible.	
• Telephone numbers and address of district/ tehsil headquarter and locals should be with the warning group.	• Contact with different shelters and safe houses to make them ready for the emergency.	
	Shelter Group	
• Check shelters and safe houses that have been identified to shelter the affected people during disaster. Make necessary repair etc. to get them ready.	• Move stocks of food, water utensil, and medicines to the shelters and safe houses. See that enough drinking water is stored.	• The shelter or relief camps continue to house and feed evacuees until they leave for their homes.

(1)	(2)	(3)
• Stock food, water, utensils, medicines, milk powder, candles, matchboxes, kerosene etc in sufficient quantity. In the case of flood, water tank in the shelter may be kept filled with water for emergency.	• Organise space to house evacuee families.	• Replenish stocks of food, clothing and fuel wood from the govern-ment stores or 'Grain Bank" of the village or any other source.
	• Help evacuees especially, children, the disabled, pregnant women, sick and old settle in the shelter. • Ensure strict hygiene practice in the shelter. • Register evacuees and hand over identification slips to them. This will help in food and relief distribution in fair manner.	• Shelters can act as centres for distributing relief materials so that supplies are not looted or hoarded by unscrupulous people and the materials can be given against identification slips. Ensure that the vulnerable sections are also covered. • Clean and disinfect the shelter all throughout the stay and before leaving.
• Ensure health and sanitation facilities.		Help government and families in assessing damages.
	Rescue Group	
• Identifying and marking safe routes on map to reach people for their evacuation. • If available, the transportation be kept ready for evacuation. • Informing concerned officials for road repair and get it done.	• Helping vulnerable groups, collecting their belongings and evacuate and ensuring that everyone knows which shelter to go. • Securing rescue boats and rescue kits during the disaster. • Ensuring discipline during evacuation.	• Village inspection and rescuing st-randed and injured people, and transferring them to the nearest hospital or medical camp. • Restoring communication and transport.

(1)	(2)	(3)
• Preparing a rescue kit depending upon the nature of disaster e.g. in the case of flood such kit should contain; a paddle, rope, iron hooks to tow belongings and /or other rafts, container to bail out water, torches, a transistor, an anchor , a first aid kit, life jackets or tyres and other floatable objects. • Keeping some tools handy such as cutting saw blades, crowbar, hammer, nails etc., to cut the fallen trees, grills, doors, etc. to rescue people stuck under the fallen houses.	• Evacuating cattle well in advance, so that it does not get stuck on the way. • The group must be indoor before the disaster strikes and also ensure no one leaves the shelter during the disaster.	• Maintaining a 'missing persons' register and updating it after rescue trip, and assisting government in enumeration of property. • Transporting doctors and other relief materials and volunteers to the village. • Coordination with Government officials for getting things done.
	First Aid Group	
• Maintaining a list of pregnant women, infants, the disabled and sick and old in the village and ensuring their medical needs. • Keeping a first aid box with dis-infectants, water purifying tablets, antiseptics, medi-cines, bandages, splints, scissors, blades, iodine,	• Moving medicine stocks and first aid kits to the affected region. • Looking after the medical needs of the evacuees. • The group must be indoors before the disaster strikes and also ensure that no one leaves the shelter during the disaster.	• Attending to injuries and traumas of rescued people. • Informing the relief group about medical supplies that are running low. • Helping doctors and paramedicos shift the ill and the injured to hospitals. • Isolating cases with infectious diseases and prevent them from spreading

(1)	(2)	(3)
ointments, sachets, safe delivery kits, clean cloth and so on, well in advance. • Distributing basic medicines (chlorine tablets, ORS packets and so on) and demonstrating their use to families in advance.		• Providing pre-ventive medi-cation if there is a danger of epidemics spread like cholera, gastro-enteritis, dy-sentery, and malaria.
Keeping stretchers ready to bring injured people.		
	Relief Group	
• Mobilising stocks from the government and others source for e.g. water pouches, baby food, food grains, dry rations, medicine, torches, hurricane lamps and kerosene/solar cooker, firewood for shelters in advance. • Stocking temporary building materials like bamboo, rope , tarpaulin, asbestos sheets and other materials that will be needed in the post cyclone/flood , landslide , earthquake stage. • Stocking food and medicine require-ments for the various vulnerable groups.	• Moving relief supplies to the shelters. • Monitoring its stocks and make a list of things to be replenished. • The group must be indoors before the disaster strikes and also ensure that no one leaves the shelter during the disaster strike.	• After the immediate search and rescue operations just after a disaster like cyclone/flood, earthquake, landslides strikes, a lot of recovery activities have to be carried out before a village can re-vert to its usual day-to-day activities and transactions.

(1)	(2)	(3)
• Stocking food and medicine for animals. • Interacting with the other groups and help them to get their supplies. • Deciding on the quantity of relief materials to be allocated to each shelter according to the number of families they can cater to.	• Receiving stock of relief material for distribution • Replenishing stocks immediately that is running out. • Monitoring and distributing relief from all sources.	
	• Continue providing people with food, clothes, water, and medicines until they are able to fend for themselves. • Ensuring that the officials start the enumeration procedure immediately, so that building materials can be arranged immediately through revenue authorities.	
	Assessment Group	
		Assessing the extent of damages: • Lives lost: women and children at risk (orphans/destitutes/disabled) • Damage and losses to property and assets- livestock, agriculture, plantations, and so on.

(1)	(2)	(3)
		• Damage to infrastructure -roads, water supply, electricity, markets and distribution networks. *Helping in rehabilitation:* • Speeding up of the government enumeration process to assess the damage. • Helping families with the paperwork to follow compensation proceedings, especially relating to death certificates, insurance, etc. • Ensuring that the assessment and the concerned papers reach the govt. department responsible for compensation to ensure timely assistance.
	Rehabilitation Group	• Arranging for compensation from the govern-ment for partially and totally damaged houses and the lives lost. • Assessing reconstruction materials and assistance of the government officials for the families. • Helping families to rebuild houses. • Arranging for food and shelter for eld-

(1)	(2)	(3)
		erly persons, women and children at risk. • Organising village communities for proper channelising food-for-work and targeting of families: *Damaged infrastructure:* • Getting water sources in the village purified. • Accessing government services for rebuilding damaged public infrastructures and follow up action till rebuilding is completed. • Helping families access financial assistance to begin income generating activities. • Making a list highlighting the various support facilities necessary to restart the economic activities of the community, for e.g. petty traders need to reach their suppliers to restock their shops, training in new skills to begin new income generating activities. Working out ways in which such facilities can be restored and seeking the assistance of the NGOs and the government.

ignored. A disaster management planning without taking this aspect into consideration is bound to yield unsatisfactory result.

In a country, with so much diversity in all aspects and variation in type and nature of disasters and agencies to deal them, it is not advisable to recommend uniform guidelines for preparing disaster management plans in different parts of the country. To resolve such issue of multi-pronged origin and options and where more than one agency is involved to mitigate the same, management tools have been found to be very effective. Modelling technique , one of such effective management tools can be of much help in dealing the issue of disaster management planning at various levels.

Modeling technique helps in improving the performance of the implementing agencies, be it government agencies, public sector organisations or NGOs. It also help in assessing the performance level and enable the administrators to identify the gaps and shortcomings in the approach towards mitigating the same. While preparing disaster management plan, either for state, district or lower level, the main aim should be to get the maximum output from the functioning of these organisations, by improving their performance. In an organisation, the performance improvement is basically assessed in terms of timeliness and quality of service and by reducing the cost of providing such services. The techniques may be used for better planning of an organisation. In the present case, functionaries involved in disaster management i.e., various ministries and departments of state government dealing in the field, the district and other junior level administration units and local self governments can apply the same.

The modeling technique basically has three steps— recognition and analysis of the problem, identification of the variables, collection of data and lastly the model building.

Recognition of the problem is the first step of modelling technique. As discussed earlier, the disaster management planning in the country has been suffering from so many problems. Partial failure of the administration and other agencies to counter the situation results in further deterioration of the condition. Unemployment, diseases, scarcity of livelihood sources, food and water shortage, lack of shelter/housing, failure of communication and other infrastructure facilities, environmental degradation, etc., are some major problems which are being faced due to one or the other form of disasters in the area. In the recent past, mainly due to increasing population pressure and various other man-made/natural factors, the intensity and severity of disasters have increased many times and subsequently the problem of managing them has become more serious.

Critical analysis of existing policies, their implementation and other secondary data reveals that disaster management in India has many shortcomings and various important opportunities remain untouched and unexplored. The data clearly indicate that the existing policies are more concerned about the immediate relief and rescue operations. The other important aspects of disaster management, i.e., preparedness, mitigation and rehabilitation are not given due importance. Some important aspects are totally ignored. The disaster management in the country, especially in rural areas is suffering mainly from poor rehabilitation efforts, delay in relief and rescue, unscientific assessment survey, misutilisation of relief, unsuitability of the relief, poor technology and training of the people and the officials engaged in disaster management, ignorance of local needs, faulty developmental schemes, poor representation of local bodies, lack of coordination among various departments, poor monitoring and evaluation of the programmes and most significantly the total negligence of the environmental aspect and so on.

After analysing the problem the next step in formulating a model is the recognition of various variables affecting the problem. Variables in the present case are nothing but the factors influencing the disaster management in an area. In the case of natural disasters, the different variables recognised are: geological structure, topography, climate of the area; type of vegetation/forest of the region, population density, land use and development pattern, environmental conservation measures, the training level of the people and officials, the education level and knowledge of the local population about disasters, the resources available to detect and suppress the impacts of disasters etc. These variables may further be classified under four heads namely outcome, controllable, manageable and uncontrollable variables. The impacts of disasters, indicated by the loss of property and lives and deterioration of the environment represent the outcome variables. Research and development in the field of disaster management, training of the people and officials involved, land-use and development pattern of the region, people's participation, the budgetary provision for disaster management, etc. are the controllable variable. The third category of disaster is manageable disasters which represent the forest cover, the development activities affecting the natural environment, the land use pattern, etc. The natural factors including geological and topographic structures, climate, drainage pattern, vegetation and forest cover of the area, which decide susceptibility of the region to disasters constitute the uncontrollable category of variables.

The appropriate disaster management in an area should aim to reduce the impacts of natural hazards. The controllable, uncontrollable and manageable variables influence the impact of natural hazards and the performance of the disaster management authorities. To effectively deal disasters, it is required that these variables are to be managed in such a way to reduce their impact. As it is not possible to manage uncontrollable variables, the effective disaster management policy must aim to manage controllable and manageable variables.

The next steps after identification of the variables is the collection of data. Data collection is very important task and necessary care is to be taken while undertaking this job. In the present case the most important data to be collected include vulnerability of the area and the society to disasters. These will be decided by various variables like geology, climate, topography, peoples' awareness about disasters, environmental conservation and after all the development pattern of the region and society. In rural areas, the review and analysis of the earlier experience of the village about a disaster that had hit it in the past is very important and useful while preparing disaster management plan. The data about the disaster incidences and their intensity and impacts in the area for the past few years will also be required for the purpose. These data may be collected from various sources. On the basis of review of the situation, a critical analysis is to be carried out by involving all groups of stakeholders. This review should be based on the content of the discussions about what happened before, during and after the disaster in terms of warning and precautions, effects of warning, extent of severity of disaster and damage, the nature and extent of self-help, etc. The review and analysis also emphasise the drawbacks and the shortcomings that were experienced during the management of the earlier disaster. This data will be helpful for planning an appropriate disaster management plan. The knowledge about the cultural traditions, education standard, traditions, the livelihood resources etc will also be of immense utility.

Besides this, the other data required for the plan formulation will include-

(i) Data about the availability of the staff,

(ii) Data about the equipment available for forecasting and resisting the impact of disasters.

(iii) Funds resources available for disaster management activities.

Based on these data, a rough picture may be drawn about the susceptibility of the area to natural hazards. Further planning and modelling will basically be determined by this data.

Plan Preparation

Based on the data collected and the other information mentioned above, the model is prepared for the disaster management. In the disaster management there are basically three steps—pre- disaster, emergency, and post- disaster. The disaster management activities can also be divided into pre-disaster, emergency and long-term post-disaster phases, which are inter-connected and inter-independent. The pre-disaster stage activities include the preparedness and mitigation aspect in a better and planned manner. The next phase involves rescue and relief operations. The third stage, post-disaster refers to rehabilitation.

Disasters are the direct consequence of the vulnerability and, therefore, the main objective of an appropriate disaster management model should be to reduce the same. Vulnerability of a region or society along with various other factors is also decided by its developmental pattern. Therefore, the basic aim of an appropriate disaster management model should be to control and monitor the developmental pattern in such a way that it ultimately leads to vulnerability reduction. Along with the developmental pattern, while formulating a plan for disaster management, equal importance is to be given to other variables also. Research and development, information and education of the society, availability of the resources, environmental conservation, population control and improving socio-economic condition of the society also play an important role in deciding the vulnerability. On the whole, these variables are to be given due importance in the plan formulation.

Prevention is better than cure, this is true in the context of disaster management also and for effective and long-term strategy, priority is to be given to the preventive measures, which will automatically reduce the vulnerability and increase resistance against the impacts of natural hazards

The ultimate aim of the model is two dimensional (i) to increase the performance of the disaster management functionaries; and (ii) decrease the vulnerability of the region and the society to disasters that is controlled by different variables. The chances of controlling uncontrollable variables are negligible, hence the modelling technique and approach in the present case must aim at managing the controllable variables, so that the outcome variable, i.e., the impact of the disasters is minimised. In the present case among the controllable variable—research and training, awareness of the people and the functionaries, resources to mitigate and manage disasters, environmental conservation, people participation, land use and development pattern, etc.—are to be managed in such a way so that the vulnerability of the society and the region is reduced. These variables may be controlled by using the best technique of monitoring and evaluation.

For better results of the functionaries involved in disaster management, there is an urgent need for their review on the basis of modern principles of accounting and budgeting.

The other modern accounting techniques, which can be used for performance measurement are—appropriate supervisory and management techniques and performance auditing. Both these techniques can be successfully used for the performance analysis of the implementing agencies, i.e., the state government, the district administration and other bodies. The supervisory and the management techniques that apply to operating more efficiently, economically and effectively include planning, executing and controlling. Controls are developed at each stage of planning to ensure that the action at the executing stage accomplishes the results contemplated from the agreed upon plans. Operational controls are needed to measure the accomplishment of the plans at the operational stage. Management controls are needed to measure the accomplishment of various plans developed at the organisational stage. And effectiveness controls are needed to assure the development of appropriate goals of the organisation and the appropriate timing for the accomplishment of these goals.

For the disaster mitigation programmes, the implementing agencies such as various state government departments, district and lower level administration and other agencies (government and non-government both) are to be made accountable for setting appropriate goals. The developing standard are needed to accomplish these goals for effectively carrying out those standards and for developing those organisational and operational standards for economical and cost efficient operations.

ANNEXURES

ANNEXURE - I

PEOPLE KILLED AND AFFECTED BY DISASTER

Country ranking according to percentage of people killed and affected by disaster	Annual Average number of people killed and affected by disaster (1992-2001)	Percentage of population killed and affected by disaster
Malawi	1,664,760	13.00
Antigua and Barbuda	7,669	11.80
Cambodia	1,333,771	10.42
Kiribati	8,400	10.24
Guyana	79,721	9.97
Djibauti	58,592	9.77
Iran	6,419,570	9.28
Zimbabwe	1,065,136	8.59
Swaziland	76,209	8.47
Australia	564,982	8.28
Philippines	5,809,986	7.83
China, People's Republic of	97,783,301	7.73
Eritrea	268,886	7.68
Cuba	820,661	7.33
Belize	14,524	7.26
Mongolia	180,528	7.22
Palau	1,201	6.32
Moldova, Republic of	265,460	6.17
Handuras	368,180	5.84
Tajikistan	347,186	5.79
Lao, People's Democratic Rep.	294,078	5.66
Zambia	573,427	5.62
Ethiopia	3,334,266	5.43
Fiji	43,081	5.39
Bangladesh	7,178,115	5.33
Somalia	424,822	5.05
Kenya	1,501,496	5.00
Mozambique	887,676	4.96
Korea, Democratic People's Rep.	1,026,964	4.65
India	46,060,125	4.64
Nicaragua	209,491	4.28
Armenia	160,492	4.22
Vietnam	2,770,612	3.59
Nigeria	374,950	3.57
Papua New Guinea	163523	3.48
El Salvador	210,807	3.40

Annexure-I (*Contd.*)

Country ranking according to percentage of people killed and affected by disaster	Annual Average number of people killed and affected by disaster (1992-2001)	Percentage of population killed and affected by disaster
Thailand	2,105,918	3.40
St. Kitts and Nevis	1,299	3.33
Afghanistan	704,979	3.33
Haiti	261,494	3.27
Sudan	932,513	3.07
Azerbaijan	245,332	3.07
Hong Kong (China)	200,914	3.00
Mauritania	76,950	2.96
Micronesia, Federated States of	2,880	2.88
Tanzania, United Republic of	895,089	2.61
Namibia	44,320	2.61
Lesotho	50,375	2.52
Sri Lanka	442,459	2.37
Tonga	2,302	2.33
Georgia	122,083	2.30
Madagascar	354,838	2.29
Solomon Islands	8,888	2.22
Lithuania	78,007	2.11
Costa Rica	81,541	2.09
Pakistan	2,732,032	1.99
Burundi	114,364	1.82
Rwanda	127,198	1.79
Vanuatu	3,552	1.78
Botswana	24,430	1.63
Chad	123,257	1.62
Spain	607,019	1.52
Benin	83,539	1.37
Dominican Republic	102,520	1.25
Peru	294,198	1.17
Bolivia	88,199	1.09
Paraguay	53,077	0.98
Brazil	1,206,957	0.72
Jordan	33,067	0.69
France	395,311	0.67
Togo	28,191	0.64
Ghana	116,920	0.62
Uganda	125,381	0.55
Colombia	229,307	0.55
Kyrgyzstan	26,461	0.55

Annexure-I (*Contd.*)

Country ranking according to percentage of people killed and affected by disaster	Annual Average number of people killed and affected by disaster (1992-2001)	Percentage of population killed and affected by disaster
Dominican Republic	,391	0.55
Ukraine	248,244	0.50
Senegal	44,226	0.48
Uzbekistan	117,453	0.48
Sierra Leone	20,099	0.47
SyrianArab Republic	65,850	0.42
Nepal	93,543	0.42
Cape Verde	1,632	0.41
Kazakhstan	64,446	0.40
Eduador	49,004	0.40
Iraq	80,812	0.36
Indonesia	690,107	0.33
Turkey	207,885	0.32
Lebanon	10,414	0.31
Gambia, The	3,890	0.30
Venezuela	69,571	0.29
Mexico	277,577	0.28
Guinea	22,692	0.28
Congo	7,922	0.27
Chile	37,091	0.25
Guatemala	25,724	0.23
Central African Republic	7,965	0.22
Argentina	80,264	0.22
Japan	277,948	0.22
Greece	21,658	0.20
Netherlands	30,607	0.19
Canada	57,532	0.19
Tavalu	17	0.17
Yemen	28,367	0.16
Korea, Republic of	73,021	0.16
Seychelles	124	0.16
Russian Federation	224,535	0.15
Albania	4,652	0.15
Burkina Fasco	16,438	0.15
Hungary	14,596	0.15
Angola	18,238	0.14
Morocco	37,627	0.13
St. Lucia	113	0.11
Bahamas	321	0.11

Annexure-I (*Contd.*)

Country ranking according to percentage of people killed and affected by disaster	Annual Average number of people killed and affected by disaster (1992-2001)	Percentage of population killed and affected by disaster
Romania	23,640	0.11
United States of America	292,511	0.10
Czech Republic	10,216	0.10
South Africa	42,011	0.10
Slovakia	4,809	0.09
Myanmar	41,845	0.09
Nigeria	96,786	0.09
Uruguay	2,820	0.09
Yugosalavia, Federal Republic of	8,330	0.08
Poland	24,158	0.06
Belarus	6,353	0.06
Macedonia, Former Yugosalv Rep.	1,174	0.06
Cyprus	437	0.05
United Kingdom	30,361	0.05
Algeria	14,676	0.05
Guinea Bissau	544	0.05
Italy	23,836	0.04
Panama	1,032	0.04
Malayasia	7,538	0.03
Egypt	20,513	0.03
St. Vincent and Grnadines	30	0.03
Germany	24,769	0.03
Mauritius	331	0.03
Congo, Democratic Republic of	12,907	0.03
Liberia	702	0.03
Grenada	21	0.02
Jamaica	539	0.02
Norway	640	0.01
Mali	1,600	0.01
New Zealand	478	0.01
Austria	1,045	0.01
Ireland	423	0.01
Iceland	32	0.01
Switzerland	663	0.01
Bhutan	182	0.01
Equatorial Guinea	35	0.01
Bulgaria	680	0.01
Estonia	110	0.01
Croatia	356	0.01

Annexure-I (*Contd.*)

Country ranking according to percentage of people killed and affected by disaster	Annual Average number of people killed and affected by disaster (1992-2001)	Percentage of population killed and affected by disaster
Malta	28	0.01
Trinidad and Tobago	62	0.00
Cameroon	617	0.00
Bosnia and Herzegovina	157	0.00
Israel	228	0.00
Singapore	144	0.00
Slovenia	70	0.00
Comoros	24	0.00
Portugal	309	0.00
Belgium	292	0.00
Saudi Arabia	479	0.00
Bahrain	14	0.00
Kuwait	20	0.00
Turkmenistan	47	0.00
United Arab Emirates	23	0.00
Cote d'Ivoire	69	0.00
Libya	20	0.00
Maldives	1	0.00
Sweden	26	0.00
Gabon	3	0.00
Surinam	1	0.00
Tunisia	12	0.00
Latvia	2	0.00
Finland	4	0.00
Denmark	1	0.00
Luxembourg	0	0.00
Barbados	0	0.00
Marshall Islands	0	0.00
Oman	0	0.00
Samoa	0	0.00
Sao Tome and Principe	0	0.00

ANNEXURE - II

TOTAL NUMBER OF REPORTED DISASTERS, BY TYPE OF PHENOMENON AND BY YEAR (1992 TO 2001)

	1992	1993	1994	1995	1996	1997	1998	1999	2000	2001	Total
Avalanches/ landslides	14	22	8	15	24	13	22	15	29	21	183
Droughts/ famines	31	14	9	16	8	18	34	30	47	46	253
Earthquakes	24	14	22	25	11	14	16	33	30	26	215
Extreme temperatures	7	4	10	13	5	13	13	8	31	22	126
Floods	57	82	80	88	69	77	90	112	152	156	963
Forest/scrub fires	8	2	13	7	5	15	16	22	30	14	132
Volcanic eruptions	5	6	6	4	5	4	4	5	5	6	50
Windstorms	74	101	66	59	62	67	73	85	100	96	783
Other natural disasters	1	4	1	4	2	3	2	2	4	2	25
Total technological disasters	147	175	191	170	207	201	215	299	331	323	2,259
Total	368	424	406	401	398	425	485	611	759	712	4,989

Source : World Disaster Report, 2002

ANNEXURE - III

TOTAL NUMBER OF PEOPLE REPORTED KILLED BY DISASTERS, BY CONTINENT AND BY TYPE OF PHENOMENON (1992 TO 2001)

	Africa	Americas	Asia	Europe	Oceania	HHD1	MHD2	LHD3	Total
Droughts/famines	6,384	41	271,051	0	98	0	1,081	276,493	277,574
Earthquakes	784	3,463	52,440	20,998	71	8,316	62,020	7,420	77,756
Floods	9,243	35,848	50,034	1,362	20	2,191	78,661	15,655	96,507
Windstorms	1,252	23,359	34,895	712	229	3,445	50,110	6,892	60,447
Total technological disasters	21,890	12,438	42,814	9,204	601	10,557	51,621	24,769	86,947
Total	40,076	79,293	463,681	35,994	3,319	27,464	261,133	333,766	622,363

Source : World Disastar, 2002

ANNEXURE - IV

TOTAL NUMBER OF PEOPLE REPORTED KILLED BY DISASTERS, BY TYPE OF PHENOMENON AND BY YEAR (1992 TO 2001)

	1992	1993	1994	1995	1996	1997	1998	1999	2000	2001	Total
Avalanches/landslides	1,070	1,548	280	1,497	1,129	801	994	351	1,099	692	9,461
Droughts/Famines	2,571	0	0	54,000	54,000	54,530	57,875	54,029	370	199	277,574
Earthquakes	3,936	10,113	1,242	7,966	582	3,076	7,412	21,870	204	21,355	77,756
Floods	5,367	5,930	6,504	7,525	8,040	6,602	11,186	34,366	6,307	4,680	96,507
Windstorms	1,355	2,965	4,064	3,774	3,649	5,330	24,552	11,899	1,129	1,730	60,447
Total technological	7,453	9,489	9,151	7,428	9,252	7,968	8,548	8,740	10,187	8,731	86,947
Total	22,264	30,312	21,873	83,949	77,033	79,411	116,083	132,099	20,266	39,073	622,363

Source : World Disaster Report, 2002

ANNEXURE - V

TOTAL NUMBER OF PEOPLE REPORTED AFFECTED BY DISASTERS, BY CONTINENT AND BY YEAR (1992 TO 2001) IN THOUSANDS

	1992	1993	1994	1995	1996	1997	1998	1999	2001	2001	Total
Africa	21,747	16,500	11,234	9,533	4,282	7,136	10,738	14,362	23,043	18,378	136,954
Americas	3,429	1,970	2,722	1,027	2,200	2,170	18,180	5,008	1,246	11,225	49,279
Asia	50,894	162,254	168,145	256,863	207,141	56,229	315,006	188,605	229,636	140,067	1,774,841
Europe	372	1,380	909	8,220	30	679	621	6,549	2,907	777	22,444
Oceania	1,849	5,158	5,914	2,682	652	1,230	328	151	7	32	18,003
High human development	2,220	6,044	8,247	11,192	2,238	1,090	1,858	4,706	984	798	39,377
Medium human development	42,523	147,331	165,961	233,338	196,087	55,386	317,237	194,881	229,087	150,410	1,732,241
Low human development	33,549	33,888	14,715	33,795	15,980	10,968	25,778	15,088	26,870	19,271	229,901
Total	78,292	187,262	188,923	278,325	214,305	67,444	344,873	214,675	256,941	170,478	2,001,519

Source : World Disaster Report, 2002

ANNEXURE - VI

TOTAL AMOUNT OF DISASTER ESTIMATED DAMAGE, BY CONTINENT AND BY YEAR (1992 TO 2001) IN MILLIONS OF US DOLLARS (2001 PRICES)

	1992	1993	1994	1995	1996	1997	1998	1999	2000	2001	Total
Africa	288	11	513	192	125	8	357	770	154	318	2,736
Americas	57,431	27,113	35,613	25,932	13,931	9,588	20,140	13,686	3,357	9,725	216,516
Asia	7,589	17,028	14,758	180,579	33,688	28,385	31,146	28,271	16,964	13,487	371,895
Europe	3,068	1,906	12,215	14,353	192	10,667	2,709	38,008	8,520	739	92,376
Oceania	2,571	1,746	2,028	1,483	1,057	257	194	904	519	141	10,901
High human development	62,279	27,308	49,176	192,319	12,907	19,695	15,129	41,472	11,108	7,546	438,940
Medium human development	7,278	19,799	15,219	11,686	32,424	28,953	36,947	40,145	11,522	16,359	220,331
Low human development	1,390	698	732	18,535	3,662	257	2,469	22	6,884	505	35,152
Total	70,947	47,804	65,127	222,539	48,993	48,905	54,546	81,639	29,514	24,410	694,424

Source : World Disaster Report, 2002

ANNEXURE - VII

TOTAL AMOUNT OF DISASTER ESTIMATED DAMAGE, BY CONTINENT AND BY TYPE OF PHENOMENON (1992-2001) IN MILLIONS OF US DOLLARS (2001 PRICES)

	Africa	Americas	Asia	Europe	Oceania	Total
Avalanches/ landslides	0	1,290	439	28	0	1757
Drought/famines	417	3,516	12,688	10,787	5,096	32,505
Earthquakes	339	39,611	170,119	27,233	314	237,615
Estreme temperatures	1	8,419	4,497	1,073	0	13,990
Floods	967	36,422	119,167	34,532	862	191,950
Forest/scrub fires	4	3,641	20,941	200	257	25,043
Volcanic eruptions	0	10	1	22	480	513
Windstorms	828	117,899	41,508	16,800	3,755	180,790
Other natural disasters	6	121	0	0	124	250
Total technological disasters	175	5,587	2,533	1,702	14	10,011
Total	2,736	216,516	371,895	92,376	10,901	694424

Source : World Disaster Report, 2002

ANNEXURE - VIII

TOTAL AMOUNT OF DISASTER ESTIMATED DAMAGE BY TYPE OF PHENOMENON AND BY YEAR (1992 TO 2001) IN MILLIONS OF US DOLLARS (2001 PRICES)

	1992	1993	1994	1995	1996	1997	1998	1999	2000	2001	Total
Earthquakes	824	1,118	31,721	154,597	597	5,355	412	33,380	147	9,465	237,615
Floods	7,061	30,061	23,101	30,244	27,977	12,781	32,866	14,112	10,991	2,755	191,950
Windstorms	54,119	10,863	5,959	28,268	14,124	8,241	15,936	25,088	9,929	8,263	180,790
Total technological disaster	1,010	2,298	1,359	1,472	2,976	33	193	216	444	10	10,011
Total	70,947	47,804	65,127	222,539	48,993	48,905	54,546	81,639	29,514	24,410	694,424

Source : World Disaster Report, 2002

ANNEXURE - IX

MAJOR NATURAL CATASTROPHES OF 20TH CENTURY

SN.	Date	Place	Nature	Fatalities	Econ. loss (Us$m)
1.	8.9.1900	USA	Hurricane	6,000	30
2.	18.4.1906	USA, San Francisco	Earthquake	3,000	624
3.	20.12.1908	Italy, Messina	Earthquake	85,926	116
4.	13.1.1919	Italian, Avezzano	Earthquake	32,610	29
5.	16.12.1920	China, Gansu	Earthquake	235,000	25
6.	1.9.1923	Japan Yokohama	Earthquake	142,800	2,800
7.	July-Aug 1931	China, Yangtzekiang	Flood	140,000	
8.	30.5.1935	Pakistan, Quetta	Earthquake	35,000	25
9.	10-22.9.1938	USA, New England States	Hurricane	600	300
10.	25.1.1939	China, Concepcian	Earthquake	28,000	100
11.	25.12.1939	Turkey, Erzincan	Earthquake	32,740	20
12.	16.10.1942	Bangladesh, India	Cyclone	61,000	
13.	Feb, 1953	The Netherlands, UK	Storm surge	1,932	3,000
14.	Aug, 1954	China, Dongting	Flood	40,000	
15.	20-27.9.1959	Japan, Honsu	Typhoon	5,10	600
16.	29.2.1960	Morocco, Agadir	Earthquake	12,000	120
17.	7-12.9.1965	USA FL, LA	Hurricane, Betsy	75	1,420
18.	12.1.1970	Bangladesh, India, Chitgaon, Khulna	Cyclone, Storm surge	300,000	63
19.	31.5.1970	Peru, Chimbote	Earthquake, Landslide	67,000	550
20.	2-4.1.1976	Central & West Europe	Capella gale	82	1,300
21.	4.2.1976	Guatemala	Earthquake	22,084	1,100
22.	22-28.7.1976	China	Earthquake	290,000	5,600
23.	19.9.1985	Mexico, Mexico city	Earthquake	10,000	4,000
24.	13-14.11.1985	Columbia, Armero	Volcano	24,740	230
25.	9-17.9.1988	USA, Caribbean	Hurricane	355	3,000
26.	17.10.1989	USA, CA, San Francisco	Earthquake,	68	6,000
27.	7.12.1988	Armania, Spitak	Earthquake,	25,000	14,000
28.	25.1-1.3.1990	West Europe	Winter Storm	230	14,800
29.	29-30.4.1991	Bangladesh	Cyclone Storm surge	139,000	3,000

Annexure-IX (*Contd.*)

SN.	Date	Place	Nature	Fatalities	Econ. loss (Us$m)
30.	26-28.9.1991	Japan, Kayushu,	Typhoon	62	6,000
31.	23-27.8.1992	USA, FL, LA	Hurricane, Andrew	62	30,000
32.	30.9.1993	India, Maharastra, Khillari	Earthquake,	9,475	280
33.	17.1.1994	USA, CA, LA	Earthquake,	61	44,000
34.	17.1.1995	Japan, Kobe	Earthquake,	6,348	>100,000
35.	May-Sep, 1998	China, Yangtzekiang, Songhua	Flood	3,650	30,000
36.	25.10-8/11/1998	Honduras, Nicaragua	Hurricane Mitch	9,200	5,500
37.	17.8.1999	Turkey, Koaceli, Izmit	Earthquake,	17,000	13,000
38.	20.9.1999	Taiwan, Taichung	Earthquake,	2,400	>11,000

Source : Munich Re Topics 2000, Munich Re Group

ANNEXURE - X

SIGNIFICANT NATURAL DISASTERS OF WORLD DURING 1999 AND 2000

SN.	Date	Event	Region	Deaths	Eco. Losses (US$m)
1.	Jan-March, 1999	Avalanches	Switzerland, Australia, Germany	100	600
2.	1-4.1.,1999	Winter storm, tornadoes	USA, Canada	18	1.000
3.	13-16.1,1999	Winter storm, Ice storm	USA, Canada	-	700
4.	25.1, 1999	Earthquake	Colombia	1.185	1.500
5.	14.4, 1999	Hailstorm	Australia	1	1.500
6.	3-7.5, 1999	Tornadoes	USA	51	2.000
7.	20-23.5, 1999	Cyclone	Pakistan, India	644	20
8.	12-28.5, 1999	Floods	Germany, Switzerland	10	850
9.	Juen-July, 1999	Floods	China	800	8.000
10.	17.8, 1999	Earthquake	Turkey	17.2	12.000
11.	7.9, 1999	Earthquake	Creece	138	4.150
12.	14-16.9, 1999	Hurricane Flood	USA, Bahamas	61	4.000
13.	20.9, 1999	Earthquake	Taiwan	2.47	14.000
14.	21.9-15.10, 1999	Flood,	Mexico Landslide	500	230
15.	22-25.9, 1999	Typhoon Bart	Japan	26	5.000
16.	29.10-11, 1999	Cyclone 05B	India	15.000*	2.500*
17.	3-4.12, 1999	Winter storm Anatol	Western & Northern Europe	20	800
18.	13-16.12, 1999	Floods, landslides	Veneuela	20.000*	15.000*
19.	26.12, 1999	Winter strom Lothar	Central Europe	100	7.500*
20.	27.12, 1999	Winter storm Martin	France, Spain, Switzerland	30	2.000*
21.	Jan-Apr., 2000	Winter damage	Mongolia: S, W	7	80

Annexure-X (*Contd.*)

SN.	Date	Event	Region	Deaths	Eco. Losses (US$m)
22.	Jan. - Dec, 2000	Drought	Afghanistan Pakistan, India, Tajikistan	35	590
23.	1-5.1, 2000	Floods, landslides	Brazil : SE	26	
24.	14.1, 2000	Earthquakes	China : SW	5	75
25.	15-19. 1, 2000	Forest fires	South Africa : Cape town region	10	
26.	22-25.1, 2000	Winter storm	USA:AL, GA, L A, NC, SC, TN, VA, NY, PA, MAD	4	350
27.	29-30.1, 2000	Winter Storm Kerstin	Germany : N. De nmar	4	100
28.	February, 2000	Frost	Kenya : SW		
29.	Feb.- March 2000	Floods, tropical Cyclone Eline	Mozambique. South Africa. Botswana. Swaziland. Zimbabwe. Malawi. Zambia	>1,000	660
30.	5.2.2000	Hailstrom	Argentina : C. Santa Isabel		20
31.	27.2-13.3, 2000	Tropical cyclone Steve	Australia : NE	1	90
32.	2.3, 2000	Tropical cyclone Gloria	Madagascar : W,N	130	
33.	9-16.3,2000	Floods	Czech Republic C,W	80	
34.	10.3, 2000	Tropical Cyclone Mona	Tonga : C		4
35.	10.3, 2000	Tornadoes	USA : TX, Fort Worth, LA	5	650
36.	31.3-13.4, 2000	Volcanic eruption : Mt. Usu	Japan : N, Hokkaido, Abuta		
37.	2.4, 2000	Tropical cyclone Hudah	Madagascar : NE, Mozambique :C	>23	

Annexure-X (*Contd.*)

SN.	Date	Event	Region	Deaths	Eco. Losses (US$m)
38.	6-10.4	Floods	Romania: C,W, Hungary : E, Ne. Serbia	10	100
39.	May, 2000	Freeze, frost	Ukraine. Belarus		115
40.	May-June, 2000	Floods	China: SE, C	410	960
41.	May-June,2000	Drought	Iran: C,E,S		3,500*
42.	May-Sept,2000	Forestfire, drought	USA: AZ, CA, CO, ID, FL, MT, NV, NM, OR, TX, UT, WA, WY	9	>1,000
43.	4.5,2000	Earthquake, tsunami	Indonesia:E	41	30
44.	17-19.5,2000	Severe storm, Tornadoes, floods	USA: CT, IA, IL, IN, NJ, NY, OH, PA, WI, NE, MN, WY, CO	1	300
45.	24.5,2000	Hail	Japan:C		350
46.	27.5,2000	Hail	Austria: NW, Upper Austria		20
47.	28.5,2000	Winter storm Ginger	Germany. Belgium. Netherlands	6	200
48.	June-July, 2000	Heat wave, drought	Eastern Europe, Europe Southeastern	70	300
49.	4.6.2000	Earthquake	Indonesia:W	130	6
50.	12-26.6,2000	Severe strom, floods	Chile: N, S, C, esp. Santiago, Valparaiso		15
51.	17.6,2000	Earthquake	Icwlands: S, Hella		20
52.	3-7.7,2000	Hailstorms	Austria: C,SE,W	2	125
53.	5-13.7,2000	Forest fircs, heat wave	Greece : S,W,E,S		25

Annexure-X (*Contd.*)

SN.	Date	Event	Region	Deaths	Eco. Losses (US$m)
54.	6-9.7,2000	Typhoon Kirogi (Ditang)	Philippines Japan, Taiwan	44	300
55.	14.7,2000	Tornado	Canadad : W, Alberta, Red Deer	10	13
56.	21-25.7, 2000	Floods	Sweden:C,N		8
57.	Aug.-Oct.,2000	Floods	India:E,N, NE. Nepal:C	1,550	1,200
58.	22-23.8,2000	Typhoon Bills	Taiwaj:S	11	135
59.	30.31.8, 2000	Typhoon Prapiroon (No. 12)	South Korea. North Korea: NE,E		42
60.	SEpt.-Oct.,2000	Floods	Cambodia, Vietnam, Loas, Thailand	>900	460
61.	Sept.-Oct.,2000	Floods	Bangladeh: W,Se	130	500
62.	13-19.9, 2000	Floods	Japan, South, Korea, Russia	25	1,500
63.	29.9-3.10,2000	Hurricane Deith	Belize, Mexico. Nicaragua, Honduras, Guatemala	21	280
64.	Oct-Nov.,2000	Floods	Great Britain: England, Wales	10	>1,500
65.	6.10,2000	Earthquake	Japan:W, Tottori		150
66.	13-20.10,2000	Floods, landslides	Italy Switzerland. France	38	8,500
67.	28-31.10,2000	Typhoon Xangsane	Philippines. Taiwan	103	70
68.	16-23.1,2000	Floods	Australia:E		250
69.	26-27.11,2000	Winter strom	Moldavia:N,C	30	
70.	16-17.12,2000	Severe strom, tornadoes	USA: AL, CT, FL, GA, KY, MA, MS, NC, NJ, NY, PA, RI, SC, TE	12	500

Source : Munich Re Topics 2001; Munich Re Group

ANNEXURE - XI

NUMBER OF DISTRICTS, BLOCKS AND VILLAGES

S. No.	States/Uts	Nos. of District	Number of Block (as on 31-1-2001)	Number of Village Inhabited	Number of Village Un-habited	Area in Sq. kms.
1.	Andhra Pradesh	23	330	26586	1414	275045
2.	Arunachal Pradesh	13	54	3649	—	83743
3.	Assam	23	214	24685	905	78438
4.	Bihar	37	535	67513	10184	173877
5.	Chhatisgarh	16	146	—	—	—
6.	Goa	2	11	360	9	3702
7.	Gujarat	25	230	18028	481	196024
8.	Haryana	19	114	6759	229	44212
9.	Himachal Pradesh	12	72	16997	2391	55673
10.	Jammu and Kashmir	14	119	6445	260	222236
11.	Jharkhand	18	219	—	—	—
12.	Karnataka	27	175	27066	2127	191791
13.	Kerala	14	152	1384	—	38863
14.	Madhya Pradesh	45	313	71526	4694	443446
15.	Maharashtra	35	320	40412	2613	307713
16.	Manipur	9	34	2182	30	22327
17.	Meghalaya	7	39	5484	145	22429
18.	Mizoram	8	30	698	87	21081
19.	Nagaland	8	52	1216	9	16579
20.	Orissa	30	314	46989	4068	155707
21.	Punjab	17	138	12428	367	50362
22.	Rajasthan	32	237	37889	1921	342239
23.	Sikkim	4	8	447	6	7096
24.	Tamil Nadu	30	385	15822	958	130058
25.	Tirpura	4	38	855	1	10486
26.	Uttaranchal	13	95	—	—	—
27.	Uttar Pradesh	70	809	112803	11147	294411
28.	West Bengal	18	341	37910	2979	88752
29.	A.N. Islands	2	3	504	43	8249
30.	Chandigarh	1	1	25	—	114
31.	D.N. Haveli	1	1	71	—	491
32.	Delhi	9	7	199	10	1483
33.	Daman and Diu	2	2	24	—	112
34.	Lakshadweep	1	9	7	16	32
35.	Pondicherry	4	3	263	1	492
	Total	595	5550	587226	47095	3287263

Source : Ministry of Rural Development

ANNEXURE - XII

PROVISIONAL POPULATION 2001

Population Distribution, Percentage Decadal Growth, Sex Ratio, Population Density and Literacy Rate

India/States/ Union Territories	Population 2001			%age decadal growth		Sex ratio (females per 1000 male)		Population density (per sq. km.)		Literacy rate 2001		
	Persons	Males	Females	1981-1991	1991-2001	1991	2001	1991	2001	Persons	Male	Females
1	2	3	4	5	6	7	8	9	10	11	12	13
INDIA	1,027,015,247	531,277,078	495,738,169	23.86	21.34	927	933	267	324	65.38	75.85	54.16
Jammu & Kashmir	10,069,917	5,300,574	4,769,343	30.34	29.04	896	900	77	99	54.46	65.75	41.82
Himachal Pradesh	6,077,248	3,085,256	2,991,992	20.79	17.53	976	970	93	109	77.13	86.02	68.08
Punjab	24,289,296	12,963,362	11,325,934	20.81	19.76	882	874	403	482	69.95	75.63	63.55
Chandigarh	900,914	508,224	392,690	42.16	40.33	790	773	5632	7903	81.76	85.65	76.65
Uttaranchal	8,479,562	4,316,401	4,163,161	24.23	19.2	936	964	133	159	72.28	84.01	60.26
Haryana	21,082,989	11,327,658	9,755,331	27.41	28.06	865	861	372	477	68.59	79.25	56.31
Delhi	13,782,979	7,570,890	6,212,086	51.45	46.31	827	821	6352	9294	81.82	87.37	7500
Rajasthan	56,473,122	29,381,657	27,091,465	28.44	28.33	910	922	129	165	61.03	76.46	44.34
Uttar Pradesh	166,052,859	87,466,301	78,586,558	25.55	25.08	876	898	548	689	57.36	70.23	42.98

(Contd...)

Annexure-XII (*Contd.*)

1	2	3	4	5	6	7	8	9	10	11	12	13
Bihar	82,878,796	43,153,964	39,724,832	23.38	28.43	907	921	685	880	47.53	60.32	33.57
Sikkim	540,493	288,217	252,276	28.47	32.98	878	875	57	76	69.68	76.73	61.46
Arunachal Pradesh	1,091,117	573,951	517,166	36.83	26.21	859	901	10	13	54.74	64.07	44.24
Nagaland	1,988,636	1,041,686	946,950	56.08	64.41	886	909	73	120	67.11	71.77	61.92
Manipur	2,388,634	1,207,338	1,181,296	29.29	30.02	958	978	82	107	68.87	77.87	59.07
Mizoram	891,058	459,783	431,275	39.77	29.18	921	938	33	42	88.49	90.69	86.13
Tripura	3,191,168	1,636,138	1,555,030	34.33	15.74	945	950	263	304	73.66	81.47	65.41
Meghalaya	2,306,069	1,167,840	1,138,229	32.86	29.94	955	975	79	103	63.31	66.14	60.41
Assam	26,638,407	13,787,799	12,850,608	24.24	18.85	923	932	286	340	64.28	71.93	56.03
West Bengal	80,221,171	41,487,694	38,733,477	24.73	17.84	917	934	767	904	69.22	77.58	60.22
Jharkhand	26,909,428	13,861,277	13,048,151	24.03	23.19	922	941	274	338	54.13	67.94	39.38
Orissa	36,706,920	18,612,340	18,094,580	20.06	15.94	971	972	203	236	63.61	75.95	50.97
Chhatisgarh	20,795,956	10,452,426	10,343,530	25.73	18.06	985	990	130	154	65.18	77.86	52.04
Madhya Pradesh	60,385,118	31,456,873	28,928,245	27324	24.34	912	920	158	196	64.11	76.08	50.28
Gujarat	50,596,992	26,344,053	24,252,939	21.19	22.48	934	921	211	258	69.97	80.5	58.06
Daman and Diu	158,059	92,478	65,581	28.62	55.59	969	709	907	1411	81.09	88.4	70.37
Dadra and Nagar Haveli	220,451	121,731	98,720	33.57	59.20	952	811	282	449	60.03	73.32	42.99
Maharashtra	96,752,247	50,334,270	46,417,977	25.73	22.57	934	922	257	314	77.27	86.27	67.51
Andhra Pradesh	75,727,541	38,286,811	37,440,730	24.20	13.86	972	978	242	275	61.11	70.85	51.17
Karnataka	52,733,958	26,856,343	25,877,615	21.12	17.25	960	964	235	275	67.04	76.29	57.45
Goa	1,343,998	685,617	658,381	16.08	14.89	967	960	316	363	82.32	88.88	75.51
Lakshadweep	60,595	31,118	29,477	28.47	17.19	943	947	1616	1894	87.52	93.15	81.56

(*Contd...*)

Annexure-XII (*Contd.*)

1	2	3	4	5	6	7	8	9	10	11	12	13
Kerala	31,838,619	15,468,664	16,369,955	14.32	9.42	1036	1058	749	819	90.92	94.2	87.86
Tamil Nadu	62,110,839	31,268,654	30,842,185	15.39	11.19	974	986	429	478	73.47	82.33	64.05
Pondicherry	973,829	486,705	487,124	33.64	20.56	979	1001	1683	2029	81.49	88.89	74.13
Andaman and Nicobar Islands	356,265	192,985	163,280	48.07	26.94	818	846	34	43	81.18	86.07	75.29

1. The population of India includes the estimated population of entire Kachchh district, Morvi, Maliya-Miyana and Wankaner talukas of Rajkot district, Jodiya taluka of Jamnagar district of Gujarat State and entire Kinnaur district of Himachal Pradesh where population enumeration of Census of India, 2001 could not be conducted due to natural calamities.
2. For working out the population density of India and Jammu and Kashmir the entire area and population of those areas of Jammu and Kashmir which are under illegal occupation of Pakistan and China have not been taken into account.
3. The literacy rates for India have been worked out by excluding the population and number of literates of areas affected by natural calamities of Gujarat and Himachal Pradesh as per details given in Note 1 above.
4. While working out the percentage decadal growth of population of Jammu and Kashmir the population figures for 1991 have been worked out by interpolation as 1991 Census could not be held there owing to disturbed conditions.
5. Figures shown against Himachal Pradesh have been arrived at after including the estimated figures of entire Kinaur district of Himachal Pradesh where the population enumeration of Census of India 2001 could not be conducted due to natural calamity.
6. Figures shown against Gujarat have been arrived at after including the estimated figures of entire Kachchh district, Morvi, Maliya-Miyana and Wankaner talukas of Rajkot district, Jodiya taluka of Jamnagar district of Gujarat State where the population enumeration of Census of India, 2001 could not be conducted due to natural calamity.
7. Literacy rates shown against Himachal Pradesh and Gujarat do not include areas affected by natural calamities, the details of which are given in Note 1 above.

Source : Ministry of Rural Development

ANNEXURE - XIII

RURAL URBAN DISTRIBUTION OF POPULATION — INDIA AND STATES/UNION TERRITORIES : 2001

States/UTs	T/R/U	Population Persons	Males	Females	Percent Urban Population
1	2	3	4	5	6
INDIA	T	1,027,015,247	531,277,078	495,738,169	27.78
	R	741,660,293	381,141,184	360,519,109	
	U	285,354,954	150,135,894	135,219,060	
State/Union Territory*					
1 . Jammu & Kashmir	T	10,069,917	5,300,574	4,769,343	24.88
	R	7,564,608	3,925,846	3,638,762	
	U	2,505,309	1,374,728	1.130,581	
2. Himachal Pradesh	T	6,077,248	3,085,256	2,991,992	9.79
	R	5,482,367	2,754,251	2,728,116	
	U	594,881	331,005	2,638,76	
3. Punjab	T	24,289,296	12,963,362	11,325,934	33.95
	R	16,043,730	8,500,647	7,543,083	
	U	8,245,566	4,462,715	3,782,851	
4.. Chandigarh*	T	900,914	508,224	392,690	89.78
	R	92,118	56,837	35,281	
	U	808,796	451,387	357,409	
5. Uttaranchal	T	8,479,562	4,316,401	4,163,161	25.59
	R	6,309,317	3,143,380	3,165,937	
	U	2,170,245	1,173,021	997,224	
6. Haryana	T	21,082,989	11,327,658	9,755,331	29.00
	R	14,968,850	8,017,622	6,951,228	
	U	6,114,139	3,310,036	2,804,103	
7. Delhi*	T	13,782,976	7,570,890	6,212,086	93.01
	R	963,215	533,219	429,996	
	U	12,819,761	7,037,671	5,782,090	
8. Rajasthan	T	56,473,122	29,381,657	27,091,465	23.38
	R	43,267,678	22,394,479	20,873,199	
	U	13,205,444	6,987,178	6,218,266	
9. Uttar Pradesh	T	166,052,859	87,466,301	78,586,558	20.78
	R	131,540,230	69,096,765	62,443,465	
	U	34,512,629	18,369,536	16,143,093	
10. Bihar	T	82,878,796	43,153,964	39,724,832	10.47
	R	74,199,596	38,510,686	35,688,910	
	U	8,679,200	4,643,278	4,035,922	
11. Sikkim	T	540,493	288,217	252,276	11.10
	R	480,488	255,386	225,102	
	U	60,005	32,831	27,174	

Annexure-XIII (*Contd.*)

1	2	3	4	5	6
12. Arunachal Pradesh	T	1,091,117	573,951	517,166	20.41
	R	868,429	453,560	414,869	
	U	222,688	120,391	102,297	
13. Nagaland	T	1,988,636	1,041,686	946,950	17.74
	R	1,635,815	846,651	789,164	
	U	352,821	195,035	157,786	
14. Manipur	T	2,388,634	1,207,338	1,181,296	23.88
	R	1,818,224	923,428	894,796	
	U	570,410	283,910	286,500	
15. Mizoram	T	891,058	459,783	431,275	49.50
	R	450,018	233,718	216,300	
	U	441,040	226,065	214,975	
16. Tripura	T	3,191,168	1,636,138	1,555,030	17.02
	R	2,648,074	1,359,288	1,288,786	
	U	543,094	276,850	266,244	
17. Meghalaya	T	2,306,069	1,167,840	1,138,229	19.63
	R	1,853,457	939,803	913,654	
	U	452,612	228,037	224,575	
18. Assam	T	26,638,407	13,787,799	12,850,608	12.72
	R	23,248,994	11,983,157	11,265,837	
	U	3,389,413	1,804,642	1,584,771	
19. West Bengal	T	80,221,171	41,487,694	38,733,477	28.03
	R	57,734,690	29,606,028	28,128,662	
	U	22,486,481	11,881,666	10,604,815	
20. Jharkhand	T	26,909,428	13,861,277	13,048,151	22.25
	R	20,922,731	10,660,430	10,262,301	
	U	5,986,697	3,200,847	2,785,850	
21. Orissa	T	36,706,920	18,612,340	18,094,580	14.97
	R	31,210,602	15,711,853	15,498,749	
	U	5,496,318	2,900,487	2,595,831	
22. Chhatisgarh	T	20,795,956	10,452,426	10,343,530	20.08
	R	16,620,627	8,290,983	8,329,644	
	U	4,175,329	2,161,443	2,013,886	
23. Madhya Pradesh	T	60,385,118	31,456,873	28,928,245	26.67
	R	44,282,528	22,975,256	21,307,272	
	U	16,102,590	8,481,617	7,620,973	
24. Gujarat	T	50,596,992	26,344,053	24,252,939	37.35
	R	31,697,615	16,289,423	15,408,192	
	U	18,899,377	1,005,463	8,844,747	
25.Daman & Diu*	T	158,059	92,478	65,581	36.26
	R	100,740	63,576	37,164	
	U	57,319	28,902	28,417	
26. Dadra & Nagar Haveli*	T	220,451	121,731	98,720	22.89
	R	169,995	91,887	78,108	
	U	50,456	29,844	20,612	

Annexure-XIII (*Contd.*)

1	2	3	4	5	6
27. Maharashtra	T	96,752,247	50,334,270	46,417,977	42.40
	R	55,732,513	28,443,238	27,289,275	
	U	41,019,734	21,891,032	19,128,702	
28. Andhra Pradesh	T	75,727,541	38,286,811	37,440,730	27.08
	R	55,223,944	27,852,179	27,371,765	
	U	20,503,597	10,434,632	10,068,965	
29. Karnataka	T	52,733,958	26,856,343	25,877,615	33.98
	R	34,814,100	17,618,593	17,195,507	
	U	17,919,858	9,237,750	8,682,108	
30. Goa	T	1,343,998	685,617	658,381	49.77
	R	675,129	339,626	335,503	
	U	668,869	345,991	322,878	
31. Lakshadweep*	T	60,595	31,118	29,477	44.47
	R	33,647	17,196	16,451	
	U	26,948	13,922	13,026	
32. Kerala	T	31,838,619	15,468,664	16,369,955	25.97
	R	23,571,484	11,450,785	12,120,699	
	U	8,267,135	4,017,879	4,249,256	
33. Tamil Nadu	T	62,110,839	31,268,654	30,842,185	43.86
	R	34,869,286	17,508,985	17,360,301	
	U	27,241,553	13,759,669	13,481,884	
34. Pondicherry*	T	973,829	486,705	487,124	66.57
	R	325,596	163,586	162,010	
	U	648,233	323,119	325,114	
35. Andaman & Nicobar Islands*	T	356,265	191,985	163,280	32.67
	R	239,858	128,837	111,021	
	U	116,407	64,148	52,259	

Notes :

1. The total, rural and urban population of India includes the estimated total, rural and urban population of entire Kachchh district, Morvi, Maliya Miyana and Wankaner taluks of Rajkot district, Jodiya taluka of Jamnagar district of Gujarat state and estimated total and rural population of entire Kinnaur district of Himachal Pradesh where population enumeration of Census of India, 2001 could not be conducted due to natural calamities.
2. The Figures of total, rural and urban population of Himachal Pradesh state have been arrived at after including the estimated total and rural population of entire Kinnaur district where population enumeration of Census of India, 2001 could not be conducted due lo natural calamity.
3. The figures of total, rural and urban population of Gujarat state have been arrived at after including the estimated total, rural and urban population of entire Kachchh district, Morvi, Maliya-Miyana and Wankaner taluks of Rajkot district, Jodiya taluka of Jamnagar district where population enumeration of the Census of India, 2001 could not be conducted due to natural calamity.

Source : Minisry of Rural Development, GOI

ANNEXURE - XIV

POVERTY AND RELATED STATISTICS

State-specific Poverty Lines in 1999-2000
(Rs. per capita per month)

	State	Rural	Urban
1.	Andhra Pradesh	262.94	457.04
2.	Assam	365.43	343.99
3.	Bihar	333.07	379.78
4.	Gujarat	318.94	474.41
5.	Haryana	362.81	420.02
6.	Himachal Pradesh	367.45	420.02
7.	Karnataka	309.59	511.44
8.	Kerala	374.79	477.06
9.	Madhya Pradesh	311.34	481.65
10.	Maharashtra	318.63	539.71
11.	Orissa	323.92	473.12
12.	Punjab	362.68	388.15
13.	Rajasthan	344.03	465.92
14.	Tamil Nadu	307.64	475.06
15.	Uttar Pradesh	336.88	416.29
16.	West Bengal	350.17	409.22
17.	Delhi	362.68	505.45
	All India #	327.56	454.11

The poverty line (implicit) at all-India level is worked out from the expenditure class-wise distribution of persons and the poverty ratio at all-India level. The poverty ratio at all-India level is obtained as the weighted average of the state-wise poverty ratio.

Source : Ministry of Rural Development, Govt. of India

ANNEXURE - XV

POVERTY AND RELATED STATISTIC

Poverty lines as per the new official methodology
(Rs. Monthly per capita)

	States	Urban				
		1973-74	1977-78	1983-84	1987-88	1993-94
	1	2	3	4	5	6
1.	Andhra Pradesh	53.96	69.05	106.43	151.88	278.14
2.	Arunachal Pradesh	*	*	*	**	*
3.	Assam	50.26	61.38	97.51	126.6	212.42
4.	Bihar	61.27	67.27	111.08	150.25	238.59
5.	Goa	59.48	73.99	126.47	189.17	328.56
6.	Gujarat	62.17	72.39	123.22	173.18	297.22
7.	Haryana	52.42	66.94	103.48	143.22	258.23
8.	Himachal Pradesh	51.93	66.32	102.26	144.1	253.61
9.	Jammu and Kashmir	37.17	55.41	99.62	148.38	*
10.	Karnataka	58.22	68.85	120.19	171.18	302.89
11.	Kerala	62.78	67.05	122.64	163.29	280.54
12.	Madhya Pradesh	63.02	74.04	122.82	178.35	317.16
13.	Maharashtra	59.48	73.99	126.47	189.17	328.56
14.	Manipur	*	*	*	*	*
15.	Meghalaya	*	*	*	*	*
16.	Mizoram	*	*	*	*	*
17.	Nagaland	*	*	*	*	*
18.	Orissa	59.34	72.41	124.81	165.04	298.22
19.	Punjab	51.93	65.07	101.03	144.98	253.61
20.	Rajasthan	59.99	72	113.35	165.38	280.85
21.	Sikkim	*	*	*	*	*
22.	Tamil Nadu	51.54	67.02	120.3	165.82	296.63
23.	Tirpura	*	*	*	*	*
24.	Uttar Pradesh	57.37	69.66	110.23	154.15	268.65
25.	West Bengal	54.81	67.05	105.91	149.96	247.53
26.	A. N. Islands	*	*	*	*	**

Annexure-XV (*Contd.*)

1	2	3	4	5	6
27. Chandigarh	*	*	*	*	**
28. D. N. Havali	59.48	73.99	126.47	189.17	328.56
29. Damman & Diu	*	*	*	*	**
30. Delhi	67.95	80.17	123.29	176.91	309.48
31. Lakshadweep	*	*	*	*	**
32. Pondicherry	*	*	*	*	**
ALL INDIA#	56.76	70.33	115.65	162.16	281.35

* In the Expert Group poverty ratios for these states have not been calculated separately, but has been adopted from those of other states. The details are as follows :

1. Poverty Ratio of Assam is used for Sikkim, Arunachal Pradesh, Meghalaya,Mizoram, Manipur, Nagaland and Tripura.
2. Poverty Ratio of Tamil Nadu is used for Pondicherry and A & N Island.
3. Poverty Ratio of Kerala is used for Lakshadweep.
4. Poverty Ratio of Goa is used for Daman & Diu.
5. Urban Poverty Ratio of Punjab is used for both rural and urban poverty of Chandigarh.
6. In 1993-94, Poverty Ratio of Himanchal Pradesh is used for Jammu & Kashmir.
7. Since poverty ratio is estimated from the consumption expenditure distribution and the poverty lines, it is preferable that the poverty lines of these states may be equated to that of the state whose poverty ratio is adopted.

\# The poverty line (implicit) at all-India level is worked out from the expenditure class-wise distribution of persons and the poverty ratio at all-India level. The poverty ratio at all-India level is obtained as the weighted average of the state-wise poverty

Source : Ministry of Rural Development

ANNEXURE - XVI

NUMBER AND PERCENTAGE OF POPULATION BELOW POVERTY LINE BY STATES - 1999-2000

State/UTs	Rural		Urban		Combined	
	No. of persons (in lakh)	%age of persons	No. of persons (in lakh)	%age of persons	No. of persons (in lakh)	%age of persons
1	2	3	4	5	6	7
1. AndhraPradesh	58.13	11.05	60.88	26.63	119.01	15.77
2. Arunachal Pradesh	3.08	40.04	0.18	7.47	3.98	33.47
3. Assam	92.17	40.04	2.38	747	94.55	36.09
4. Bihar	376.51	44.03	49.13	32.91	425.64	42.06
5. Goa	0.11	1.35	0.59	7.52	0.07	4.04
6. Gujarat	39.8	13.17	28.09	15.59	67.89	14.07
7. Haryana	11.94	8.27	5.39	9.99	17.34	8.74
8. Himachal Pradesh	4.84	7.94	0.29	4.63	5.12	7.63
9. Jammu and Kashsmir	2.97	3.97	0.49	1.98	3.46	3.48
10. Kamataka	59.91	17.38	44.49	25.25	104.04	20.04
11. Kerala	20.97	9.38	20.07	20.27	41.04	12.72
12. Madhya Pradesh	217.32	37.06	81.22	38.44	298.54	37.43
13. Maharashtra	125.12	23.72	102.87	26.81	227.99	25.03
14. Manipur	6.53	40.04	0.66	7.47	7.19	28.54
15. Meghalaya	7.89	40.04	0.34	7.47	8.23	33.87
16. Mizoram	1.04	40.04	0.45	7.47	1.86	19.47
17. Nagaland	5.21	40.04	0.28	7.47	5.49	32.67
18. Orissa	143.69	48.01	25.4	42.83	169.09	47.15
19. Punjab	10.02	6.35	4.29	5.75	14.49	6.16
20. Rajasthan	55.06	13.74	26.78	19.85	81.83	15.28
21. Sikkim	2	40.04	0.04	7.47	2.05	36.55
22. Tamil Nadu	80.51	20.55	49.97	22.11	130.43	21.12
23. Tripura	12.53	40.04	0.49	7.47	13.02	34.44
24. Uttar Pradesh	412.01	31.22	117.88	30.89	529.89	31.15
25. West Bengal	180.11	31.85	33.38	14.86	213.49	27.02
26. A. & N. Islands	0.58	20.55	0.24	22.11	0.82	20.99
27. Chandigarh	0.06	5.75	0.45	5.75	0.51	5.75

Annexure-XVI (*Contd.*)

1	2	3	4	5	6	7
28. D.&N.Haveli	0.3	17.57	0.03	13.52	0.33	17.14
29. Daman & Diu	0.01	1.35	0.05	7.52	0.06	4.44
30. Delhi	0.07	0.04	11.42	9.42	11.49	8.23
31. Lakshadweep	0.03	0.38	0.08	20.27	0.11	15.6
32. Pondicherry	0.64	20.55	1.77	22.11	2.41	21.67
ALL INDIA	1932.43	27.09	670.07	23.62	2602.05	2610

1. Poverty Ratio of Assam is used for Sikkim, Arunachal Pradesh, Meghalaya.Mizoram, Manipur, Nagaland and Tripura.
2. Poverty line of Maharashtra and expenditure distribution of Goa is used to estimate poverty ratio of Goa.
3. Poverty Line of Himachal Pradesh and expenditure distribution of Jammu & Kashmir is used to estimate poverty ratio of Jammu &Kashmir
4. Poverty Ratio of Tamil Nadu is used for Pondicherry and A & N Island.
5. Urban Poverty Ratio of Punjab is used for both rural and urban poverty of Chandigarh.
6. Poverty line of Maharashtra and expenditure distribution of Dadra & Nagar Haveli is used to estimate poverty ratio of Dadra & Nagar Haveli
7. Poverty Ratio of Goa is used for Daman & Diu.
8. Poverty Ratio of Kerala is used for Lakshadweep.
9. Urban Poverty Ratio of Rajasthan may be treated as tentative.

Source : Ministry of Rural Development GOI

ANNEXURE - XVII

NUMBER AND PERCENTAGE OF POPULATION BELOW POVERTY LINE — ALL INDIA

Item	1993-94	1999-2000
RURAL		
Number of Poor (million)	244.03	193.24
Percentage below poverty line	37.27	27.09
URBAN		
Number of Poor (million)	76.34	67.01
Percentage below poverty line	32.36	23.62
COMBINED		
Number of Poor (million)	320.37	260.25
Percentage below poverty line	35.97	23.10

Notes :

1. Estimate of Poverty, Govt. of India, P.I.B. 11th March, 1997.
2. Poverty Estimates for 1999-2000, Govt. of India, P.I.B., 22nd February, 2001

Source: Planning Commission

ANNEXURE - XVIII

NUMBER AND PERCENTAGE OF B.P.L. CENSUS FOR 9TH PLAN-STATE-WISE

(As on 17-3-2001) (Provisional)

States		Total No. of rural families	No. of rural families below	%age of families below	Total No. of rural families	No. of rural families	%age of families below	%age of rural population
	1	2	3	4	5	6	7	8
1.	Andhra Pradesh	1,04,84,028	41,84,628	39.91	1,00,03,000	43,48,525	43.47	15.92
2.	Arunachal Pradesh	1,02,852	80,627	78.39	1,08,817	86,646	79.63	45.01
3.	Assam	36,07,241	21,64,416	60.00	31,96,041	19,82,008	62.01	45.01
4.	Bihar	1,89,33,813	93,99,281	49.64	1.14,80,451	62,49,372	54.42	58.21
5.	Goa	1,35,816	23,101	17.00	1,37,837	62,927	45.65	5.34
6	Gujarat	55,87,768	19,80,879	35.45	48,04,235	26,18,940	54.51	22.18
7	Haryana	20,74,615	5,03,019	24.25	17,10,440	6,28,860	36.77	28.02
8.	Himachal Pradesh	10,36,996	2,86,112	27.59	9,05,671	2,59,175	28.62	30.34
9.	Jammu & Kashmir	10,47,251	6,06,545	57.92	11,75,860	7,28,648	61.97	30.34
10.	Karnataka	64,79,832	22,02,756	34.00	58,48,262	33,07,706	56.56	29.88
11.	Kerala	NR	NR		55,81,799	17,86,874	32.01	25.76
12.	Madhya Pradesh	1,16,51,082	51,11,874	43.87	86,08,104	55,50,757	64.48	40.64
13.	Maharashtra	1,10,10,022	38,60,675	35.07	1,00,75,029	77,65,384	77.82	37.93
14.	Manipur	3,65,670	2,46,980	67.54	2,27,816	1,53,489	67.37	45.01
15.	Meghalaya	2,82,362	1,56,646	55.48	2,55,984	1,53,853	60.10	45.01

Annexure-XVIII (*Contd.*)

1	2	3	4	5	6	7	8
16. Mizoram	1,10,570	74,154	67.07	1,15,490	67,572	58.51	45.01
17. Nagaland	1,46,615	88,541	60.39	1,47,603	65,344	44.27	45.01
18. 0rissa*	67,90,202	44,45,736	65.50	52,23,124	41,10,434	78.70	49.72
19. Punjab	23,30,725	6,50,209	27.90	26,86,349	10,74,130	39.98	11.95
20. Rajasthan	67,68,541	20,97,560	30.99	62,66,763	19,48,554	31.09	26.46
21. Sikkim	NR	NR		62,961	50,886	80.82	45.01
22. Tamil Nadu	93,88,118	27,37,921	29.16	83,02,958	31,46,112	37.89	32.48
23. Tripura	5,95,397	3,97,798	66.81	4,76,334	3,50,476	73.58	45.01
24. Uttar Pradesh	2,04,30,204	75,41,494	36.91	NR	NR	NR	42.28
25. West Bengal	1,10,76,586	49,18,296	44.40	95,99,236	44,19,686	46.04	40.80
26. A. &N. Islands	NR	6,421		3,315	1,455	43.89	32.48
27. Dadra & N. Haveli	26,237	17,231	65.67	26,200	17,323	66.12	51.95
28. Daman & Diu	10,735	395	3.68	9,046	4,640	51.29	5.34
29. Lakshadweep	8,625	885	10.26	6,940	3,270	47.12	25.76
30. Pondicherry	1,33,555	63,262	47.36	1,00,467	46,871	46.65	32.48
All India	13,06,15,558	538,47,442	41.23	9,71,46,132	5,09,89,917	52.49	37.27

Source: Ministry of Rural Development, GOI

ANNEXURE - XIX

STATE-WISE PERCENTAGE OF POPULATION BELOW POVERTY LINE (MODIFIED EXPERT GROUP)

Sl.No.	State	1973-74	1977-78	1983	1987-88	1993-94
1.	Andhra Pradesh	48.41	38.11	26.53	20.92	15.92
2.	Arunachal Pradesh	52.67	59.82	42.60	39.35	45.01
3.	Assam	52.67	59.82	42.60	39.35	45.01
4.	Bihar	62.99	63.25	64.37	52.63	58.21
5.	Goa	46.85	37.64	14.81	17.64	5.34
6.	Gujarat	46.35	41.76	29.80	28.67	22.18
7.	Haryana	34.23	27.73	20.56	16.22	28.02
8.	Himachal Pradesh	27.42	33.49	17.00	16.28	30.34
9.	Jammu & Kashmir	45.51	42.86	26.04	25.70	30.34
10.	Karnataka	55.14	48.18	36.33	32.82	29.88
11.	Kerala	59.19	51.48	39.03	29.10	25.76
12.	Madhya Pradesh	62.66	62.52	48.90	41.92	40.64
13.	Maharashtra	57.71	63.97	45.23	40.78	37.93
14.	Manipur	52.67	59.82	42.60	39.35	45.01
15.	Meghlaya	52.67	59.82	42.60	39.35	45.01
16.	Mizoram	52.67	59.82	42.60	39.35	45.01
17.	Nagaland	52.67	59.82	42.60	39.35	45.01
18.	Orissa	67.28	72.38	67.53	57.84	49.72
19.	Punjab	28.21	16.37	13.20	12.60	11.95
20.	Rajasthan	44.76	35.89	33.50	33.21	26.46
21.	Sikkim	52.67	59.82	42.60	39.35	45.01
22.	Tamil Nadu	57.43	57.68	53.99	45.80	32.48
23.	Tripura	52.67	59.82	42.60	39.35	45.01
24.	Uttar Pradesh	56.53	47.60	46.45	41.10	42.26
25.	West Bengal	73.16	68.34	63.05	48.30	40.80
26.	A & N Islands	57.43	57.68	53.99	1.29	32.46
27.	Chandigarh	27.96	27.32	23.79	45.80	11.35
28.	Dadra & Nagar Haveli	46.85	37.64	14.81	14.67	51.95
29.	Daman & Diu	—	—	—	—	5.34
30.	Delhi	24.44	30.19	7.66	57.11	1.90
31.	Lakshadweep	59.19	51.48	39.03	29.10	25.76
32.	Pondicherry	57.43	57.68	53.99	45.80	32.48
	All India	56.44	53.07	45.65	39.09	37.27

Source: Planning Commision estimates as quoted in Malhotra (1997)

Annexure XIX (Contd...)

Dev et al (1991)		World Bank (1997)		Planning Commission		Expert Group		
Year	%	Survey period		Year	%	Year	Est. I	Est. II
(1)	(2)	(3)	(4)	(5)	(6)	(7)	(8)	(9)
1961-62	38.22	Aug 51-Nov52	47.37	1972-73	54.10	1973-74	56.44	56.44
1963-64	45.33	Apr 52-Sep 52	43.87	1977-78	46.13	1977-78	53.07	53.07
1964-65	45.73	Dec 52-Mar 53	48.21	1983	32.73	1983	45.61	45.65
1965-66	47.21	May53 -Sep 53	54.13	1987-88	28.73	1987-88	39.06	39.09
1966-67	56.09	Oct 53-Mar 54	61.29	1993-94	19.24	1993-94	37.27	37.27
1967-68	55.79	Jul 54-Mar 55	64.24					
1968-69	50.50	May55-Nov 55	51.83					
1969-70	49.12	Dec 55- May 56	48.34					
1970-71	45.39	Aug 56-Feb 57	58.86					
1972-73	42.90	Mar 57-Aug 57	62.11					
1973-74	44.88	Sep 57-May 58	55.16					
1977-78	40.21	Jul 58-Jun59	53.26					
1983	32.85	Jul 59-Jun 60	50.89					
1986-87	25.58	Jul 60- Aug 61	45.40					
		Sep 61-Jul62	47.20					
		Feb 63-Jan 64	48.53					
		Jul 64-Jun 65	53.66					
		Jul 65 - Jun 66	57.60					
		Jul 66- Jun 67	64.30					
		Jul 67-Jun 68	63.67					
		Jul 68-Jun 69	59.00					
		Jul 69- Jun70	57.61					
		Jul 70- Jun 71	54.84					
		Oct 72-Sep 73	55.36					
		Oct 73-Jun 74	55.72					
		Jul 77-Jun 78	50.60					
		Jan 83-Dec 83	45.31					
		Jul 86-Jun 87	38.81					
		Jul 87- Jun 88	39.23					
		Jul 88-Jun 89	36.06					
		Jul 89- Jun 90	34.30					
		Jul 90- Jun 91	36.43					
		Jul 91- Dec 91	37.42					
		Jan 92- Dec 92	43.47					
		Jul 93- Jun 94	36.66					

Sources : Ministry of Rural Development

ANNEXURE - XX

THE CONSTITUTION (SEVENTY-THIRD AMENDMENT) ACT, 1992

AN ACT *Further to amend the Constitution of India*

BE it enacted by Parliament in the Forty-third Year of the Republic of India as follows:-

1. (1) This Act may be called the Constitution (Seventy-third Amendment) Act, 1992. **Short title and commencement**

   (2) It shall come into force on such date as the Central Government may, by notification in the Official Gazette, appoint.

2. After Part VIII of the Constitution, the following Part shall be inserted, namely:- **Insertion of new Part IX**

PART IX
THE PANCHAYATS

243. In this Part. unless the context otherwise requires,- *Definitions*

(a) "district" means.-a district in a State;

(b) "Gram Sabha" means a body consisting of persons registered in the electoral rolls relating to a village comprised within the area of Panchayat at the village level:

(c) (c) "intermediate level" means a level between the village and district levels specified by the Governor of a State by public notification to be the intermediate level for the purposes of this Part;

(d) "Panchayat" means an institution (by whatever name called) of self-government constituted under article 243B. for the rural areas',

(e) "'Panchayat area'.' means the territorial area of a Panchayat:

(f) "population" means the population as ascertained at the last preceding census of which the relevant figures have been published:

(g) "village" means a village specified by the Governor by public notification to be a village for the purposes of this Part and includes a group of villages so specified.

243A. A Gram Sabha may exercise such powers and perform such functions at the village level as the Legislature of a State may by law, provide. **Gram Sabha**

243B. (1) There shall be constituted in every State, Panchayats at the village, intermediate and district levels in accordance with the '' provisions of this Part,

Constitution of Panchayats

(2) Notwithstanding anything in clause (1), Panchayats at the intermediate level may not be constituted in a State having a population not exceeding twenty lakhs.

243C, (1) Subject to the provisions of this Part. the Legislature of a State may, by law. make provisions with respect to the composition of Panchayats:

Provided that the ratio between the population of the territorial area of a Panchayat at any level and the number of seats in such Panchayat to be filled by election shall, so far as practicable, be the same throughout the State.

(2) All the seats in a Panchayat shall be 'filled by persons chosen by direct election from territorial constituencies in the Panchayat area and: for this purpose, each Panchayat area shall be divided into territorial constituencies in such manner that the ratio between the population of each constituency and the number of seats allotted to it shall, so far as practicable, be the same throughout the Panchayat area.

(3) The Legislature of a State may, by law, provide for the representation—

(a) of the Chairpersons of the Panchayats at the village level, in the Panchayals at the intermediate level or, in the case of a State not having Panchayats at the intermediate level, in the Panchayats at the district level:

(b) of the Chairpersons of the Panchayats at the intermediate level, in the Panchayats at the district level;

(c) of the members of the House of the People and the members-of the Legislative Assembly of the State representing constituencies which comprise wholly or partly a Panchayat area at a level other than the village level, in such Panchayat;

(d) of the members of the Council of Sates and the members of the Legislative Council of the State, where they are registered as electors within

(i) a Panchayat area at the intermediate level, in Panchayat at the intermediate level;

(ii) a Panchayat area at the district level, In Panchayat at the district level.

(4) The Chairperson of a Panchayat and other members of a Panchayat whether or not chosen by direct election from territorial constituencies in the Panchayat area shall have the right to vote in the meeting of the Panchayats.

(5) The Chairperson of-

(a) a Panchayat at the village level shall be elected in such manner as the Legislature of a State may, by law, provide: and

(b) a Panchayat at the intermediate level or district level shall be elected by, and from amongst, the elected members thereof.

2430 (1) Seats shall be reserved for- **Reservation of Seats**

(a) the Scheduled Castes: and

(b) the Scheduled Tribes,

in every Panchayat and the number of seats so reserved shall bear, as nearly as may be, the same proportion to the total number of seats to be filmed by direct election in that Panchayat as the population of the Scheduled Castes in that Panchayat areas or of the Scheduled Tribes in that Panchayat area bears to the total population of that area and such seats may be allotted by rotation to different constituencies in a Panchayat.

(2) Not less than on'-third of the total number of seats reserved under clause (1) shall be reserved for women belonging to the Scheduled- Castes or, as the case may be, the Scheduled Tribes

(3) Not less than one-third (including the number of seats reserved for women belonging to the Scheduled Castes and the Scheduled Tribes) of the total number of seats to be filled by direct election in every Panchayat shall be reserved (or women and such seats may be allotted by rotation to different constituencies in a Panchayat.

(4) The offices of the Chairpersons in the Panchayats at the village or any other level shall be reserved for the Scheduled Castes, the Scheduled Tribes and women in such manner as the Legislature of a State may, by law, provide:

Provided that the number of offices of Chairpersons reserved for the Scheduled Castes and the Scheduled Tribes in the Panchayats at each level in any State shall bear, as nearly as may be, the same. proportion to the total number of such offices in the Panchayats at each level as the population of the Scheduled Castes in the State or of the Scheduled Tribes in the State bears to the total population of the State:

Provided further that not less than one-third of the total number of offices of Chairpersons in the Panchayats at each level shall be reserved (or women:

Provided also that the number of offices reserved under this clause shall be allotted by rotation to different Panchayats at each level.

(5) The reservation of seats under clauses (1) and (2) and the reservation of offices of Chairpersons (other than the reservation for women) under clause (4) shall cease to have effect on the expiration of the period specified in article 334.

(6) Nothing in this Part shall prevent the Legislature of a State from making any provision for reservation of seats in any Panchayat or offices of Chair persons in the Panchayats at any level in favour of backward class of citizens.

243E. (1) Every Panchayat, unless sooner dissolved under any law for the time being in force, shall continue for five years from the date appointed for its first meeting and no longer.

Duration of Panchayats etc.

(2) No amendment, of any taw for the time being in force shall have the effect of causing dissolution of a Panchayat at any level, which is functioning immediately before such amendment, till the expiration of its duration specified in clause (1).

(3) An election to constitute a Panchayat shall be completed-

(a) before the expiry of its duration specified in clause (1):

(b) before the expiration of a period of six months from the date of its dissolution:

Provided that where the-remainder of the period for which the dissolved Panchayat would have continued is less than six months, it shall not be necessary to hold any election under this clause for constituting the Panchayat for such period.

(4) A Panchayat constituted upon the dissolution of a Panchayat before the expiration of its duration shall continue only for the remainder of the period for which the dissolved Panchayat would have continued under clause (1) had it not been so dissolved.

243F. (1) A person shall be disqualified for being chosen as, and for being, a member of a Panchayat- **Disqualificatons for membership**

(a) if he is so disqualified by or under any law for the time being in force for the purposes of elections to the legislature of the State concerned: Provided that no person shall be disqualified on the ground that he is less than twenty-five years of age, if he has attained the age of twenty-one years:

(b) if he is so disqualified by or under any law made by the Legislature of the State.

(2) If any question arises as to whether a member of a Panchayal has become subject to any of the disqualifications mentioned in d+use (1). the question shall be referred for the decision of such authority and in such manner as the Legislature of a Stale may, by law, provide.

Disqualifications for membership

243G. Subject to provisions of this Constitution, the Legislature of a State may, by law, endow the Panchayats with such powers and authority as may be necessary to enable them to function as institutions of self-government and such law may contain provisions for the devolution of powers and responsibilities upon Panchayats at the appropriate level, subject to such conditions as may be specified therein, with respect to :

Powers, authority and responsibilities of Panchayats

a) the preparation of plans for economic development and social justice: and
b) the implementation of schemes for economic development and social justice as may be entrusted to them including those in relation to the matters listed in the Eleventh Schedule.

Powers to impose taxes by, and Funds of, the Panchayats

243H. The Legislature of a State may, by law,-

(a) authorise a Panchayat to levy, collect and appropriate such taxes, duties, funds and fees in accordance with such procedure and subject to such limits;
(b) assign to a Panchayat such-taxes, duties, tolls and fees levied and collected by the State Government for such purposes and subject to such conditions and limits; and
(c) provide for making such grants-in-aid to Panchayats from the Consolidated Fund of the State; and provide for constitution of such Funds for crediting all moneys received, respectively, by or on behalf of the Panchayats and also for the withdrawal such moneys there from as may be specified in the law.

Constitution of Finance Commission to review financial positions

243-I (1) The Governor of a State shall, as soon as may be within one year from the commencement of the Constitution (Seventy-third Amendment) Act.-1992, and, thereafter at the expiration of every fifth- year, constitute a Finance Commission to review the Financial position of the Panchayats and to make recommendations to the: Governor as to-

(a) the principles which should govern-

(i) The distribution between the State and the Panchayats of the net proceeds of the taxes, duties, - tolls and fees livable by the State, which may be divided between them under this Part and the allocation between the Panchayats at all levels of their respective shares, of such proceeds;
(ii) the determination of the taxes, duties, tolls and fees .which may be assigned to, or appropriated by, the Panchayats; and
(iii) the grants-in-aid to the Panchayats from the Consolidated Fund of the State;

(b) the measures needed to improve the financial position of the Panchayats; and

(c) any other matter referred to the Finance Commission by the Governor in the interests of sound finance of the Panchayats.

(2) The Legislature of a State may, by law, provide for the composition of the Commission, the qualifications, which shall be requisite for appointment as members thereof, and the manner in which they shall be selected.
(3) The Commission shall determine their procedure and shall have such powers in the performance of their functions as the Legislature of the State may, by law, confer on them.
(4) The Governor shall cause every recommendation made by the Commission under this article together with an explanatory memorandum as to the action taken thereon to be laid before the Legislature of the State.

Audit of accounts of Panchayats

243J. The Legislature of a State may, by law, make provisions with respect to the maintenance of accounts by the Panchayats and the auditing of such accounts.

Elections to the Panchayats

243K. (1) The superintendence, direction and control of the preparation of electoral rolls for, and the conduct of, all elections to the Panchayats shall be vested in a State Election Commission consisting of a State Election Commissioner to be appointed by the (governor.
(2) Subject to the provisions of any law made by the Legislature of a State, the conditions of service and tenure of office of the State Election Commissioner shall be such as the Governor may by rule determine:
Provided that the State Election Commissioner shall not be removed from his office except in like manner and on the like grounds as a Judge of a High Court and the conditions of service of the State Election Commissioner shall not be varied to his disadvantage after his appointment.
(3) The Governor of a State shall, when so requested by the State Election Commission, make available to the State Election Commission such staff as may be necessary for the discharge of the functions conferred on the State Election Commission by clause (1).
(4) Subject to the provisions of this Constitution, the Legislature of a State may, by Law, make provision with respect to all matters relating to, or in connection with, elections to the Panchayats.

Application to Union Territories

243L. The provisions of this Part shall apply to the Union territories and shall in their application to a Union territory, have effect as if the references to the Governor of a State were references to the Administrator of the Union territory appointed under article 239 and references to the Legislature or the Legislative Assembly of a State were references, in relation to a Union territory having a Legislative Assembly, to that Legislative Assembly:

Provided that the President may, by public notification, direct that the provisions of this Part shall apply to any Union territory or part thereof subject to such exceptions and modifications as he may specify in the notification.

Part not to apply to certain areas

243M. (1) Nothing in this Part shall apply to the Scheduled Areas referred to in clause (1), and the tribal areas referred to in clause (2), of article 244.

(2) Nothing in this Part shall apply to-

(a) the States of Nagaland, Meghalaya and Mizoram:

(b) the hill areas in the State of Manipur for which District Councils exist under any law for the time being in force.

(3) Nothing in this Part-

(a) relating to Panchayats at the district level shall apply to the hill areas of the District of Darjeeling in the State of West Bengal for which Darjeeling Gorkha Hill Council exists under any law for the time being in force;

(b) shall be construed to affect the functions and powers of the Darjeeling Gorkha Hill Council constituted under such law.

(4) Notwithstanding anything in this Constitution,-

(a) the Legislature of a State referred to in sub-clause (a) of clause (2) may, by law; extend this Part to that State, except the areas, if any, referred to in clause (1), if the Legislative Assembly of that State passes a resolution to that effect by a majority of the total membership of that House and by a majority "of not less than two-thirds of the members of that House present and voting;

(b) Parliament may, by law, extend the provisions of this Part to the Scheduled Areas and the tribal areas referred to in clause (1) subject to such exceptions and modifications as may be specified in such taw, and no such law shall be deemed to be an amendment of this Constitutions for the purposes of article 368.

Continuance of existing laws and Panchayats

243N. Notwithstanding anything in this Part, any provision of any law relating to Panchayats in force in a State immediately before the commencement of the Constitution (Seventy-third Amendment) Act, 1992, which is inconsistent with the provisions of this Part, shall continue to be in force until amended or repealed by a competent legislature or other competent authority or until the expiration of one year from such commencement, whichever is earlier:

Provided that all the Panchayats existing immediately before such commencement shall continue till the expiration of their duration, unless sooner dissolved by a resolution passed to that effect by the Legislative Assembly of that State or, in the case of a State having a Legislative Council, by each House of the Legislature of that State.

Bar to interference by courts in electoral matter

243-O. Notwithstanding anything in this Constitution-
(a) the validity of any law relating to the delimitation of constituencies or the allotment of seals to such constituencies made or purporting to be made under article 243K, shall not be called in question in any court:
(b) no election to any Panchayat shall be called in question except by an election petition presented to such authority and in such manner as is provided for by or under any law made by the Legislature of a State..

Amendment of Article 280

3. In clause (3) of article 290 of the Constitution, after sub clause (b), the following sub-clause shall be inserted, namely:-
"(bb) the measures needed to augment the Consolidated Fund of a State to supplement the resources of the Panchayals in the State on the basis of the recommendations made by the Finance Commission of the State;"

Addition of Eleventh Schedule

4. After the Tenth Schedule to the Constitution, the following Schedule shall be added, namely:-

ELEVENTH SCHEDULE
(Article 243G)

1. Agriculture, including agricultural extension
2. Land improvement, implementation of land reforms, land consolidation and soil conservation
3. Minor irrigation, water management and watershed development
4. Animal husbandry, dairying and poultry

5. Fisheries
6. Social forestry and farm forestry
7. Minor forest produce
8. Small scale industries, including food processing industries
9. Khadi, village and cottage industries
10. Rural housing
11. Drinking water
12. Fuel and fodder
13. Roads, culverts, bridges, ferries, waterways and other means of communication
14. Rural electrification, including distribution or' electricity
15. Non-conventional energy sources
16. Poverty alleviation programme
17. Education, including primary and secondary schools
18. Technical training and vocational education
19. Adult and non-formal education
20. Libraries
21. Cultural activities
22. Markets and fairs
23. Health and sanitation, including hospitals, primary health centres and dispensaries
24. Family welfare
25. Women and child development. "... Social welfare including welfare of the handicapped and mentally retarded
26. Welfare of the weaker sections, and in particular, of the Scheduled Castes and the Scheduled Tribes
27. Public distribution system
28. Maintenance of community assets."

ANNEXURE - XXI

STATUS OF PANCHAYATI RAJ INSTITUTIONS — SELECTED INDICATORS (FEBRUARY 2002)

Status/Uts	Holding of Panchayat Election	Constitution of District Planning Committee (DPC)	Status of State Finance Commission Recommen-dation	Devolution of funds, Functions, and Functionaries in Respect of 29 Subjects (At.243G)	Status of DRDA/ZP Linkage
Andhra Pradesh	GP elections held in August, 2001, while Intermediate and District Panchayats elections held in July, 2001.	Not constituted.	Accepted 54 recom-mendations fully, with some modifications and 19 not accepted at all. Second SFC Constituted.	Funds-05 Functions-17 Function-aries-02	DRDA & ZP not merged, Collector is Chairperson of DRDA and President of ZP is Vice-Chairman.
Arunachal Pradesh	Elections not held.	Constituted.	Not constituted	Not applicable yet.	Not yet.
Assam	Elections held in January, 2001.	Not constituted, so far.	Re-com-mendat-ions accepted in part,	No action taken yet.	Not transferred.
Bihar	Election held in April, 2001.	No	Report awaited.	Funds- Functions -20 Functionaries-	Not merged.
Goa	GP - in 1997	No information	Report under consideration	No information available	Merger under consideration.
Gujarat	GP- December. 2001. PS& DP - in December, 2000.	Not constituted.	Received but not yet been placed before Legislature for consideration	No information available	Not merged.

(Contd.)

Annexure XXI (*Contd.*)

Haryana	Elections held in March, 2000.	Only in 16 districts.	Accepted major recommendations.	Funds-0 Functions -16 Functionaries-0	Not merged.
Himachal Pradesh	Elections held in December, 2000.	Only in 5 districts out of 12.	Accepted. Second SFC constituted.	Funds -2 Functions - 23 Functionaries -7	Merged and headed by President of Zila Parishad.
Jammu & Kashmir	73rd Constitutional Amendment Act has yet to be extended to State. However, Ministry of Home Affairs has requested the Government of J& K to seek the views of the State Legislature to extend the provisions of the 73 Constitutional Amendment Act 1992 to the State. Panchayat elections in some part were held in January -February, 2001 according to State Panchayati Raj Act.				
Karnataka	GP - February, 2000. PS & DP - July 2000.	Only in 5 districts.	Accepted major recommendations.	Funds -29 Functions -29 Functionaries -29	Merged.
Kerala	September, 2000	Yes	Accepted and implemented. Second SFC constituted.	Funds -15 Functions -29 Functionaries - 15	Merged and headed by President of Zilla Parishad.
Madhya Pradesh	January, 2000.	Yes	Accepted. SFC constituted.	Funds - 10 Functions - 23 Functionaries - 9	Merged.
Maharashtra	GP - October, 1997. PS & DP - March, 1997.	No	Major recommendations accepted.	Funds - 18 Functions - 18 Functionaries - 18	Against merger of DRDA with ZP.
Manipur	GP & DP - January, 1997.	Yes in 2 out of 4 districts.	Accepted	Funds - 0 Functions -22 Functionaries -4	No information available.

Annexure XXI (*Contd.*)

STATUS OF PANCHAYATI RAJ INSTITUTIONS — SELECTED INDICATORS (FEBRUARY 2002)

Status/Uts States	Holding of Panchayat Election	Constitution of District Planning Committee (DPC)	Status of State Finance Commission Recommendation	Devolution of funds, Functions, and Functionaries in Respect of 29 Subjects (At.243G)	Status of DRDA/ZP Linkage
Meghalaya Mizoram Nagaland	73rd Constitutional Amendment Act does not applicable as the traditional system of local self government exist in these States				
Orissa	January 1997. Elections in Schedule V area invalid.	Only in 6 districts.	Accepted.	Funds - 5 Functions - 25 Functionaries - 3	Merged and headed by Chairperson of ZP.
Punjab	GP - June 1998 PS & DP - election are due.	Not yet.	Accepted.	Funds -5 Functions -25 Functionaries -3	Not merged.
Rajasthan	January, 2000.	Yes	Accepted. Second SFC constituted.	Funds - 0 Functions -29 Functionaries - 0	Merged.
Sikkim	October, 1997.	Yes	Accepted. Second SFC constituted.	Funds -24 Functions -24 Functionaries -24	Status not reported.
Tamil Nadu	October, 2001.	Yes	Accepted. Second SFC constituted.	Funds -0 Functions -29 Functionaries -0	Status not cleared.

Annexure XXI (*Contd.*)

Tripura	July, 1999.	Yes	Accepted. Second SFC constituted.	Funds -0 Functions - 12 Function-aries -0	Status difficult to define.
Uttar Pradesh	June, 2000.	Yes	Accepted. Second SFC constituted.	Funds - 12 Functions - 13 Function-aries -9	Merged and headed by President of ZP.
West Bengal	In 1998.	Yes	Accepted	Funds -12 Functions -29 Function-aries -12	Merged and headed by President of ZP.
Chattisgarh	January, 2000.	Yes	Not set up.	Funds -10 Functions -23 Function-aries -09	Merged.
Jharkhand	Election due. Reported that election will be held in Sept., 2002	Not Con-stituted.	Not set up	No information available	
Uttaranchal	Term of Panchayat expired in December, 2001. State Panchayati Raj Act has yet to be notified.	Not Con-stituted.	Report awaited.	Funds - 12 Functions -13 Function-aries -9	
Union Territories					
Andaman & Nicobar Is.	September, 2000.	Yes	Under con-sideration.	Funds - 6 Functions - 6 Function-aries 6	Merged and headed by Chairperson of ZP.
Chandigarh	GP - January, 1999. ZP - July, 2000. PS - not held so far.	No	SFC Report awaited.	No information available	Not applicable.

Annexure XXI (*Contd.*)

STATUS OF PANCHAYATI RAJ INSTITUTIONS — SELECTED INDICATORS (FEBRUARY 2002)

Status/Uts States	Holding of Panchayat Election	Constitution of District Planning Committee (DPC)	Status of State Finance Commission Recommendation	Devolution of funds, Functions, and Functionaries in Respect of 29 Subjects (At.243G)	Status of DRDA/ZP Linkage
Daman & Diu	September, 2000.	Yes	Under Consideration.	Funds - 5 Functions - 9 Functionaries -3	Merged and headed by ZP President.
Dadra & Nagar Haveli	October, 2000.	Yes	Under Consideration.	Funds - 0 Functions -3 Functionaries - 3	No DRDA exists.
Delhi	NCT Delhi had repealed the Panchayat Raj Act and sought abolition of the Panchayati Raj Institutions (PRIs) System. However,it is now considering adopting the 73rd Amendment Act and reviving the Panchayats.				
Lakshadweep	December, 1997 - January, 1998	Yes	Under consideration.	Funds - Functions -6 Function--aries	No DRDA exists.
Pondicherry	Elections have not been held in the UT, as the matter relating to the validity of provisions pertaining to reservation for backward classes in the Pondicherry Panchayati Raj Act was subjudice. The Judgement of the Chennai High Court had become available and the UT Administration filed a clarificatory application in the Chennai High Court. On a similar issue pertaining to Tamil Nadu, the Hon'ble High Court at Chennai had passed Orders making it possible for Tamil Nadu Government to hold elections. The Ministry of Rurual Development has advised the UT Administration to take appropriate action to hold panchayat elections at the earliest on the same lines.				

Source : Planning Commission.

ANNEXURE - XXII

STATE-WISE NUMBER OF ELECTED PANCHAYAT REPRESENTATIVES IN THE THREE TIERS SHOWING BREAKUP INTO SC/ST AND WOMEN

Sl. No	States/UTs	Gram Panchayat				Intermediate Panchayat				District Panchayat			
		SC	ST	Women	Total	SC	ST	Women	Total	SC	ST	Women	Total
1	2	3	4	5	6	7	8	9	10	11	12	13	14
1	Andhra Pradesh	38,674	15,304	78,000	230529	789	803	5,420	14,644	128	66	363	1,093
2	Arunachal Pradesh	Arunachal Pradesh Panchayati Raj Act not yet passed											
3	Assam			5,469	30,360			669	2.564				845
		Figures not current, Fresh elections due since October, 1997											
4	Bihar				116036				11611				1.161
5	Goa			468	1,281								35
6	Gujarat	4,739	9,550	21,351	123470	279	561	1,275*	3,814	57	114	254	761
7	Haryana	12,128	0	16,704	54,346	536	0	858	2.43	66	0	182	226
8	Himachal Pradesh	3,824	672	6,016	18,264	280	74	558	1,661	46	14	84	252
9.	Jammu & Kashmir	73rd Amendment not applicable in the State, State proposes adopting 73rd Amendment											
10	Karnataka	17,918	7,575	35,305	80,627	601	169	1,343	3,340	165	47	335	919
11	Kerala				10,270				1,547				300
12	Madhya Pradesh	68,924	157191	160077	474770	1,316	2,795	3,031	9,105	151	294	338	1,008
13	Maharashtra	40,766	35,150	101182	303545	409	453	1,174	3,524	206	232	587	1,762
14	Manipur	35	44	555	1,556	0	0	0	0	1	2	22	61

Annexure XXII (*Contd.*)

1	2	3	4	5	6	7	8	9	10	11	12	13	14
15	Meghalaya												
16	Mizoram	Traditional councils perform duties of Local Govt. 73rd Amendment not applicable in these States											
17	Nagaland												
18	Orissa	7,394	11,823	27,036	81,077	478	809	1,754	5,260	85	131	284	854
19	Punjab	23,814	0	26,939	75,473	Elections due							
20	Rajasthan	17,902	15.616	33,566	112897	943	804	1,740	5,494	177	154	33	1,028
21	Sikkim	40	298	326	873	0	0	0	0	6	40	28	92
22	Tamil Nadu	18,886	686	31,548	125852	1,358	41	2,295	6,499	137	3	22	648
23	Tripura	1,237	704	1,809	5,421	48	26	67	196	15	7	24	70
24	Uttar Pradesh	101939	867	120591	799780	9,126	135	13,865	59,991	389	7	634	2,687
25	West Bengal	13,644	3,319	17,883	49,225	2,354	582	2,997	8,520	200	50	243	716
26	A & N Islands	—	—	229	667	—	—	25	—	—	—	10	30
27	Chandigarh	Current Figure not available											
28	D. & N. Haveli	3	103	46	135	—	—	—	—	—	11	4	16
29	Daman &Diu	1	17	25	63	—	—	—	—	1	3	5	15
30	NCT Delhi	NCT Government propose conduct of Panchayat elections											
31	Lakshadweep	0	79	30	79	0	0	0	0	0	22	8	22
32	Pondicherry				120								16
	Total	3,71,868	2,58,998	6,85,155	26,96,716	18,517	7,252	37,071	1,40,200	1,830	1,197	3,460	14,617

Source : Panchayati Raj Scheme M/o RD

GLOSSARY

Aftershocks : Follow-up earthquakes that occur after the first earthquake and are usually of less intensity.

Anganwadi: Locally developed women and child welfare centres.

Avalanche: An event where a mass of snow , rock and ice falls down a mountain.

Alluvial fan: A fan shaped deposit of sediment built by a stream where it emerges from an upland or a mountain range into a broad valley of plain.

Asthenosphere: The earth layer lying below lithospere. It is probably soft and yielding to plastic flow.

BIMARU States: Stands for Bihar, M.P. , Rajasthan, and U.P.. Name coined by WHO, UNICEF in view of the poor condition of the states.

Bio-diversity: It is a variety of different species, genetic variability among individuals within each species and variety of ecosystems.

Bio-mass: Amount of vegetation in any form in an area.

Boulder: A rock piece or fragment more than 25.6 cm. in diameter.

Capillary action: The phenomenon, caused by surface tension effects, whereby a liquid such as water rises up a narrowtube placed in the liquid.

Continental Drift : The theory that the continents have moved in relation to one another.

Controls: The need to control the activities of the enterprise. It includes identifying where targets have or have not met so that the reasons for the failure to achieve the target can be identified.

Crust: The outermost layer of the earth.

Debris flow: Rapid downward movement of rock, soil and mud.

Deciduous: A plant that sheds its leaves regularly or annually within a year of their production.

Disaster: An occurrence of a severity and magnitude that normally results in deaths, injuries and property damage and that can not be managed through the routine procedures and resources of government.

Disaster management: A collective term encompassing all aspects of planning for and responsible to disaster, including both pre- and post-disasters activities.

Discharge: Rate of flow of water.

Drainage pattern: An integrated system of tributaries which collect and funnel surface water to common water body i.e. lake, ocean etc.

Earthquake: The shaking, rolling and sudden shock of the earth's surface. They occur due to pressure release from internal activities in the earth. The rock movement along broken surfaces or volcanic activities are major causes of earthquake.

Eco-system: It is a community of organisms interacting with one other and with the chemical and physical factors making up their environment.

Emergency: An extraordinary situation where there are serious and immediate threat to human life as a result of disaster, imminent threat of disaster, cumulative process of neglect, and socio-economic condition etc.

Flash flood: A dangerous and sudden flood that threatens lives and property and usually occurs after heavy rain. May occur after an ice jam breaks up or after a dam breaks.

Fold: Bend or flexure in a rock.

Fossil: Naturally preserved remains or evidences of past life giving idea about it.

Geo- hydrological: Related to natural water bodies of earth surface.

Gram Sabha: A village council body elected by the villagers.

Hail: Rain that has been frozen many times on the way to the ground, creating a lumpy ball of ice.

Hazard: A rare or extreme natural or human made event that threatens to adversely affect human life, property or activity to extreme causing disaster.

Hazard Assessment: The process of estimating for defined areas, the probabilities of the occurrence of potentially damaging phenomenon of given magnitude within a specified period of time.

Hazard Mapping: the process of establishing geographically where and to what extent particular phenomena are likely to pose a threat to people, property, infrastructure and economic activities.

Heat flow: The flow of heat from the interior of the earth.

Human Development Index (HDI): Index reflecting the state of human development for the society as a whole.

Human Poverty Index (HPI): Index, capturing the state of the deprived of the society.

Ice storm: Freezing rain that creates a dangerous sheet of ice that is quarter inch thick or greater.

Lava: Hot molten rock that reaches the surface through volcanic esuption.

Lightening: A sudden visible flash of energy and light caused by electrical discharges during a thunder storm.

Lithosphere: The relatively solid zone of Earth., which include the continental crust, the oceanic crust, the part of the mantle lying above the asthensphere.

Magma: A mobile silicate melt, which can contain crystals and dissolved gases as well as liquid.

Mantle: The zone of Earth's interior between the base of the crust and the core.

Mitigation: Refers to measure which can be taken to minimize the destructive and disruptive effects of hazards and thus lessen the magnitude of disaster.

Physiography: The study of the surface features and landforms of the Earth.

Plate: A broad segment of the lithosphere that floats on the underlying asthenosphere and moves independently of the other plate.

Plate tectonics: The Theory of global dynamics in which the lithosphere is believed to be broken into individual plates that move in response to convection in the upper mantle. The margins of the plates are sites of considerable geological activities.

Poverty Line: It is the minimum required consumption expenditure level of items such as food, clothing, shelter, transport, and health care, which meets the average per capita daily calorie requirement of 2400 calories in rural areas and 2100 calories in urban areas.

Post Disaster Assessment: The process of determining the impact of a disaster or event on a society, the needs for the immediate, emergency measures to save and sustain the lives of survivors, and the possibilities for expediting recovery and development.

Preparedness: Measures to ensure the readiness and ability of a society to forecast and take precautionary measures in advance of an imminent threat, and to respond to and cope with the effects of a disaster by organising and facilitating timely and effective rescue, relief and appropriate post- disaster assistance.

Quartzite: A metamorphic rock, composed mainly of silica.

Richter scale: A scale used to measure the intensity of earthquake, created by Charles F. Richter.

Risk: The expected loss caused by a particular phenomenon.

Risk Assessment: The process of determining the nature and scale of loss and damage due to a disaster, which can be anticipated in particular area during a specified period of time.

Risk mapping: The presentation of risk assessment on a map, showing the level of expected losses, during a particular time period, as a result of particular hazard or vulnerability.

Rock fall: The most rapid type of mass movement in which rocks ranging from large masses to small fragments are loosened from the ace of a cliff.

Runoff : Water that flows over the land surface.

Sex Ratio: Number of females per 1000 males.

Seismic: Pertaining to earthquake or to waves produced by natural or artificial earthquakes.

Shear Force: The tagential component of stress is generally called shearing stress or shear.

Strain: The deformation of rocks caused by stress. It may be dilation, a change in volume; distortion, a change of shape, or both.

Stress: Stress is the system of internal forces with a body which is established as a reaction to an external force tending to change the shape or volume of the body. Any stress system can be resolved into two forces acting in opposite directions on either side of a plane- the plane of maximum stress. Geologists tend to use the word stress to describe effects arising from external forces.

Strike: The bearing (the compass direction) of a horizontal line on bedding plane, a fault plane or some other planar structural feature.

Strike Slip Fault: Fault in which the movement of the broken rock bodies is in the direction of the strike of the fault.

Thrust: A low angle fracture surface in rock bodies along which the broken parts move miles away due to earth's interior forces.

Vulnerability: The extent to which an individual community , sub-group, structure, service, or geographic area is likely to be damaged or disrupted by the impact of a particular disaster or hazard.

OTHER DISASTER RELATED TERMINOLOGY

Disaster:

"…. A serious disruption of the functioning of a society, causing widespread human material, or environmental losses which exceed the ability of the affected society to cope using its own resources." The United Nations defines disaster as fabric and normal functioning of a society (or community). "It is an event or a series of events which gives rise to casualties and/or damage or loss of property, infrastructure, essential services or means of livelihood on a scale that is beyond the normal capacity of the affected communities to cope with unaided.

Disaster is sometimes also used to describe a "catastrophic situation in which the normal patterns of life (or eco-systems) have been disrupted and extraordinary emergency interventions are required to save and preserve human lives and/or the environment."

Risk is a measure of the expected losses due to a hazard event of a particular magnitude occurring in a given area over a specific time period . Risk is a function of the probability of particular occurrences and the losses each would cause. The level of risk depends upon:

* Nature of the hazard
* Vulnerability of elements which are affected
* Economic value of those elements

Hazards and vulnerability

A disaster is the product of a hazard such as earthquake, flood or windstorm coinciding with a vulnerable situation, which might include communities, cities or village. If we manage to nullify vulnerability, the disaster will automatically reduce.

$$\text{Disaster} = \text{Hazard} \times \text{vulnerability}$$

Hazards are defined as "Phenomena that pose a threat to people,

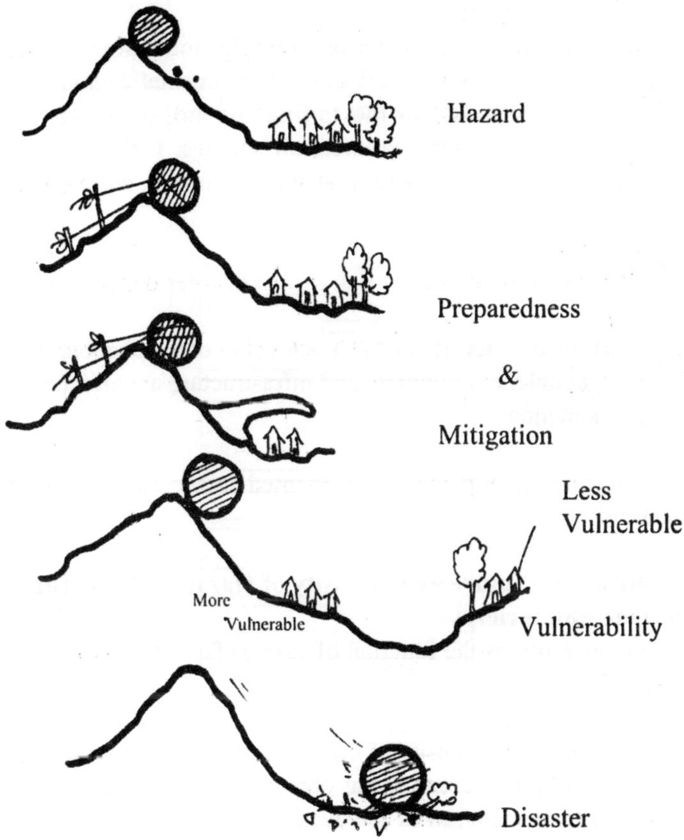

structures or economic assets and which may cause a disaster. They could be either man-made or naturally occurring in our environment." A **natural hazard** pertains "to a natural phenomenon which occurs in proximity and pose a threat to people, structures and economic assets caused by biological, geological, seismic, hydrological or meteorological conditions or processes in the natural environment."

There are four types of hazardous events that put societies at risk:

(a) Those based in **nature**: Earthquakes, droughts, floods, avalanches, etc.

(b) Those based in **violence**: War, armed conflict, physical assault, etc.

(c) Those based in deterioration: Declining health, education and other social services; environmental degradation etc.

(d) Those based in the failings of industrialised society: Technological failures, oil spillage, factory explosions, fires, gas leakage, transport collisions, atomic radiation leakage.

The extent of damage or risk from a disaster depends on:

1. The impact, intensity and characteristics of the phenomenon, and
2. How people, environment and infrastructure are affected by that phenomenon

The relationship may be presented in the form of following equation-

Risk = f (Nature and intensity of Hazard + Vulnerability of the land and society)

vulnerability is the function of various factors, which decide the risk.

As nature and intensity of the natural hazard in most of the cases are beyond human control, the objective of risk reduction during disaster management can be achieved only by managing vulnerability. The objective of risk reduction may be achieved by-

* Disaster preparedness
* Disaster response
* Disaster recovery
* Disaster mitigation
* Sustainable development and
* Adoption to climate change.

Vulnerability

Vulnerability is defined as "the extent to which a community, structure, service, or geographic area is likely to be damaged or disrupted by the impact of particular hazard, on account of their nature, construction and proximity to hazardous terrain or a disaster prone area.

Vulnerability incorporates considerations of both the intrinsic value of the elements concerned and their functional value in contributing to communal well being in general and to emergency response and post-disaster recovery in particular. The concept of vulnerability therefore implies a measure of risk ... with the level of social and economic ability with the resulting event in order to resist major disruption or loss.

Types of Vulnerability

Physical vulnerability

Physical vulnerability relates to the physical location of people and elements at risk; buildings, infrastructure , etc., and their proximity to the hazard. For example people are only vulnerable to a flood because they live in a flood prone area and vulnerable to landslides because of their habitation on steep slopes. Physical vulnerability also relates to the technical capacity of buildings and structures to resist the forces acting upon them during a hazard event.

Socio-economic vulnerability

The recent perceptions of vulnerability indicate that the degree to which a population is affected by a calamity will not purely lie in the physical components of vulnerability but also has a contextual realisation to the prevailing social and economic conditions. The impact of a disaster is determined by the event, its effects on people and their environment, as well as its consequential effect on human activities within a given society. The social and economic condition of people is also major deciding factors of the vulnerability.

The weaker sections who occupy comparatively weaker positions within the social fabric or have limited access to social services have a lessened capacity to absorb or avoid the impact of hazards. The habitations of weaker section are not strong enough to resist or withstand the adverse impacts of hazards. These weak structure without any technical know-how are easily damage by hazard, i.e., floods, earthquakes resulting into heavy life loss. These differences in capacities are exemplified in risk analysis. Its effects are seen to be directly proportionate to the poverty-gap and poverty-intensity in the society/location, as it is the weaker group that normally lives in high concentration in marginal areas (unstable slopes, flood plains) with little infrastructure and fewer resources to cope with such disasters. Research in areas affected by earthquakes indicates that single parent families, women, handicapped people, children and the aged are particularly vulnerable social groups (M. Erdik, 1993)

Disaster Preparedness and Mitigation

Disaster preparedness has been defined by the United Nations Disaster Relief Office (UNDRO) AS ".....(a series of) measures designed to organise and facilitate timely and effective rescue, relief and rehabilitation operations in case of disaster..... Measures of preparedness include among others, setting up disaster relief machinery, formulation of emergency relief plans, training of specific groups (and vulnerable communities) to undertake rescue and relief, stockpiling supplies and earmarking funds for relief operations".

Relief

Refers to the period immediately following the occurrence of a disaster when steps are taken to meet the needs of survivors with respect to shelter, water, food and medical care,

Rehabilitation

Rehabilitation includes activities that are undertaken to support the victims' return to "normal" life and re-integration into regular community functions.

Disaster Mitigation

Disaster mitigation is a "collective term used to encompass all activities undertaken in anticipation of the occurrence of a potentially disastrous event, including preparedness and long-term risk reduction measures. (UNDP, 1994)". Mitigation involves reducing the actual or probable effects of extreme disaster on man and his environment.

ABBREVIATIONS

A&Ni	—	Andaman and Nicobar Islands
APP	—	Anti Poverty Programmes
BIMARU	—	Bihar, Madhya Pradesh, Rajasthan and Uttar Pradesh.
CAPART	—	Council for Advancement of People's Action and Technology
DDP	—	Desert Development Programme
DPAP	—	Drought Prone Area Programme
DRDA	—	District rural Development Agency
EAS	—	Employment Assurance Scheme
GDP	—	Gross Domestic Production
GIS	—	Geographic Information System
HDI	—	Human Development Index
HPI	—	Human Poverty Index
HUDCO	—	Housing and Urban Development Corporation
HYV	—	High Yield Variety
IADP	—	Integrated Area Development Programme
IAY	—	Indira Awas Yojana
IDNDR	—	International Decade for Natural Disaster Reduction
IMD	—	Indian Meteorological Department
IRDP	—	Integrated Rural Development Programme
IWDP	—	Integrated Wasteland Development Programme
JFM	—	Joint Forest Management
JRY	—	Jawahar Rojgar Yojana
MLA	—	Member of Legislative Assembly
MLC	—	Member of Legislative Council
MNP	—	Minimum Need Programme
NCDM	—	National Centre for Disaster Management
NDM	—	Natural Disaster Management
NFCR	—	National Fund for Calamity Relief
NGO	—	Non Government Organisation
NIRD	—	National Institute of Rural Development
NREP	—	National Rural Employment Programme

NRSA	—	National Remote Sensing Agency
PDS	—	Public Distribution System
PRI	—	Panchayati Raj Institution
RLEGP	—	Rural Landless Employment Guarantee Programme
UT	—	Union Territories

BIBLIOGRAPHY

Abbas. N. and Subramanian, G., 1984. Erosion and Sediment Transport in the Ganga River Basin. *Indian Jour. Hydrol.*, 69; 173-82.

Annan, Kofi. 1999. *Introduction to Secretary General's Annual Report on the Work of the Organisation of United Nations*, 1999.

Arya A.S., 1998. *Earthquake Disaster Mitigation*, Programme Components, Indian Institute of Public Administration.

Bahuguna, V. K. and Satendra, 2002. Fire Situation in India, International Forest Fire News. *http://www2.ruf.uni-freiburg.de/fireglobe/iffn_26content*

Bajpai, A., 1997. *Panchayati Raj and Rural Development*, Sahitya Prakashan, New Delhi.

Bansal, R. C. and Mathur, H. N. 1976. Landslides — the nightmare of roads. *Soil Conservation Digest*, 4(1):36-37.

Bell, F.G., 1999. *Geological Hazards*, E&FN Spon, London.

Bhatt , C. P., 1999. Impact of Natural Disasters on the Environment and Development; Examples from Himalaya and Eastern and Western Ghats, *Himalayan Research Centre*, Dehradun, In Sharma, V. K. (Ed.) *Disaster Management*, NCDM, IIPA, New Delhi.

Carter Nick , W. 1992. *Disaster Management (Disaster Managers Handbook)*, Asian Development Bank, Manila.

Celly, R. K. and Gupta, T. N., 1999. *Dimension of Natural Disaster Management in India*: Special issue, World Disaster Reduction Day.

Gaur, V.K. 1999. Earth Quake Hazard in the Himalaya, *Time News Letter*, Dehradun.

Gautam, Ashutosh,1994. *Earthquake - A Natural disaster*, Ashish Publshing House, New Delhi.

Government of India, 1999. *India Rural Development Report-1999*, National Institute of Rural Development, Hydrabad.

Government of India, 1991-92 to 2000-2001. *Annual Reports*, Ministry of Agriculture and Cooperation, Govt. of India publications.

Government of India, 1999. *Transferring Rural India : Programme for Change*, Ministry of Rural Development, Government of India, New Delhi.

Government of India, 1999, *IDNDR, Indian Experience and Initiatives*, Ministry of Agriculture and Cooperation, Govt. of India publications.

Government of India, Contingency Action Plan for Natural Calamities , unpublished report of Ministry of Agriculture and Cooperation, N.D. M. Division, New Delhi.

Government of India, 2000. Vulnerability Atlas of India, Building Material and Technology Promotion Council, Ministry of Urban Development.

Government of India, 2000. *State of Forest Report-1999*, Forest Survey of India, Ministry of Environment and Forest, Dehradun.

Government of India, 2002. *High Powered Committee Report on Disaster Management*, Department of Agriculture and Cooperation.

Government of India, 2002. *National Human Development Report-2001*, Planning Commission, Government of India.

Gupta, M. C *et al.*, 2001. *Manuals on National Disaster Management in India*, National Centre for Disaster Management, IIPA, New Delhi.

Gupta, H. K. and Rastogi, B. K. 1975. *Dams and Earthquakes*, Elsevier, Amsterdam, 229 p.

Hemmedy, A.K.R., 1996. *Earthquake*, National Book Trust India, New Delhi.

Indira Gandhi National Open University, 1999, *Course Material for Foundation Course in Disaster Management*, New Delhi.

International Federation of Red Cross and Red Crescent Societies, 1996. *World Disaster Report*, Oxford University Press.

International Federation of Red Cross and Red Crescent Societies, 2002. *World Disaster Report*, Oxford University Press.

Kovach Robert L., 1995. *Earth's Fury*, Prentice-Hall, Englehood Cliffs, New Jersey.

Lewis, J., 1999. *Development in Disaster - Prone Places,* International Technology Publications Ltd., London.

Morten Ron L., 1996. *Music of the Earth*, Plenum Press, New York and London.

Munchener Ruck, 2000. *Topics 2000*, Natural Catastrophes — the Current Position, Munich Re Group, Germany.

Munchener Ruck, 2001. *Munich Re Topics*, Annual Review of Natural Catastrophes 2000, Munich Re Group, Germany.

Nain, Huang, 1982. Enginerring geological analysis method for the forecast of reservoir-induced seismicity. *Proc.4th Intern. Egg. Geol. Congr.* Oxford & IBH, New Delhi.

Praksh Indu, 1994. *Disaster Management*, Rasthra Prahari Prakashan, New Delhi.

Rawat, A. S. and Sharma, R. 2000. *Managing floods in Eastern Uttar*

Pradesh (A study in community perspective) Centre for Development Studies, U. P. Academy of Administration, Nainital.

Rawat, R.B.S. and Satendra, 2002. Role of forestry in Disaster Mitigation in Himalaya, *Proc. of Silver Jubilee National Seminar on Geodynamics and Environment Management in Himalaya*, H.N. B. Universiity, Garhwal.

Ross Simon, 1988. *Hazard Geography*, Longman.

Saklani P.S.& Satendra (1986) Strain Estimation of Narender Nagar; *Current Trends in Geology, IX Himalayan Thrust and Associated Rocks*, P.S.(Ed), pages 71-87.

Satendra, 1985. *Geology of a part of Lesser Garhwal Himalaya*, Unpublished Ph. D. thesis submitted to University of Delhi.

Satendra, 1989, *Prithvi (The Earth)*, National Book Trust of India, New Delhi.

Satendra, 1998. Forest Fire- Problem and Solution, *Kurukshetra*, Government of India publication, New Delhi.

Satendra, 1999. Slope Failure Caused valley damming in Madhya Maheshwar Valley, Garhwal Himalaya; *Proc. National Workshop on Rehabilitation Problem of Ookhimath Landslide affected Villagers*, H.N.B. University, Garhwal, Uttranchal.

Satendra, 2000. The turmoil beneath- How the landslide of the 1998 kind be prevented in Garhwal, *Down to Earth*, Centre for Science and Environment, New Delhi.

Satendra, 2001. Disaster and Development, *Silver Jubilee issue of Employment News*, Publication Division, Ministry of Information and Broadcasting, New Delhi.

Satendra, 2001. Managing Disasters, *Down to Earth*, Centre for Science and Environment, New Delhi.

Satendra, 2002. Forest Fire Prevention and Control in Himalaya, *Proc. of Silver Jubilee National Seminar on Geodynamics and Environment Management in Himalaya*, H.N. B. University, Garhwal, Uttranchal.

Satendra, 2002. Forest Fire, *Employment News (20-26 April)*, Publication Division, Ministry of Information and Broadcasting, New Delhi.

Satendra, 2002. Droughts, *Employment News (2-9 August)*, Publication Division, Ministry of Information and Broadcasting, New Delhi.

Sharma, V. K., 1999. Function of Disaster Management Organisation and Methodology to cope with Disasters in India, In Sharma (Ed.), *V. K Disaster Management*. National Centre for Disaster Management IIPA, New Delhi.

Singh, J. S. and Saxena, A. K. , 1980. Analysis of forest grazing and vegetation in parts of Kumaun Himalaya, *Ind. Jour. Range Mangement*, 1(1).

Singh, P. *et al.*, 2000. *Disaster Response in India*, A Joint Study Initiative by The Center of Excellence in Disaster Management and Humanitarian Assistance and The Foreign Military Studies Office.

Sinha, A. and Sharma, V.K., 1999. *Cultural and Prevention, Natural Disaster Management: India*; National Centre for Disaster Management (IIPA) and Natural Disaster Management Division, Ministry of Agriculture, Government of India.

Sinha, R.K. (Ed.), 1995. *Environment- Employment, Rural Poverty*, Commonwealth Publishers, New Delhi.

Swanston, D. N. and Swanson, F. J. 1978. Timber harvesting, mass erosion and sheepland forest geomorphology in the Pacific north-west. In: Coastes, D. R. (Ed), *Geomorphology and Engineering*, Halsted, Stroudsburg (Pennsylvania) pp. 199-221.

Suresh, V., 1999.: Rehabilitation of the Housing Stock in the Earthquake Affected Areas of Chamoli and Rudra Prayag. *Special issue, World Disaster Reduction Day.*

Turner Berry, A. and Nick, F. Pidgeon, 1977. *Man made Disasters.* Butterworth- Heineman: Oxford.

United Nations, 2001. Natural Disasters and Sustainable Development : Understanding the links between development , environment and natural disasters, *http://www.unisdr.org.*

Valdiya, K. S., 1987. *Environmental Geology - Indian context*; Tata-Mc Graw Hill publishing company limited, New Delhi. 32.

Valdiya, K. S., 1984. *Aspects of Tectonics: Focus on South Central Asia*, Tata Mc Graw Hill, New Delhi, p 319.

Valdiya, K. S., 1998. *Dynamic Himalaya*, Universities Press (India) Ltd., Hydrabad.

Index